" Nancy Peacock grew up in a world that 'was a corset of restrictions and rules. Church. School. My mother.' Her memoir is a moving ode to a life frayed by time and circumstance and relationships, a moving ode to a journey that took her to Wildwood, which was 'like a mother who would always welcome [her] home.' Nancy Peacock is a magnetic storyteller. *Wildwood* is profoundly observed, vividly peopled, and impeccably written."

—**Judy Goldman**, author of *The Rest of Our Lives*

" There is a heartbreaking innocence in seventeen-year-old Nancy Peacock's decision to marry her humdrum boyfriend so that they can live together as hippies, free from the conventions of their parents. The reader can see what dreamy, desperate young Nancy cannot: she is trading one prison for another.

Four years into a punishing marriage, Nancy moves with her husband to Wildwood, a rustic enclave of small, hand-built houses on the outskirts of Chapel Hill. Here she comes alive. She chops wood, builds fires, chinks cabin walls, bakes bread, gathers wildflowers for Coke-bottle bouquets. Through the sheer physical work of making a home, she comes home to herself. Wildwood saves her, and, for a while, her marriage. In time, the memory of Wildwood will fuel her writing.

Frank, lyrical, absorbing, *Wildwood* conjures a lost paradise. I could not put the book down and did not want it to end."

—**Kim Church**, author of *Byrd*

" The first word that comes to mind when I think about Nancy Peacock's memoir is *agency*. The lack of it in her early adult life and the journey to being a woman who embraces agency and self-value are what make the writing of this tale so remarkably poignant and relatable.

—**Beverly Donofrio**, author of *Riding in Cars with Boys*, *Looking for Mary*, and *Astonished*

Wildwood

Nancy Peacock

LYSTRA BOOKS
& Literary Services

ISBN 979-8-9935520-1-9 paperback
ISBN 979-8-9935520-2-6 e-book
Library of Congress Control Number 2026901078

Book design by Kelly Prelipp Lojk.
Author photo by Grace Camblos.

LYSTRA BOOKS
&c Literary Services

Published by Lystra Books & Literary Services, LLC
391 Lystra Estates Drive
Chapel Hill, NC 27517
lystrabooks@gmail.com

For Ellen

ALSO BY NANCY PEACOCK

FICTION

Life Without Water

Home Across the Road

The Life and Times of Persimmon Wilson

NONFICTION

*A Broom of One's Own: Words on Writing,
Housecleaning and Life*

PROLOGUE

I knew what I had to do. I had to kill it. I had to kill it all. I had to tear up my writing. I had to stop putting words on paper. I had to fold up my dream of being a writer and put it in the place of all childhood dreams—the place where Puff the Magic Dragon went to die. Where swings are stilled. Where balls go flat, and dolls' eyes are blacked out. The place where Weebles wobble and actually do fall down.

Instead of being a writer, I would be the thing I was raised to be, the thing my mother always pushed me toward, the thing I'd tried to avoid. I would be a good girl, and I would be a good wife, even if it killed me.

My first glimpse that something was possible other than the world I lived in, the girdled world of suburbia, church, and school, came in August of 1969. The glimpse arrived in a flickering reflection in the sliding glass door behind my brother's shoulder during dinner, the reflection of the television behind me, airing the *CBS Evening News* with Walter Cronkite.

The news was always on during family dinners, and at age fifteen I'd watched plenty of world events in the glass behind my brother. I'd seen people stumble out of a firebombed bus. I'd seen firemen turn high-pressure hoses on children. I'd seen the faces of four young girls killed when their church was bombed. When I was in fourth grade, President Kennedy was assassinated, and three civil rights workers vanished in Mississippi, their bodies found forty-four days later in an earthen dam. When I was in eighth grade, Martin Luther King Jr. was assassinated, and a few months later, Robert Kennedy. Every night, the reflection in the glass behind my brother showed American soldiers in Vietnam, wading through rice paddies holding their guns above their heads. I saw grass-roofed huts being set on fire and peasants sitting on the ground crying. I saw planes flying over that country, spreading a defoliant called Agent Orange that stripped the jungle of itself.

Closer in, the world I lived in was a corset of restrictions and rules. Church. School. My mother. Things were supposed to be a certain way, but the world Walter Cronkite reported on did not reflect that. Things were not orderly. Things were not okay, and although the turmoil did not touch me directly, I wasn't immune to it. I didn't like what I heard and saw on the news. The world out there seemed both real and unreal to me, ridiculous, and incredibly dangerous, and even as a child I realized the danger was greater for some people than for others. This wasn't a world I wanted to participate in, so I never turned around to watch the television during dinner.

But just before I was about to enter tenth grade, on Monday, August 18, 1969, I twisted in my chair at the table to see for myself what Walter Cronkite was talking about. He sat in front of a map with a star pointing out the location of White Lake, NY, where something called the Woodstock Music and Art Fair had taken place. Three hundred thousand people had shown up for this rock concert held on a dairy farm, far more than anyone had expected.

The coverage flipped to the ground showing a sea of trash and mud, a traffic jam of cars rolling slowly by packed with people on every surface. The people looked tired and dirty, but happy. They smiled and flashed the peace sign—two fingers held up in a V. A wicked guitar rift sounded before fading away to commentary.

By the time I heard about it, the Woodstock Music and Art Fair was over, but the world I briefly saw that night on TV seemed as far away from the suburban dinner table I sat at and the church I'd attended the day before, farther away than Vietnam or even the moon, where Neil Armstrong had planted an American flag just the month before.

When the *Life Special Edition: Woodstock Music Festival* arrived on the magazine rack in our local drug store, I dug into my pocket for babysitting money and bought it. The only footage I'd seen of the festival was on our black-and-white TV, and now, as I gazed at these color pictures it seemed impossible to me that I hadn't added color to those brief views. At home I paged through the images again and again. I could not get enough of these people in their flowing, colorful clothes, their dancing, and communal sense of self, their sense of fun and absurdity. Even the rain and mud were taunted and played with.

How did they do it? How did they refuse the rigidity? The suits and ties. The briefcases and shiny shoes. The binding dresses and rigid pointy bras.

I was especially fascinated with the women, the women who bloomed like morning glories across the pages of my *Life Special Edition*. They were nothing like the women in my world. Nothing like the women at the beauty parlor with their pink frocks and sculpted locks. Nothing like the women in church, buttoned up and righteous and doing the Lord's work of cutting up white bread into tiny pieces for communion. They were nothing like the women on TV shows who vacuumed in heels and never broke a sweat. They were certainly nothing like my beleaguered mother, heavily sighing every day at the stove.

Maybe this was a way to become a woman. Maybe this was a way to avoid my fate as a traditional wife and mother. Maybe this was a way to not tie myself down with children.

I could see that my mother's children—me, my sister, and my two brothers—were the source of her unhappiness. She could never escape us. We vexed her with our needs. Due to us she didn't have a minute to herself, as she often said, and I could see it was true. There was always something Mom had to tend to. As if putting breakfast, lunch, and dinner on the table, as if meal-planning and buying the groceries for the week, as if keeping a family of six in clean clothes were not enough, there would also be a broken vase during roughhousing, a skinned knee, a late school project, a bored and whiny child, and the million daily minutia of running a household and raising four children. I saw clearly that my mother was trapped. I saw it as clearly as I saw the advertisements and shows on TV that said she should be happy.

Worse for my mother than our physical needs were our emotional needs, our needs for guidance through the world of school and society and the future we'd have to navigate, the needs the TV mothers met so effortlessly. But not my mother. If she couldn't wipe it up, clean it up, cook it up, or serve it up, she didn't know what to do with it, so she opted for not listening to us, or not believing us if she did listen. My mother opted for lying, denying, dismissing, blaming, and if a problem really needed a serious answer, telling us to talk to God, not her.

But I didn't see God or the church comforting my mother or giving her any sort of reprieve. From what I gleaned from my forced attendance, my mother's ensnarement in marriage and motherhood was God's plan for her. It's not that she hadn't chosen to marry my father, and it's not that she hadn't chosen to have children or didn't love us, but I could see her straining against the tether and boredom and relentlessness of it all. If she went to church for comfort, she didn't get it there. Instead, she got blame. The church told her that it was her privilege to wipe our noses and serve us, and that any sourness she felt at any given time wasn't God's fault, it was her own. She just needed to step up her game with Him. Pray more. Be more devout. Believe harder.

But my mother believed pretty damn hard already. She was a preacher's daughter. Her father left the Catholic Church to become a Methodist minister. I was glad I never met him. I was suspicious of her adoration of him, the way she pointed to his picture on the shelf above her very messy desk and told me again and again, "That's my father." The story of his ministry always followed.

He must have been strict. He must have convinced her that an unrepentant soul would burn in hell forever, and he must have painted hell in technicolor gore. He must have defeated her spirit, cast her female body as inherently bad and, without the supervising presence of a man, dangerous. In turn, and with the help of society and the church, she passed all these lessons on to me. I absorbed them as easily as I absorbed the differences I saw in my mother and the women on TV. I absorbed the message that a woman should be happy with wifedom and motherhood, but my mother was not. And I didn't think I would be either. And for that, I think we both felt shame.

I questioned many things, but I knew better than to ask questions out loud. In school asking a question only proved your ignorance. At home a question would attract ridicule and teasing from my older siblings. To question the church and God was the worst of all. This would invite my mother to lean over me, grip the arms of my chair, trapping me there. Her face only inches from mine, she would hiss something about blasphemy, impiety, and never taking "the Lord's name in vain," three things I did not understand, but what was the point in asking?

Sometimes though, a question just slipped out of me like breath. Three years before Woodstock, in the summer of 1966, Walter Cronkite told us during dinner of man named Richard Speck who broke into a townhouse in Chicago and killed eight women, all of them nursing students, raping one. He kept them in a room, taking them out one by one to stab or strangle. The only witness escaped by hiding under a bed. In Speck's murderous frenzy, he lost count.

My mother paid as much attention to the news as I did. She never turned around to watch. It was the background to the dinner she served, the meal she'd planned and cooked for hours, the vegetables she'd chopped, the meat she'd seared, the spaghetti sauce she'd simmered. If she resented the news being on during dinner, she never said so. Throughout the violence and strife and conflict I saw reflected in the sliding glass door, my mother never paused serving the mashed potatoes and reminding us to take our elbows off the table, but when the story of Richard Speck killing eight women aired, she stopped everything. She put down the bowl she held. She clasped her hand over her mouth. "How awful," she said.

"What?" I asked because I'd never seen this in her. Something about this story had hit her hard, and always looking for clues and truth, I wanted to know what it was.

Mom took her hand away from her mouth, but she didn't register having heard me. "How awful," she breathed out again.

"What?" I asked. "What is it?"

Meaning, why now? Why this reaction to this story now? Why does this violence affect you when all that other violence has gone unremarked upon?

"What is rape?" I asked.

She heard me this time. I could tell by the way she didn't reply, by the way she turned away from the TV and picked up a serving spoon and slapped some squash onto my plate.

"I don't like squash," I said.

"Oh, you do too," she said, and she put even more squash on my plate. This was what she said and did every time I told her I didn't like squash.

But even though things seemed to return to normal—the news droning on, my mother denying my likes and dislikes because they were inconvenient—I could tell she was disturbed. I could also tell there would be no forthcoming information.

Ditto for the time a man followed me around the public library when I was twelve. I was alone, as I often was on Saturday mornings at the library, and at first, I thought it must be my imagination. I tested my theory by moving around all different places within the stacks. My suspicion was confirmed when I saw his hairy fingers prying books aside from the next stack over, so he could peer at me. I went straight to the pay phone in the lobby and called Mom to come pick me up. I waited inside the library for her, surrounded by people, instead of sitting outside on a rock wall where I would have been alone. When she drove up, I rushed out and hopped in the car.

"You didn't stay long," she said.

"No," I agreed, knowing I couldn't tell her about the man in the library. Mostly, I feared her saying that I must have imagined it. Just like the squash, I didn't know my own mind.

But I hadn't imagined it, and I didn't know what the man might have wanted with me. From what I could tell from TV shows, men liked pretty women. Grown women. Sexy women. I wasn't any of those things. I was just a kid, alone in the library. That night at dinner, with the safety of the entire family around me, during a commercial break in the news, I casually said, "A man followed me around in the library today."

There was a small, silent pause. It was as though I hadn't spoken. I was used to this. I often went unheard. But then I felt my mother suddenly move beside me. Her chair scraped back across the floor, and then her face was in my face, just as if I'd taken the Lord's name in vain again.

"Why didn't you tell the librarian?" she crisped out. "I don't understand why you didn't tell the librarian. You didn't even tell me."

I recoiled from her. I knew when I was being blamed. In this case it was not for attracting him, but for not handling the situation the way she thought I should have. But I didn't know what the situation was.

"What did he want?" I asked.

But my mother went on. "Why didn't you tell the librarian?"

"What did he want?" I asked again.

She still leaned over me. "Why didn't you tell the librarian? You should have told the librarian. Why didn't you tell the librarian?"

"I don't know," I finally whispered.

But why would I have told the librarian? I lived in a world where grownups mostly did not believe what children said. I lived in a world where the women I knew sphinctered up and would not talk whenever a child bumped into an uncomfortable topic. I could see them looking knowingly over my head at each other. I could see them trying to distract me, dismiss me, avoid the subject at hand. In a nutshell, I didn't trust women. I trusted men more, although I didn't know many.

In my neighborhood, the men went to work, the homes and streets emptied of them throughout the week. I only knew these men on weekends. Besides my own father, there were the other fathers in the neighborhood, each with their own characteristics—one who blew a bugle to call his kids in for dinner, another who was an artist and painted pictures that weren't of anything, a third who filled the family's above-ground pool every summer with a trickling water hose. There were a few male teachers in school, most notably in the arts and music. And there was the minister in church whose hand I shook because I had to, before running off to play with my brother in the cemetery.

Aside from the minister, whose agenda was to deliver God's message, the men in my life seemed, for the most part, loose, direct, and guileless.

My father went to work as a chemist every weekday. On weekends he gardened, turned his compost pile, played the organ in church, and fixed his children breakfast every Saturday morning. He was ten times easier to be around than my mother.

Every Saturday morning, I found Di-Da, as we called him, sitting at the table reading a book with the waffle iron and a bowl of batter beside him, waiting for his children to get up one by one. I can't remember a Saturday morning when my breakfast wasn't with him alone. He'd look at me as I wandered in, still in my pajamas, rubbing sleep out of my eyes. "Hey honey," he'd say. "Do you want a waffle?"

Yes. Of course I wanted a waffle.

Di would put his book down and fire up the waffle iron, pour the batter, serve me, and we'd sit and talk while I ate. I was mostly quiet, but this too was easy. I never felt pressure from my father to reveal something, or to make something different from what it was. He might ask if I wanted to go with him to find rocks for the wall he was building. And then I'd sit in the front seat of the grey station wagon with the red interior, letting the world slide by. When we stopped somewhere to pick up rocks, he told me what size he needed. "At least this big," he'd say, holding his hands apart. "Larger is fine, but let me know if you find something too large for you to move." And off we'd go, working peacefully side by side.

In the summer of 1969, the summer America landed men on the moon, the summer of Woodstock, the summer before I started tenth grade, my mother started pushing a book onto me. I was four years old when 'Twixt Twelve and Twenty by Pat Boone was published, but my mother clung to the raft of its alleged relevancy, as though it could save her from my pending adolescence.

"He has good things to say about being a teenager," she said, handing it to me. "You should read it."

I obediently took the proffered book, but the cover told me everything I needed to know about it—Pat Boone's scrub-a-dub-dub face mooning above a sketch of three teenagers—two boys flanking a girl who wore a wide-skirted dress typical of the 1950s.

I could easily predict the offered advice.

Be well-groomed, showing pictures of a clean-cut teenage boy combing his bristly short hair and a girl with a perfect, perky ponytail.

Be well-dressed, showing boys in neatly pressed slacks and girls in flaring skirts.

Go to church, showing boys and girls holding Bibles and looking up.

No thank you. Pat Boone would condemn the very times in which I lived. Pat Boone would tell me God's opinions on dancing, long hair on boys, miniskirts on girls, the civil rights movement, and the protests against the Vietnam War. Youth was not supposed to have an opinion. Youth was supposed to sit in the soda shop and say things like "Jeez" and "Golly." Youth was not supposed to be what youth so clearly was.

Pat Boone's book sat unopened on the bedside table while I lay in my room, looking through my magazine with pictures of Woodstock. There was no advertising in this special edition, no pictures of a woman fawning over her new stove or vacuum cleaner or washing machine. No pictures of women with their heads under bullet-shaped silver hair driers or fretting over the condition of their skin or lips or hips or breasts. No insinuation that whatever unhappiness a woman felt, it was due to her inability to attract a man or keep a husband interested or have soft hands after having washed a mountain of dishes. There was no message that a woman's unhappiness was due to her own inability to follow the rules. There didn't seem to be any rules at Woodstock, yet there had been something that kept the crowd harmonious and peaceful.

What's more, it seemed a big secret, one of many kept from me, that women could have as much fun as men. They could take off their clothes and go swimming in a pond, just like the men. They could dance with their arms in the air, hair flying. They could slide down a muddy hill with bystanders cheering at the distance they traveled. And the men I saw pictured at Woodstock didn't seem to mind one bit. The judgment I felt in church and school was absent. Gone. Vanished.

My mother ignored Woodstock. She was too busy to notice or care about my fascination with it. If she did notice, she likely dismissed it as a fad. Her children were just children.

Not formed. Their minds were sieves. Nothing there was especially worth paying attention to. Woodstock for my mother was just another news story, a thing that thrummed in the background of her world as so many news stories did.

But for me it thrummed in the foreground. This was my path. This was the way to avoid my mother's fate of traditional wifedom and motherhood. I'd join the movement. I'd become a hippie. I'd denounce the bullshit. Fuck yeah.

2.

It was easy. I wasn't the only student who returned to school from the summer of '69 completely transformed. The air in my high school crackled with drugs and music and hormones. Guitars sang out in the common area between the classrooms and the cafeteria, where students were allowed to smoke and where the grass was beaten down to nothing from our feet and the seats of our pants. The scent of cigarettes and patchouli oil and incense drifted out amongst the guitar chords. Girls' hips and breasts swayed as they danced. Softly whiskered boys struck wooden matches on the zippers of their jeans and cupped their hands around the flame to light a smoke. Some of these boys could even flick a match to flame with nothing but a thumbnail, a trick that dazzled me.

They were spellbinding—these beautiful boy-men clad in jeans and denim jackets and leather boots with colorful bandanas in their pockets and their hair spilling over their collars. I drank them in. I longed to have one of these magical creatures put his arms around me.

And now, because I was a hippie, because I was a member of a small but vibrant circus in school calling ourselves "the freaks," the attention of a boy felt more possible than it ever had before. Talking to boys no longer depended on having

13

the right clothes or combing my hair the right way or wearing makeup or being coy. These were the things my mother,
in her quest to keep her youngest child a child, never guided
me in. She refused to acknowledge my developing body. Except for "the talk" about the mechanics of marital sex—stress
on marital, not stress on pleasure—I'd received no counsel.
In junior high, I picked up the razor and, not knowing any
better, dry-shaved my legs. She would not teach me how
to do this. I was too young, she said again and again. Thirteen. Fourteen. Nearly fifteen. She would never teach me to
soap the skin first or use lotion. I learned these techniques
through talk with girls at school.

But now it really didn't matter. I'd leapt over her. I'd leapt
over all the top secret, classified information that women
knew, but did not share in unmarried company. I'd landed
smack dab in the middle of the sexual revolution. Smack dab
in the middle of the carousel. Smack dab in the middle of
make love, not war.

I didn't need the guidance of the previous generation.
Their secrets were moot. I didn't need their whisperings,
their elder knowledge, their unhelpful twitters, their knowing glances at each other. They'd taught me nothing so far
but lessons that never felt right, things that I determined
might be lies. Fuck them.

I tossed my copies of *Seventeen* and *Calling All Girls* magazines in the trash. For years, I'd been desperately reading
articles about how to attract a boy. They all said the same
thing. Pat Boone could have written them.

*Find out what he likes and do a little research on the sub-
ject so you can converse with him. Be well-groomed. Show him
that you care about your appearance. Let him do most of the
talking—no one likes a "motor mouth."*

Every article, after dishing out advice about how to cater to the needs of boys, ludicrously ended with: *Above all, be yourself.*

Well, now I had a self to be. I'd joined the damn circus. I wasn't straight and boring. I was a freak, and the world loosened. I guzzled the intoxicating hooch of revolution. I turned that bottle up and gulped and did not take a breath.

Skipping school with my new friend Becky, we discovered the PTA Thrift Shop, where I could finally afford to buy my own clothes and not depend on hand-me-downs from the family next door or the annual school shopping trip with my mother, during which we argued, and she held firm that I must wear what she picked out and not what I wanted. Ha! With the discovery of the PTA Thrift Shop, I reached over and took those reins right out of her hands.

The wide-open style of funk made finding clothes at the thrift shop a grand adventure.

The women who priced the used clothing hadn't yet caught on to the fact that hippies were putting together spirited wardrobes from out-of-style clothes, and so the most fantastic, freak-approved attire was ridiculously cheap. Plowing through something called The Costume Barrel, I found a beautiful black shirt from the '40s, with a starburst pattern of silver beads across the collar and bodice, costing only a quarter. With tip money from my job scooping ice cream at the Dairy Bar, I bought long silver chains of necklaces, scarves, a knitted top with daisies, a long black skirt, a funky leather bag. The possibilities were endless, and I reveled in them.

Every morning I put together a new ensemble. A long skirt held together with safety pins, a striped knit shirt paired with a man's plaid wool vest, a floppy yellow hat.

"I don't think you should wear that to school," my mother sang, as I sailed out the door in a dress she said looked like a slip.

I'd finally figured out to just ignore her objections. It was easier to do what I wanted, rather than advocate for my preferences. Advocating for my preferences only gave her power, and I was done with that. Apparently, she knew it and, except for bleats of verbal protest, accepted it, and this was because my sister's adolescence preceded mine. In a sense, my sister walked point for me, and it wore my mother down.

My mother and I entered an unspoken pact. I wouldn't put anything that she judged overly sinful in her face, and she wouldn't go looking. My mother would not search my room or my pocketbook, as she'd done with my sister. She would not ask too many questions. She would swallow my lies. And for my part, I would not make her cry. I would protect her from her own emotions.

My mother's crying was theatrical, and I hated sitting in witness of it. All that keening. All that over-the-top emotion, so large and on display that there was no room for anyone else's emotion. This was never truer than during my sister's adolescence when she ran away to New York with her boyfriend and another couple.

During the time she was missing, my mother served us dinner every night, as always. The meal was well-rounded, straight out of a home-economics textbook—a meat, three vegetables, glasses of iced tea sweating on the plastic tablecloth. You could have taken a picture of it just as it was laid out on the table, and you'd have never seen my mother pushing her plate forward and her chair back after the blessing. You'd have never seen her lay her head on the table and cry while we silently ate. You'd have never seen my father turning his attention to the TV, to Walter Cronkite delivering the news, to the helicopter blades in the Vietnam War chop-chop-chopping the air as we cut our meat and vegetables and my mother cried. I hated my mother's sobbing, not because I felt sorry for her, but because I wanted to eat my meatloaf in peace.

So, my mother sputtered and whinged over my clothing choices, and I shrugged them away. Every weekday, I dodged her opinions and ignored her eruptions. It was easy because I had somewhere to be, and if I spent time in conflict with her, I'd be late to school. And if I missed the bus or my ride, she'd have to drive me there. But on Sundays, I didn't have this situation on my side, and my mother dug in with her agenda, and her agenda, capital A, was that I should go to church, capital C.

My siblings had moved away from home by now, the boys gone to college and my sister separated from her husband and living in Atlanta. I was alone with my parents, and Sundays were a test of wills between my mother and me, with my father remaining silent and waiting on the sidelines until time to leave for church. My mother insisted that when I turned sixteen, I could make up my own mind about church. Until then, I had to go. She railed about it. Bombed me with her emotions. Pushed God out in front of her. Threw the covers off my body. Harangued me to get up. Reminded me that I needed to get dressed so we wouldn't be late. Complained about my choice of clothes. Refused to leave with me wearing my burgundy dress with the tiny glinting mirrors embroidered on it. Stomped and railed until I changed. And then we were off to church, primed for God's word. What the fuck?

I don't have a lot of sympathy for my mother here. My siblings had been allowed to make up their minds about church at age thirteen, and when each of them, one by one, chose the option of not attending, my mother moved the goalpost. Sixteen was the new thirteen. The age at which her youngest could decide her own spiritual future. And it all had to do with how my mother identified, and how she might look to the congregation, and maybe to God, if all her children decided church wasn't for them.

Our church was conservative. My parents chose it more for its architecture than its philosophy, a quaint little white country church that reminded them of Alabama, where they'd grown up and we'd moved from. The cars in the parking lot were plastered with George Wallace for President stickers, but even though my parents, especially my mother, thought Wallace was awful, this was where they went for spiritual sustenance.

In church I sat on a hard pew and stared out the window at a tree. I always looked at that tree, and it was as though the tree looked back at me, providing me with the spiritual nurturing that was missing inside the building. It was a beautiful tree. An oak, with squirrels scampering up its trunk and moss growing at its roots and birds flitting from branch to branch. I wanted to be out there, in nature, alone.

And then finally, I was sixteen, the magic age, and predictably, I didn't go to church anymore. I stayed home and smoked dope down in my brother's dark room and then went upstairs and sat on the large screened-in back porch that overlooked the woods. I would be sufficiently un-high by the time my parents came home, but I discovered they couldn't tell anyway. Teachers couldn't tell either. Or so we told ourselves.

It was likely because so many students showed up to school drugged-out and falling asleep at their desks that the administration announced that roll call would only be taken during homeroom. This provided the opportunity to skip school while also maintaining a record of perfect attendance. We showed up for homeroom and then left in droves. Sometimes we stayed for a class we liked and then left. There was no real pattern to who would be in school one day and who wouldn't.

During lunch, if we were staying in school for the day, we often walked to a field behind the football stadium. A copse of woods with a small brook bordered the field, which was planted with hay. In the center the hay had been tramped down into a circle, a nearly invisible path leading to it. It was a magical place.

I was sure it had been created by some brilliant boy. Who else would have thought to do such a thing but a brilliant boy? Brilliant boys were doing all kinds of wild, interesting stuff in my school. They had the best artwork, the best music, the most imaginative poems, the best performances in class. They owned the world, and I wanted a part of it.

In the hayfield, we sat in the circle, passing a joint around.

Camaraderie. Friends. Fellow rebels. The girls weren't mean and gossipy. The guys were easy friends. Yet I always watched enviously as a girl leaned against a boy in the hayfield, his arm snaking around her possessively as he kissed her neck.

I wanted to be possessed that way. I wanted to be chosen. I wanted to be wanted. I longed for it. I longed for it badly, but even though I was a part of the tribe, loose and willing, I didn't land on any boy's radar that way. I was just there, an accepted but chaste member of the tribe. I could make people laugh. I could do improv and mimic our teachers. I was trusted to never turn anyone in to the authorities for smoking dope or skipping school. But I could not attract a boy, and to be unable to find a partner in such a wide-open sexual environment proved to me my unworthiness.

Perhaps the rules of engaging with a boy that the teen magazines had touted applied even here, in the midst of a revolution, in the midst of a tramped-down circle in a hay-field, in the midst of doing illegal drugs in a coed setting. Perhaps I didn't know how to show availability without displaying desperate neediness.

And needy, I was. Neediness needled me, pricked my skin, brought droplets of invisible blood to my surface, where they leaked out, souring the air around me. The only solace would be a boy. I wanted a boy to take physical hold of me. I wanted a boy to lean me against a locker and trap me there, maybe shoving his denim-clad thigh into my crotch and demanding a kiss. What would that be like?

One day I was skipping school with a group of friends. We were in a car, having just finished off a joint when someone said, "Strickland," alerting us to our principal heading up the hill to the student parking lot. We dove under blankets conveniently stashed in the backseat and hid, perfectly still, while Mr. Strickland walked around and tried the locked doors and knocked on the windows, saying, "I know you're in there." We didn't budge.

My blanket mate was a boy named George. It was hotter than hot under that blanket, but I didn't mind. I could feel George's bare arm against mine, the length of his body close, his legs against my legs. After the knocking stopped, he was the first to whisper, "I think he's gone." He was the first to bravely poke his head out from under our blanket to check. He threw the blanket off and said, "Coast clear." I instantly missed his body. I wanted him to reach for my hand. I wanted him to not fling the blanket off so quickly. I wanted to not feel like an untouchable.

"How was school today?" my mother asked when I came home.

"Fine," I said, as I headed to my room to play records and stand before the mirror taking inventory of my physical flaws, the reasons I was sure I had no boyfriend, the reasons George had thrown our blanket off so quickly. I was too tall, too small breasted, I didn't have a pretty face.

"Did you do your homework?" Mom called after me.

"I did it in school," I hollered back. A lie as easy as skipping classes, and one my parents were perfectly willing to accept. After all they saw no visible plummet in my grades due to my new lifestyle.

My grades had always been bad. Even though I studied, I couldn't retain what I read in textbooks. I rarely passed tests. Going all out for an F was easier than studying for a string of Ds, so why not just forget trying?

When I brought a report card home for her to sign, my mother performed her disappointment in me as always, but it was a temporary moment, just something for me to endure. A brief bit of discomfort as she sternly told me I needed to do better. Then she signed the report card, handed it back to me, and the moment was over. In the past, she'd brought up summer school every now and then. Perhaps I should attend, she said. Bring my grades up. I adamantly refused. Give up my summer? To go to school? To voluntarily enter the hallways with the grey, slamming lockers? To voluntarily enter a classroom and squeeze my long, tall body into the too-small desk? No. Absolutely not, as my mother often said to us.

Although my grades were dismal, there were two classes that I did not fail and rarely skipped. Creative Writing and

English. I had the best teachers in these classes. In English, my teachers welcomed different opinions about the motivation of a character in a novel we'd been assigned. Discussion was encouraged. Here was a chance to think and express instead of regurgitating memorized facts.

One of my creative writing teachers turned out all the lights and had us lie on the floor, listen to a rainstorm, and then in the final moments of class, list the sensations we'd felt. Another had us make up a lie and try to pass it off as truth, then write about it. Our stories were read out loud in class, our desks ringed into a circle. Our work was discussed, critiqued, considered, and valued.

Despite being convinced I wasn't pretty and was stupid, I was equally convinced I could be a writer. There seemed to be room for me at that table. I gathered from some of the biographies I'd read that writers didn't always do well in the confinement of school.

Oddly, it was my mother, my straight-laced Bible-thumping mother, who inadvertently gave me the subversive act of writing in the form of a Christmas gift when I was eight – a small five-year diary. The book had a red fake-leather cover, gold embossed lettering across the front, and a tiny little lock with a tiny little key. I remember sounding out the gold lettering and asking her, "What is a d-i-a-r-y?"

"It's a place to write your thoughts," she answered.

"Who reads it?" I asked.

"No one reads it but you," she assured me. "It's private. Open it."

I can still feel the little key inserted into the little lock. I can still hear that unconvincing click. I knew that lock was a useless gewgaw. It was child's play, but a place to write down my thoughts appealed to me. My thoughts, by necessity, were held in most of the time. Speaking them out loud would invite either being ignored or being made fun of. My thoughts needed a place to get out, a way to live somewhere besides in my overcrowded mind, where they'd grown large and numerous.

When I opened the little book, my mother pointed to a page divided into five spaces by thin gold lines. "Each one of these spaces is meant to be written in daily, for the next five years."

My mother greatly miscalculated the enormity of her youngest daughter's thoughts. Nothing I had to say could fit in one of those little spaces. I had so much to say that even a whole page couldn't hold it. I finished entries on pieces of notepad paper taped on as extensions. Sometimes the add-ons were three or four or five pieces of paper taped together, folded accordion-style and locked in with the little gold key. I kept the diary hidden behind a stack of books: a biography of Betsy Ross; a copy of *Pippi Longstocking*; a Nancy Drew mystery, purchased with my own allowance because Mom wouldn't buy me a Nancy Drew book. She disapproved of the main character's independence, although Pippi seemed to get away with it, perhaps because she seemed cartoonish, while Nancy Drew seemed like a serious, sharp, and capable young woman who had no mother and didn't go to church.

I wrote in my diary nightly, sitting in bed with it, printing tiny so I could fill those tiny pages with my words, with what I had to say about the world I lived in.

It wasn't long after receiving the diary that my mother's mother came to stay with us. This was a yearly event until she passed away when I was ten. We called my grandmother Gala, and she was on rotation from staying with my mother's sisters and brother.

Gala was too frail to traverse the stairs between the guest room and the floor above, where the kitchen and main living area were. To accommodate her, my sister moved out of the room we shared, into the guest room downstairs, and Gala moved in with me for three months.

Gala was senile. She shuffled and talked to herself and looked out the window and muttered and muttered and muttered and muttered. I hated sharing a room with her.

Each year, before Gala arrived, I lobbied to let my sister share a room with her instead of me. Let me move downstairs, I begged. And each year my mother said, "That's a good idea. We'll do that next year, but this year it's already arranged."

"You said that last year," I reminded her.

"I did no such thing," she said. And then, without any sense of irony or shame, she would say, "But it's a good idea. We'll do it next year, but this year it's already arranged. Okay?"

Not only was I powerless to change this, but I was also powerless to be heard and powerless to understand why my mother lied to me every single year, why she thought I wouldn't notice or care. In my twin bed, in the corner of the room, as far away from Gala's bed as it could be, I wrote in my little red diary in large block letters, "I HATE GALA. I HATE GALA. I HATE GALA."

I was a child with nowhere to spew my feelings except onto the page, and the page, thankfully, held it all.

The diary never lied to me, the way my mother did. The diary never tried to dupe me, like her. The diary never dismissed me. The diary never silenced me. The pages never judged me, never told me not to think something, never implied to me that I wasn't a good girl, never threatened me with hell or held the carrot of heaven out as a future reward. The diary never told me whom to love or whom to hate. My needs and thoughts were never inconvenient here.

Within the year, I had filled my five-year diary. To replace it, I stapled paper between sheets of cardboard and made my own booklets. I wrote my name on the front and hid them in various places in my room. By the time I was in high school, a part of that vibrant, wonderful, whacky circus of hippies, I not only kept a journal, but I also wrote poetry and stories. I kept it all in a spiral-bound notebook I carried with me in my oversized fringed leather purse.

This, then, is who I was—a writer, a hippie, and a young girl anxious for love, to whom no one was attracted. I was surrounded by girls with boyfriends. I was surrounded by boys with girlfriends. I was surrounded by sex, drugs, and rock and roll. I was available, willing, primed, ready, and living in a fertile, wild environment, an ongoing fertility festival with birth control, and yet, no one noticed me that way. No one saw me as a potential mate, even for a night. And when finally, someone did, I was ready to bet the bank on him. I would hold on, and not let go. I would invest all my unworthiness and desperation into him, no matter what.

3.

The students were packed into the upstairs and downstairs lobbies of the school, waiting for the bell that would allow us into the hallways and on to our homerooms. Becky and I were standing against a brick wall, the loud buzz of hundreds of conversations and joking all around us. I remember that I was joking about how great it would be if every single brick in that wall was a brick of hash when a boy named Calvin Powell walked up to us and said, "Hi."

"Hi," I said, and with my new-found social skills that marijuana and hippiedom had given me, I added, "Wouldn't it be great if every single one of these bricks was a brick of hash?" I ran my hand across the wall.

"Yeah," Cal said quickly, as though he hadn't heard me at all, or as though the point of his presence was not conversation, but something else. "Do you want to go out Saturday night?" he said in a rush of words, directed at me.

"Yes," I said, my one word just as rushed as his had been, as though this offer would be retracted if I waited a millisecond to respond. The bell rang and I quickly gave Cal my address, he told me when he'd pick me up, and we dispersed for roll call in homeroom.

And just like that, I had a date. I had a date with a boy I barely knew well enough to nod hello to in the hallways. He was one of us, a fellow freak, but I'd never skipped school with him. I'd never sat out in the commons joking with him. We'd never shared a joint in the circle of tromped-down hay behind the football field.

Cal wasn't the stuff of dreams, not my dreams anyway, and my dreams included almost any boy with long hair. But Cal hadn't landed on my radar at all. There were better boys to lust after, and some of them were even taller than me. Most were not. Cal wasn't. His hair was combed in the front, but unkempt and knotted in the back. His skin was pitted, and his nose was large. He was not one of the boys who could strike a match with his thumbnail.

Saturday night he showed up wearing a pink scarf jauntily tied around his neck. I thought he looked ridiculous. John Lennon could pull this off. Mick Jagger could pull this off. Roger Daltrey could pull this off. Calvin Powell could not. I quickly closed the door behind me without inviting him in. I didn't want to go through the whole meet-my-parents scene, and they hadn't insisted. My sister's fiery adolescence had softened my mother and father's resolve to be involved with mine, so it was easy to slip out the door without introductions.

"I need to wash the car," Cal said as we walked up the brick walkway to his black Mustang.

"Okay," I said, silently thinking, *If you wanted the car washed you should have done it before you picked me up.*

Just as quickly as this criticism arose, I squashed it, berating myself for criticizing him at all, even silently. He was a boy, after all, the first I'd been able to attract. He was my fly. I was his shit.

Don't be a prig, I scolded myself. *Don't complain. Don't be so picky. You're so soda-shoppy. Just like Mom.*

Cal and I didn't say much in the car. He didn't make an effort at conversation, and neither did I. Without the props of other friends and pot, I froze, but he didn't seem to notice. He pulled into a bay at the carwash, and said, "I'll be right back."

"Okay," I said again.

I sat in the front seat watching his blurred figure circle the car as a film of pink foam slithered down the windshield. I'd never been to a carwash before. We'd always washed our car in the driveway with buckets and sponges and the garden hose. I was fascinated by the pink foam. I liked the way it blocked out the world. When Cal turned the wand to rinse, it sounded like heavy rainfall, and the pink foam on the windshield dissolved into a silvery cascade.

"Do you want to go uptown?" Cal asked, as he slid into the driver's seat.

"Sure," I said.

Cal drove us to Franklin Street, the main drag through Chapel Hill. We still didn't talk. I stared out the window as the shops and restaurants slid by. I was used to looking out car windows: on family trips, on the way to and from church, on the way to school, always a passenger, never a driver.

After mowing down a few orange cones while trying to parallel park in driver's ed and failing my driving test three times, I gave up trying to get my license. I didn't need more proof of my incompetency. When I needed to propel myself somewhere, I relied on my mother, on Becky's mother, on my feet, and on my thumb. But I didn't hitchhike at night. And I'd never been to Franklin Street after dark.

It was late spring. The weather was warm and soft. Cal parked the car, and we got out and walked toward campus. During the day, when Becky and I skipped school, the sidewalk was filled with businessmen, lawyers, students, and secretaries, while shopkeepers busily swept the stoops in front of their stores. But now, these stores were closed, and beneath their awnings, hippie vendors had spread blankets and wares. As we walked by, I admired the underground market. I eyed the offerings: used records, clothing, macramé wall-hangings, wooden boxes, handmade jewelry, hubcaps turned into fisheye mirrors.

We passed by bars, filled with longhairs, smoke and laughter and talk and loud music spilling out into the night air.

We ran into a boy we both knew from school, and he and Cal joined in a hippie handshake involving linked fingers and thumbs landing together in solidarity. The boy joined us, walking in the opposite direction he'd been heading when we met. We ran into more kids I knew from school, and as Cal and I walked down the street, a tribe magically assembled itself around us. We ended up sitting in a row on the rock wall dividing UNC campus from town.

Someone suggested we pool our money for a bottle of Boone's Farm Apple Wine. I dug into my fringed purse, and Cal dug into his pocket, and we produced some coins, as did others. The designated purchaser of this wine, the one we all agreed was least likely to get carded, went off on his mission and soon returned triumphant. We piled down on the ground behind the wall, out of sight of any cops walking the beat, and passed the bottle from hand to hand. I hated alcohol, but I wanted to be cool, so I enthusiastically turned the bottle up in a pretend gulp, blocking most of the wine with my tongue. Someone produced a joint, which got lit and passed along, each of us cupping it out of sight of any passersby. Sufficiently high now, we climbed back up on the wall and watched the world go by.

The campus seemed charged differently at night. The people drifting by, some carrying books and some not, nodded to us, assuming, I hoped, that we were students at UNC, not students in high school. After all, we were, by all appearances, fellow revolutionaries and part of the scene. And we were fellow revolutionaries. We were part of the scene.

When Cal dropped me off at home, he asked if he could kiss me, and I said yes.

This was not the first time I'd said yes to a kiss, but it was the first time I'd meant it.

When I was in junior high, after multiple fights with my sister having to do with sharing a room, my parents decided to separate us, and I was finally allowed to move downstairs into the guest room, next to the boys' rooms, while my sister occupied the room next to our parents, their thinking being that it was more important to keep an eye on their eleventh-grade daughter than on me, their seventh-grade daughter. And rightly so. I wasn't up to anything except nursing my undying love for Micky Dolenz of The Monkees.

The windows in my new room were at ground level, and one night, someone knocked on the glass. I saw the silhouette of a person I assumed to be my brother, motioning me to the patio, asking me to open the sliding glass door and let him in. My brother was often up to antics, and he sometimes included me in his adventures. If he needed to be let back inside, I would do it. Of course. But when I slid the glass door open, I didn't find my brother. I found Jim, the boy who lived across the wooded ravine from us. His mother was my mother's best friend. Jim was my age, and we were not friends. In school he acted like he didn't know me and vice versa.

I'd never been taught how to back out of a situation. I'd never been taught how to say no, or even that no was an okay thing to say to anyone. If I was good, the messaging went, it was a word I would never need to use. When it came to the opposite sex, if I just behaved myself, a boy would never need to be told no, because he would never ask. I was ignorant about what he might ask for, but I was smart enough to feel vulnerable here in the middle of the night, wearing only my blue flannel nightgown with nothing underneath, after I had mistakenly opened the door for a boy I did not like.

"Can I kiss you?" Jim asked, without greeting.

"Okay," I answered, not wanting this at all, but not knowing how to back out of it.

He leaned in. His tongue roamed around inside my mouth, fat and beery and gross.

He pulled back and said, "I'll be back later."

"Okay," I said again.

And then he was gone. I closed and locked the door.

There was no way I was climbing the stairs and telling my parents what just happened. No way I was willing to risk causing my mother her predictable anguish when it came to her girl children. She'd sniffle. She'd howl. She'd say, "How could you? How could you?" Meaning, why did I open the door?

I couldn't explain it. If I told her it had been a mistake, I'd thought it was my brother knocking at my window, I'd be implicating him in mischief he hadn't committed.

I turned off my light and went to bed. When Jim knocked at my window again, I ignored him. He stood there, knocking for a long time. I could see his silhouette, could see him raise his knuckles to tap the glass, trying to summon me.

Tap, tap, tap. I held my breath.

Tap, tap, tap. I didn't move.

Tap, tap, tap. Tap, tap, tap.

Jim finally gave up and left. In school the next day, we ignored each other.

But now, with Cal, I'd pieced a few things together, and one of the things I'd figured out was that I did not want to die a virgin. And if I didn't get picked soon, I'd end up like Miss Williamson, the French teacher in school.

Miss Williamson was short and round, and she churned her way down the hallway between the gauntlet of students leaning against the lockers and bragged to her classes about being a "fifty-year old virgin and proud of it."

We made fun of her and joked about her sad existence. No man had ever chosen her, and she'd turned that tragedy into a club of one. I felt dangerously close to this being me. A girl no boy wanted. A tragic figure. The stuff of crazed single women in the movies and on TV. Lacking a man, a woman was capable of anything. Murder. Self-harm. Insanity. Being an embarrassment and a burden to her family. Getting too many cats.

In those days a young girl could go to the health clinic, get an examination, and a prescription for birth-control pills without parental consent and without questions, and that is exactly what I did.

At the drugstore next to the health clinic, I paid for my pills with my waitressing tips. A one-month supply cost $2.85, and every month I counted out my change and paid the pharmacist in quarters and dimes.

I kept the small yellow plastic case, its little cream-colored pills captured in a blister pack labeled with the days of the week, in my purse. Before homeroom at school, I swallowed one down at the water fountain in the hallway. On weekends I cupped one in the palm of my hand as I went to the bathroom in the mornings.

I had to be on the pill for a month before they took effect, so Cal and I waited to have sex. I appreciate the restraint and respect that Cal showed in this regard. On the other hand, it would have been nice if the month of waiting to have sex had been a month of hot and heavy necking, but it wasn't that. It was just waiting, dry time ticking by. And in the waiting, the deed became the thing. The penis inside the vagina would be the glorious thing, as exalted as boys themselves were.

But it wasn't glorious.

I was sure this was my fault. I was so sure of it, that I couldn't admit the disappointment to myself. Just as I couldn't admit to myself what a disappointment Cal was. How I wasn't really attracted to him. How I didn't love him. To admit such things would be to admit to sin, a journey straight to my mother's technicolor hell, the teaching I'd simultaneously rejected and absorbed as absolute truth. I convinced myself that, contrary to my mother's teaching, it was okay to have sex outside of marriage, but not outside of love. So, I set about trying to make myself feel about Cal what I was supposed to feel. Giddy inside. Happy to see him. Fuzzy with anticipation. Love. I tried to feel love.

4.

We went out every Saturday night. Cal picked me up in either his Mustang or on his motorcycle. We went uptown or to someone's house, but all our dates on Saturday night ended at his house, where his parents conveniently went to bed while Cal and I turned on the late-night monster movie and had sex on the carpet of the den. I wanted the sex, not because it was great, but because it was skin on skin. It was holding. It was physical closeness and as close to romance as I could get.

Our interests were chasms apart. Cal didn't read. He didn't appreciate writing and certainly not poetry. He didn't like sentimental movies. He liked his motorcycle. He liked his car. He liked his guitar. He liked getting high. Any attempted conversation about anything else only irritated him. If I mentioned a book I'd read, he'd glare at me. If I talked about wanting to search for wild asparagus, à la Euell Gibbons' book on foraging, he glared at me. Even bringing up the magnificent lightning strike on a meter cover I'd witnessed on Franklin Street, in which the lightning had balled up into little marbles rolling around on the sidewalk before dissipating, brought on a glare. He hadn't seen it. It wasn't his story.

Why was I telling him this? I went further and further inward, sharing nothing.

Yet I did not end it. I did not break it off, largely because I lacked an alternative. If another boy had stepped in and spoken for me, I'd have easily slipped away, but no one did. So what if he wasn't interested in what I had to say? So what if he glared at me to show his discomfort? So what if he probably read the CliffNotes instead of the book for English class? At least he took me somewhere on Saturday nights. At least he took me away from sitting on the scratchy brown couch in the living room watching TV with my parents. At least he took me away from my mother, whom I was still careful not to ignite into a crying jag.

At the end of the school year, Cal graduated. We spent the summer driving around, visiting people, getting high, taking long motorcycle rides out in the country. I liked the motorcycle. Nothing was expected of me on the motorcycle. Conversation was impossible, so I leaned on Cal's back and enjoyed the wind coming over his shoulder into my face.

I often didn't know where we were when we went riding on the motorcycle. Cal seemed to have an innate sense of direction and an understanding of how the country roads connected to each other. We stopped at rural gas stations for crackers and Cokes, and I enjoyed being a spectacle to the old men gathered outside. I enjoyed imagining myself as the hot young babe on the back of a cool guy's motorcycle.

In the fall I returned to school, and without college on his radar, and with an exemption from service in the Vietnam War that, when I asked about it, earned me a glare and no answer, Cal got a job on a construction site.

Now when he called on Sunday night and I asked, "How are you doing?" he replied with his words so dragged out that had they been visible they'd have left a mud trail. "Alllll riiiiiight, I gueeess, for a Sundaaay," Cal said.

"What's wrong with Sunday?" I asked.

"Tomorrow's Mondaaay," Cal said.

"Yeah?"

"I have to go back to wooork," he reminded me.

I didn't yet know how tough a low-wage menial job could be. I didn't yet know the demoralizing nature of such jobs, how trapped a person can feel, how looked-down-on one was for working with your hands, how little money one earns, how physically ground up one can be at the end of the day. So I answered with my own Monday.

"Oh. Yeah, I have to go back to school," I said, as if the two were equivalent, which they were not. I'd check into homeroom, answer roll call, but then I'd be skipping class, hitchhiking into Chapel Hill, wandering the campus, getting stoned with Becky, and eating Twinkies washed down with Cokes.

But even if this weren't true, even if I had a crummy job too, even if my feet were swollen from standing all day, it wouldn't have mattered. Cal's misery took primacy over everything else. It was easy to see that Cal was always willing to get a jump on the blues and drag everyone he could down with him. Cal's moods were sticky, and they clung to me like the beggar's lice that affixed themselves to my jeans when I walked through a field.

And still, I did not break it off. In some ways it simply seemed like an extension of my already exquisite skills at navigating my mother's fragile emotions and shuttling my needs and thoughts underground. I was primed for it, primed to be with Cal. He was a man so different from my father that they didn't seem to be of the same species. But he was so like my mother that I merely walked on new eggshells for a new person.

I wanted out of my family house, and I wanted out badly, but the only map my parents had laid out for me was college, a wedding, a brief time without children, then the first baby, followed by another and another and another. I don't know how my parents managed to maintain this fantasy for me. With grades as dismal as mine, I wasn't going to get into college. But academic prowess was never the goal. Marrying me off and having grandchildren was the ultimate reward for having kept me alive all these years.

"How many children do you want?" the old ladies at the church had always trilled.

None was not an answer. "One" would be met with dispute. "Don't you want another so he can have some company?"

The more the better. Four, six, ten, fifteen? However many children I had, their father would support us. I was never taught otherwise. I never had it impressed upon me that eventually I'd be on my own. Eventually, I might have to pay rent and bills. I had no concept of rent and bills. I'd rejected the life my parents had charted for me, but I didn't replace it with anything. Being on my own sounded blissful, but in my imagination, I lived with magical support, in a beautiful house, where my only job was to make it nice and write poetry.

I had the house already picked out. It was a large yellow Victorian house on Franklin Street beside Hardee's. The house was barely visible behind huge overgrown boxwood bushes lining the street. I'd never noticed it when accompanying my father on a run to Hardee's for hamburgers, but on foot when I skipped school with Becky, we often peered up the weed-choked driveway as we passed by on our way to the thrift shop. It had clearly been uninhabited for some time. One day we decided to go see it.

It was fall. The trees surrounding the house had lost their leaves. They'd piled up against the back door and rattled as we pushed our way through and tried the doorknob. The knob turned, and the door easily swung open. We stepped into a large kitchen with a long counter and cast-iron sink with a drainboard, a window above overlooking the back-yard. I could see remnants of a garden out back, a fence sur-rounding vegetation, a fallen down gate, a bench beneath a crepe myrtle tree with its strange, mottled bark.

There was no furniture in the kitchen, or in the rest of the house. As we walked through, our feet tracked prints through the dust on the hardwood floors. The downstairs living room had a bay window and a fireplace surrounded with green tiles. Another room across the hall also had a bay window and a fireplace surrounded with blue tiles. An ele-gant, curved staircase with a smooth banister led to several bedrooms and a bath. The bath had a clawfoot tub.

In Alabama, in the house my father grew up in, I'd bathed in a clawfoot tub, and it was the most comfortable tub in the world. Its back curved to meet the back of any human who soaked in it, so unlike the boxy bathtubs in our suburban home. I loved clawfoot tubs.

Becky and I sat in one of the bay windows, admiring the tiling surrounding the fireplace—and then we continued our walk to the thrift shop. We didn't talk about the house, but it was on my mind. And it was on my mind heavily. Mentally, I was moving in.

This was the place for me. I knew it, and I would claim it. I would sweep the dead leaves from its entrance. I would reclaim the garden. I would polish the curved banister. I would sleep in a brass bed and have tea at a round table in the kitchen with a vase of flowers always at its center. This was the future I dreamed of. This house would support me. I had no idea how I would support it. Or even that a house needed support.

Skipping school alone one day, I passed the construction site where Cal worked. I looked down into a hole next to the sidewalk, and there he was, digging around a pipe buried in mud. "Hey, Cal," I said.

He looked up. "Hey," he answered, wretchedly, and then he returned to digging.

But I kept standing there, waiting for more, and of course he kept digging. Finally, he looked up again, and said, "Go away. I'm working."

On the phone that night he said, "Don't do that again."

"Okay."

"Terry might have seen."

I knew that Terry was his boss. Cal had complained about him.

"Okay," I said. "I'm sorry."

He was right, of course, but I was hurt. And, what did I expect from Cal as I stood above him looking down in the hole he'd been tasked to muck around in? Did I really think he'd climb out and talk to me? Did I think he'd be glad to see me? Did I think he was the same person down in the hole as he was on a Saturday night? Or driving his motorcycle? Or sifting pot down the spine of a double record album so the seeds rolled out?

For Christmas that year Cal saved up enough money from that shitty, hateful construction job to buy me a long, beige leather coat with a fuzzy white lining. It was the kind of coat my mother never would have agreed to buy for me.

It fell mid-calf, was beautiful, and fit me perfectly. I don't remember what I got for him, but I remember being pleased by his gift to me. It didn't make up for the glares I received for talking about something he couldn't process or the way he mud-dragged his words or his sticky beggar's-lice moods, but it was at least a physical manifestation of what a relationship was supposed to look like.

I paired the coat with a fake fur hat I got from Kroger's for cheap. I knew I looked good in this get-up, with my long brown hair and the fake fur framing my face and the coat hugging my hips.

Senior year of high school was a good year. I skipped school every day. I smoked dope every day. Becky and I wandered the UNC campus. We walked to the thrift shop. We ate hamburgers from Hector's and bought bags of jellybeans from Rose's on Franklin Street. I wrote poems and ditties and journal entries in the notebook I always carried with me. Senior year of high school was the most spacious year of my life.

But things were changing. My friends had plans beyond high school, beyond the brick buildings and the hallways and skipping classes. Beyond Chapel Hill, beyond hanging out with me and getting high. We were largely a white-collar school, and the freaks were largely white-collar kids, and even the scrappiest dudes and the biggest potheads in our vibrant circus talked about going to college. But I didn't want to go to college. I'd had enough of tests and teachers and folding my long body into the too-small desks. I'd had enough of continuous proof of my inadequacies.

My brother said college was different than high school. The classrooms were bigger. The teachers were called professors, and the teaching was different. Better. Deeper. You had access to more knowledge in college. You learned more truthful things in college.

But not only did I not buy it, I was pissed off to hear it. If they wanted us to learn the truth, why didn't they start with the truth? Besides, I didn't need college to be a writer.

Even with Saturday night dates and being stoned 90 percent of the time, I'd already written a novel. I turned it in late as my senior project, over one hundred handwritten pages with characters whose names and hair color I managed to keep consistent. In my novel there was some conflict, not much originality, major plot holes, and the stupid premise that a guy drafted into the Vietnam War could be so morally opposed to that war that he chose not to put bullets in his gun. Despite all that, I received a B on it, my teacher being kind enough to reward the effort.

Writing was my thing, my only thing. But even my English and Creative Writing teachers didn't see it as a useful skill to take into the future. My classmates were going to college with plans to become doctors, lawyers, social workers, dentists. From my perspective they were going straight. These were straight jobs. I thought we were part of the revolution. I thought we were changing the world. But suddenly talk as we skipped school and passed a joint from hand to hand, was all about college applications, the universities that had sent acceptance letters, moving away. In the summer between high school and college, some planned to strike out on adventures, driving across America or hitchhiking through Europe. Adulthood reached out and grabbed them. Adulthood took my classmates into its "you're-old-enough-now" maw. It ate them up with freedom. They were going places and I was not.

Caught up with their own plans, my friends didn't ask what I was going to do once I graduated, but parents and teachers did. It was the only thing they could talk about. I was seventeen years old, and the question pounded relentlessly like the drums in the old Tarzan movies I'd watched with my brother.

What are your plans? What are your plans? What are your plans, plans, plans, plans?

A merciless drumbeat I would have to respond to. I was expected to have something well thought out and previously discussed with my parents to say. Something pre-approved on the conveyor belt of a young girl becoming a woman. I stood on the abyss, the drums beating behind me. Decide, the drums said. Jump. Know what you want to be and do for the rest of your life.

Writer?

No, not that.

Besides the very real message that I could not pursue writing, I received conflicting messages about what college was for. My mother hammered away at me about it. She gleefully told me I needed to go to college so I could get my M.R.S. Then she told me I could become a dental assistant. Or if I learned to type, I could at least be a secretary.

Had my mother pointed out that typing would be a useful skill for a writer to have, I'd have learned it. Had the goal been something I wanted to do, I'd have been willing to take steps toward it. But every option mentioned put writing on the back burner, writing as the thing I might do later, as a hobby, after I'd completed this other, more important, less interesting, soul-draining, adult-approved thing first.

Once again, it was my mother who had inadvertently encouraged my writing habit. When I was ten, after having read a novel set during the Civil War whose story and characters lingered and haunted me, I told her that when I grew up, I wanted to write "history novels." We were on a family trip, my father driving and my mother in the passenger seat, doling out Dixie cups of cold water from the large brown thermos at her feet to anyone who asked.

She turned around and said, "Good. That's a good thing to do."

And I sucked that up. The pride in her voice. The sound of approval. The emphatic way she'd declared my goal to be *good*. I'd never heard that from her before, and it stayed with me.

But now it had transformed from something good to something unrealistic, irrational, senseless, and fanciful. Something had happened between the time I was ten years old and wanting to write "history novels" and the time I was seventeen years old still wanting to write "history novels." The ball hadn't changed but the game had.

The pressure to go to college mounted. My parents insisted that I take the SATs. I can't imagine why they pursued this, given the report cards I brought home for their signatures. I was just barely getting out of high school, but I submitted to taking the SATs just to quiet them. My father drove me to Durham where I sat in an anonymous institutional building with scores of young people my age, all of them, I assumed, earnest about doing well and getting accepted to a university. But I just wanted to get it over with, because afterwards, Becky and I were going to see *Yellow Submarine*.

I have no idea how I scored on the SATs. It must have been very low, because no one ever brought it up again. I hadn't tried very hard on the test. I hadn't cared. Tests were my enemies. Always had been, and always would be.

I graduated. My mother asked again and again if I was sure I didn't want to don a cap and gown and attend the ceremony. I was very sure, and I was very depressed. I'd hated school, but I'd loved the freedom I found once I'd taken the leap of rejecting everything about it. And now that was over. There was no school to skip. There was no easy social life.

My friends scattered. They were gone. The people I saw now were Cal's friends. Boys who weren't going to college and had avoided the war and worked as mechanics and carpenters, or boys who were a year or two behind me in school, young and full of themselves and not yet facing the senior-year dilemma of what to do with their lives. It would be no problem for them though. Stoners that they were, they had the world by the balls.

Cal and I were equally adrift, both living in our parents' houses, and both anxious to leave. And so we hatched a plan to live together. I don't remember how it came about, how it got brought up, but I do remember that there was no fanta-sizing about where this home would be, or what it would be like.

Cal did not fantasize. Imagining a nice large kitchen or an Indian-print bedspread hanging on the wall behind our bed or wanting houseplants and a cat would only bring me glares. He knew more about the real world than I did. With his parents' co-signing he'd taken out a loan to buy his mo-torcycle. He understood the need for money, but he didn't understand the need for imagination. He could never engage in what might be. That we managed to even discuss moving in together only tells me he must have been as desperate to move into a place of his own as I was.

This would be the next step I made into adulthood. It would get me out of my parents' petri dish and into a home of my own. I could take college off the table. I could point to work and home and my relationship with Cal as what I was doing with my life.

I could decorate as I wished. Listen to music as I wished. I could go to the grocery store and buy hotdogs and fix dinner and make brownies. We could smoke dope whenever we wanted and have sex too, and we wouldn't have to hide it.

I thought that being alone with Cal in our own place would be the factor we needed for romance, for a melding of spirits and bodies. We would have sex in a real bed. No more carpet burns from sex in his parents' den while Mothra terrorized Japan. No more Mothra. No more *Creature from the Black Lagoon* swimming beneath a woman in a shimmering white bathing suit. No more *Godzilla*, *Night of the Living Dead*, *Frankenstein*, *Dracula*, *The Wolf Man*, *The Mummy*.

These movies had terrified me when my brother and I got up early on Saturday mornings to watch them, and they terrified me still. As Cal humped away on top of me during our Saturday night sex, I could never completely ignore the roaring and growling and screams that were the background to our love-making, which is what I called it. Love-making.

Sex was puzzling to me. I wanted it, and I was sure that a deeper connection to Cal could be found there, but it eluded me. The monster movies and the carpet burns didn't help. Moving in together, I reasoned, would make everything better. Having our own place. A dedicated bed. Privacy. These were things I longed for.

We decided we would each tell our parents and then confer on the next step, but I hadn't worked up the nerve to tell mine yet when Cal said to me one night, while we were sitting in his car waiting for a train to go by, "I talked to my folks. *Mother doesn't want us to live together, and you don't want to get married, so..."*

He glared at me. The train rumbled along in front of us, car after car carrying coal to the UNC power plant. That train must have had a hundred cars. The unfinished sentence hung in the air between us. My future hung there.

Mother doesn't want us to live together, and you don't want to get married, so...

There were so many ways that sentence could be finished.

So... this is a proposal?

So... we're breaking up if I say no?

So... I'm being left alone?

So... you'll do what your mother says?

So... it's all on me what happens next?

Cal's glare pressed into me. The train still rumbling along was the metaphor neatly writing itself and solidifying its own heartless reality. Everything I knew so far flashed before my eyes, and it wasn't much. My room with its single maple beds, beside my parents' room. The dope I had to keep hidden. The fact that I couldn't drive. For all his faults, for all his glares, for all his inabilities to have conversations about things I wanted to talk about, Cal had been the one thing that consistently got me away from my parents' house and their scrutiny. The caboose went by, and I said, "Okay, I'll marry you."

If Cal reached over and squeezed my hand in gratitude or love, I don't remember. I do remember the railroad-crossing bells ringing and the light flashing and the gate lifting and Cal driving over the tracks.

I did not feel bells ringing inside me. I did not feel a gate lifting. I was seventeen years old. I had only wanted to live with Cal as a way of getting out of my parents' house, and now it had become marriage.

I told my folks the next day.

"You're seventeen," my mother said.

"I'll be eighteen in a month, then I can do what I want," I said defiantly, defending the thing I really didn't want.

"Well, we'd rather you get married than live together," my father said.

And there it was. My parents would accept marriage as a viable alternative to college. I would be folded under the protective wings of Cal, a boy-man who combed the hair he saw in the mirror, but not the hair he didn't see in the mirror. What was most important to my parents was that I would not be condemned to hell. God's punishing moodiness would be appeased, God with his insatiable appetite for irreproachable and unblemished humans after he'd had the audacity to create us in his own image.

5.

My mother insisted on having enough time to throw a shower for me, and my father enough time to rent folding chairs and a candelabra for the screened-in back porch where the wedding was to be held. So, we picked a convenient Saturday in August. My mother and I shopped for invitations and shoes and ordered a cake. She and Cal's mother conferred on how many guests to invite. We sent invitations to two of Cal's friends. None of mine. Mine were off on adventures.

We proceeded as if all this was normal. As if I had made a rational decision. It was as if my parents were as anxious to get me out of the house under their terms as I was to leave under any terms at all.

When it came to my wedding, the only things I had an opinion on were my dress and the flowers. I already owned the dress, a long cream-colored muslin hippie dress, which I'd bought for eleven dollars from a headshop in town, and which my boobs did not fill. As for the flowers, I wanted exactly two. A single white rose for me and a single red rose for my only bridesmaid.

I wanted my best friend from first grade through junior high to serve as my bridesmaid. Laura and I had drifted apart when I started smoking dope, but we'd always said hello in the hallways at school, and sometimes we still talked. I loved her still, and she loved me. I called her and asked, and she agreed. She later told me that when she got off the phone, she told her mom, "Nancy's getting married." And her mother said, "What's she doing that for?"

My mother mentioned birth control several times, and every time I said I would take care of it until finally I said I had taken care of it. I showed her the yellow plastic case of pills I'd been hiding in my purse for over a year now. Another lie she was perfectly willing to swallow. And what did it matter now? I was getting married. I was going to be a wife. A sanctioned woman at last. As far as my mother was concerned, she'd done her job, delivering me intact (in her mind) to a man who would be my husband. She didn't need to believe anything else.

My mother's best friend, Jim's mother, hosted the shower for me. Because my mother had so few friends, and because my own friends were scattered and gone, the women who attended were all friends of my future mother-in-law. I had no idea who these people were. I sat on the screened-in back porch of our neighbor's house, awkwardly unwrapping gifts from strangers, strangers who imagined I needed to start my married life off with a cut crystal salad bowl rimmed with silver (I received two) and cut crystal coasters also rimmed with silver.

It was my own fault. I hadn't registered anywhere. My mother kept on pushing it. "We need to go to Belk and register." I hated the idea. I thought it sounded square, and weird, and I hadn't been to Belk Department Store since I'd found the thrift shop and started dressing myself. I had no desire to go deal with those salesclerks again, those women who never saw me in the first place. They would undoubtedly gush and congratulate me on landing a man, and I would be expected to gush and flitter as well. To go to Belk with my mother, to register for wedding gifts, would only push me harder into the deadness I felt inside. And I was fighting that deadness. Fighting it by not acknowledging it. By pretending I knew exactly what I was doing. Pretending that I was hopelessly in love with Cal. Pretend. Pretend. Pretend.

My mother twittered and gushed about the wedding and my future. She kept calling the little yellow rental house we'd found "our little love nest." I rolled my eyes. This was bullshit, but I carried the same bullshit inside me. I couldn't help but want the fairy tale my mother spun. It should be fun. It should be great. Maybe it would be. Maybe Cal would magically transform from frog to prince. He didn't.

One night he said that his friend Earl Johnson, a man whom I did not like because of his caustic humor, told Cal that he was making a big mistake marrying me. Earl predicted that I was going to make Cal miserable.

"Earl said, 'Oh, she's real nice now,'" Cal reported, "'but all that will change after you get married. You'll see. She'll be a real bitch then. She'll have you by the short hairs.'"

Cal looked at me accusingly, his usual glare, waiting for an explanation, waiting for me to convince him that Earl Johnson was wrong.

I was keeping hope on life-support, IV tubes of dead dreams running to its body, the bags of fluid slack and dry, and here Cal was glaring at me over something he'd taken in as truth from a man who lived alone with his motorcycles in a house with no running water. It was ludicrous to be asked by the man I was going to marry to defend myself against the hypothetical predictions of another man, a man whom Cal seemed to believe had a Gandalf-like bead on the world of women.

I was furious with both of them. But to show it would only prove Earl Johnson's prediction, so I delivered the requested reassurance and asked nothing in return.

A week before the wedding while at work, I tried to move a small industrial refrigerator door that was leaning up against the wall. I managed to lift it (I was strong) but ended up dropping it on my foot (I wasn't that strong). I didn't break anything, but my foot was swollen and bruised. It could not be comfortably crammed into one of the white shoes, half of the pair my mother and I had hunted down for the wedding, and yet I shoved it in. I managed to walk (not limp) down the aisle on my parents' large screened-in back porch, created by two rows of rented metal chairs on which our guests' buttocks chilled awaiting the ceremony.

Cal stood at the end of the porch between the candelabras. His brown suit was too large. The cuffs of his pants puddled to the floor. He looked as ridiculous as he did the evening of our first date with the pink scarf tied jauntily around his neck. I wore my muslin hippie dress and carried my single white rose. My hair was pulled back with two tendrils curled and sprayed into submission alongside my ears. My father walked me down the aisle and turned me over to Cal.

We spoke our vows. We cut the cake and slid it into each other's mouths. Both sets of parents were teetotalers so there was no alcohol, although there was a rented crystal punch bowl containing a brew made from ginger ale and pineapple juice.

Our honeymoon was spent in our new home, arranging what little furniture we had. My parents gave us the scratchy brown couch I'd grown up with, the one I'd always hated, and Cal's parents bought us drapes for the large front windows.

His father installed them before we moved in. I wanted to be grateful, but no one had consulted me about what I wanted in my new home. Those drapes with their huge brown and beige flowers blooming across a cream-colored background reflected my mother-in-law's tastes, not mine.

Cal and I spread the new bedspread from his parents on the bed (again with the big-ass brown and beige flowers) and shoved a trunk that had been in his teenage room in front of the scratchy brown couch. I placed the stack of silver-rimmed cut-crystal coasters on it.

My mother had used twelve years' worth of Green Stamps collected from her weekly shopping trips at the A&P to buy us a table with four matching chairs for the kitchen. The table and chairs folded like a card table, and all were padded with dark green vinyl. When I sat down in one of the chairs the air went out of the vinyl and made a little farty sound. Phffft.

It was ugly, like everything else.

I put a foil-wrapped piece of wedding cake in the freezer. My mother had handed it to me after the guests left and told me I should freeze it, and then, to celebrate our first anniversary, I should thaw it out and eat it. "It's tradition," she said, giddily, perhaps remembering her own first anniversary with my father.

Before leaving home, I slowly typed one of my poems up on the family typewriter, and once I got it right, without mistakes, I cut all the extra white paper away from it. I'd done this with the express purpose of taping it to our refrigerator, which I did now, the wedding cake chilling its fancy frosting behind the door. It was a ditty more than a poem, but a wise one and one I would now have to heed.

Could've and should've
Are words we don't use.
They only depress us
And give us the blues.
     –Nancy Powell

My married name felt strange on my tongue, strange in my mouth, and strange in my pen. At least my initials hadn't changed.

Cal tacked up some motorcycle posters in the living room, installed the stereo, and pulled the big-flowery drapes closed before plopping down on the couch and rolling a joint. I sat beside him. He lit the joint and passed it to me. I took a toke. He pulled one of the cut-crystal coasters off its stack to use as an ashtray. That was fine with me. I couldn't see any other purpose for them.

I tried to make a home out of the weird hodgepodge of domestic items we'd either inherited or been given. But what a strange mix. The couch I'd wanted to escape from, the hated huge flowers on the drapes and our bedspread, the cut crystal salad bowls rimmed with silver, the vinyl-padded table with its folding chairs. One night, for a lark, I served a salad in one of the cut crystal salad bowls rimmed with silver. I enjoyed how out of place it looked on the vinyl-padded table, as though we'd stolen it and brought it into our crummy outlaw lair. But I should have known that Cal wouldn't eat salad, from this bowl or any other. Whenever we'd gone to a fast-food place, he ordered a cheeseburger. When asked what he'd like on it, he answered, "Maybe a little salt."

I can count on my fingers the food Cal deigned to put in his mouth—all boring and bland and mostly in hues of brown and grey.

He refused anything with onions in it. Eggs were never fried or boiled or poached or baked but always scrambled, hard. He liked corned beef hash, Campbell's Chunky Beef Soup, and fried chicken, but not broiled chicken, not baked chicken, not smothered chicken, not chicken any way but fried. Vegetables were completely off limits, except for potatoes and canned green beans.

There was nothing juicy in my life anymore. I went from skipping school and smoking dope with my friends to working and coming home to ugly drapes, a scratchy brown couch, motorcycle posters and cooking dull, colorless food.

6.

My journals and notebooks, filled with my poems and short stories and my one novel that earned me a B, sat on the floor of our closet surrounded by shoes. My books lined a make-shift shelf beneath the hated drapes.

I still wrote. I still kept a journal. I still complained to the page.

In my journal I wrote of an incident that occurred a month after our wedding, in which I'd forgotten, for the first time in two years, to take my birth control pill.

I casually mentioned it to Cal while standing on the heating grate that dominated the floor of the little hallway between all the rooms.

"You better not forget," Cal said, a threatening tinge in his voice I'd never heard before. He made it clear what that threatening tinge was about. "If you get pregnant, I'll leave. I swear I will."

And then he walked into the living room and put a record on.

I was stunned. Hadn't Cal spoken vows to me just the month before? For better, for worse?

I didn't want children either. I'd seen what children did to my mother. I'd heard the heavy sighs and witnessed the constant work, the lack of time to call her own. My mother's life was the best motivation I had for birth control, and regardless of the rumors Earl Johnson and others might have filled Cal's head with, I had no intention of trapping Calvin Powell deeper into this marriage by getting pregnant.

But where the fuck was his pride? Where was his sense of honor? Of embarrassment? Of shame? He had none.

I stood in the hallway, the heating grate cutting into my bare feet. "Whipping Post" by The Allman Brothers filled my ears. I heard Cal sit down on the couch and pick up his guitar. He picked along with the song while The Allman Brothers sang about a woman doing a man wrong, about tying him to the "whipping post."

The irony is stupidly heavy here. Just like the train going by when I agreed to marry Cal. If this were fiction, I would not include it.

Fuck you, Cal, I thought. Who is tying whom to a whipping post? I popped the pill out of its blister pack and swallowed, not out of deference to him, but out of self-protection.

In an odd twist, now that I was safely married, my mother might have begun to see me as a writer. She found a used bookcase and a large oak desk and had them delivered to our house. I don't know why she suddenly saw me in need of a desk and a bookcase. These items had never been mentioned when our parents were busy furnishing our home. But like most things with my mother, there was an order in which to do things. Now that I had my M.R.S. I could be anything I wanted within that framework.

Alone in the house the day they were delivered, I pushed the furniture around in the living room. I pushed the desk into a corner. I pushed the bookcase perpendicular to it and stapled a panel of blue-print fabric on the back to create a private nook to call my own. I arranged my journals and books on the bookcase. I put pens and pencils and a Pink Pearl eraser in the narrow top drawer of the desk. And I placed my current journal on the desk, front and center. This was my house now, and there was no danger my siblings would read my private thoughts.

Shortly after getting married, we each got new jobs. Cal left the construction site and found work as a janitor at the local mall. And I, never good at waitressing, had spent a day walking Franklin Street, applying for jobs in the shops, and landing one at a new drugstore, which I will call Chain Store #1. To get to Chain Store #1, I walked from our house to the end of the road and caught a chugging orange bus, which had once belonged to the city of Atlanta, into town.

Come Thanksgiving, Cal's mother and mine began vying for our presence at their tables. We chose to go to Cal's parents' house. It was easier. I could relax there because Cal could relax there, whereas when at my parents' house, Cal answered every question from my father with "uh, uh, uh." The simplest questions. Questions that required only yes, please, or no, thank you. Or fine, thanks for asking.

"Would you like some more iced tea, Cal?"

"Uh, uh, uh, yeah, I guess so."

"How's the new job going, Cal?"

"Uh, uh, uh, okay, I guess."

Cal said "uh, uh, uh" a lot. His sister told me that when he and his family arrived at my parents' house for our wedding, my father answered the door, and Cal had said, "Uh, uh, uh, is Nancy here?"

He embarrassed me. Why couldn't he step up his game even just a little? Why couldn't he simply be warm with my parents, as I was with his?

At my parents' house it was hard not to face the huge mistake I'd made in marrying Cal. At his parents' house it was easier to ignore my feelings, to pretend this was exactly what I wanted. With his parents, there was no "uh, uh, uh."

This wasn't a real stammer. It was a fake stammer, something he did to buy himself time, to figure out how to engage.

One day on Franklin Street, soon after we were married, we were confronted with a pair of panhandlers. "Hey man, you got any spare change?"

"Uh, uh, uh," Cal said, and then he had a bright idea of how to get out of this. He pointed to me and said, "I gave all my money to her."

"Thanks a lot, Cal," I muttered, and then I shook my head at them and said no, and they moved on.

Cal never gave his money to me. I gave mine to him.

I was paid every other week. When I got home, Cal asked if I'd cashed my check, and then he asked for the money, and I handed it over. Except for bus fare for the week, I had no cash. He never slid a five back to me. There were no hamburgers or Cokes in my life anymore. No impulse purchases. No eleven-dollar hippie dresses from the headshop in town. All my money, it seemed, was needed for bills and rent. I didn't know how to pay either, so I turned it over to him to take care of, but all the same, our mailbox filled with envelopes sporting orange Past Due stickers on the front.

Having rebuffed my parents' invitation for Thanksgiving, my mother insisted that we owed them Christmas. My mother was fierce about it. We belonged to her on Christmas day.

I thought I'd left home. I thought I had my own place now. I thought I didn't belong to them anymore. But it seemed to me that the only way to end the holiday tug of war would be to either move far away from both sets of parents or to have children. If we had children, I'd have every reason to stay home Christmas morning.

But Cal had already promised he would leave me if I got pregnant. And I wasn't planning on it anyway, despite the comments from total strangers when seeing the shine of my new wedding ring.

When are you going to start your family?

Another relentless drumbeat in my life, as unfaltering as the questions about my future at the end of high school had been.

When a woman at the bank asked me this, I answered, "I don't want to have children."

She looked at me as though I'd said I killed chickens and drank their blood, as though I was a witch and should be burned at the stake, as though I was a freak of nature.

"That's selfish," she snapped.

Damn these women, and it was always women, insisting I join their club of motherhood, insisting that tying myself down with diapers and bottles and overwhelm was the only way to truly be a woman. I was young and female and married, which was all the permission they needed to assault me with talk of reproducing. These unwelcome comments swarmed and buzzed around me and bit hard.

Even if Cal hadn't promised to leave me a month after promising, at our wedding, not to leave me, I'd have done everything within my power not to procreate with him. It was easy to see that he'd be a lousy father. I'd be the one taking care of the kid, all alone. I never forgot a birth control pill again.

One day, during my lunch break at Chain Store #1, I walked across the street to the bookstore. I just intended to look. I had no money with me. But there on display was a slim, wide picture book called *Handmade Houses: A Guide to the Woodbutcher's Art* by Art Boericke and Barry Shapiro. The cover showed a wooden house with a stained-glass window and shake shingles.

I opened the book to a picture of a small cottage built on a platform surrounded by a sea of lush ferns. The house was topped with wide wooden shingles. A tall stovepipe stabbed itself into the sky, and a neat pile of firewood was stacked against one wall.

I flipped the pages again and found a clawfoot tub in a room with the overhang of a boulder making a ceiling. There were houses with windows overlooking the woods. Houses with enamel cookstoves, one of them blue. Houses with rocking chairs surrounding a brick hearth with a woodstove. And one house with a tipi-like structure at its top, windows at the zenith, a mattress covered with an Indian-print bedspread on the floor.

These houses were so different from any houses I had known that as I gazed at the pictures, I felt swept into a fable, into another world, into new possibilities, just as I'd felt swept into new possibilities when I'd watched the coverage of Woodstock four years earlier.

My parents had a charge account at the bookstore, and I took that book home, charged to them. Riding home on the bus, I looked at every picture. I went inside each house. Dark wooden floors were covered with ancient rugs, looking like magic carpets one could ride into the air. The carpets were anchored down with equally magical velvet couches or rocking chairs or handmade tables or beds built of shaved tree limbs, sanded and polished. Stained glass in stairwells cast discs of colored light on floors and walls. There were pots and pans hanging from beams, baskets filled with produce from a garden, candles and kerosene lamps and clay bowls filled with apples that sat on top of large wooden spools turned into tables.

Not a motorcycle poster in sight. No big-flowery drapes. No scratchy brown couch. No vinyl-topped table with chairs that went *pffft* when you sat down.

I was completely seduced. I wanted what I saw. I wanted a man who could and would build such a house. I wanted a garden, toiled over and harvested together. I wanted a man who would eat an apple or a salad or an eggplant. Or an artichoke.

One day, when I lived at my parents' house after my siblings had all left, my father brought home a bag of artichokes. "What are they?" I asked, eyeing the strange-looking aliens after he'd emptied the bag on the kitchen counter.

"They're thistles," my father said.

"'Tiggers don't like thistles,'" I said, quoting *Winnie-the-Pooh*.

"But Eeyore does, and I think you will too."

At the table with the red-and-white-checked plastic cloth, my father showed me how to peel the leaves off the artichokes, how to dip the end of each leaf in a bit of mayonnaise, how to scrape the meaty part off the leaves with my teeth. My father was right. I did love artichokes. How had I gone from the house of a man who would bring home artichokes to the house of a man who would not eat an apple?

I wanted a home with soul. A home like those in *Handmade Houses: A Guide to the Woodbutcher's Art*. Or like the abandoned yellow Victorian house beside Hardee's that Becky and I had walked through on one of those spacious days of skipping school.

The memory of that house, of looking out at the garden through the window over the sink, was vivid. Vivid because I'd subtracted and added so many things to it. I'd subtracted the weeds in the garden. I'd cleaned off the bench, found the flowers and nursed them back to health. I'd fixed the fence and the gate. I'd added a morning cup of tea at a round table. A soft breeze through the open door. A rumpled bed upstairs.

A bed I would make after I had my tea. I always made my bed. Home mattered to me in a way it didn't seem to matter to others I knew. Homemaking seemed square and straight and not hip. It seemed bourgeois to care about home the way I did. But here, in this book, was proof of hippies who did care about home.

I replaced my dream of the house beside Hardee's with a funky hippie house in the woods. This was what I wanted. I wanted to be away from town. I wanted to be in a place that was rustic, where inside and outside organically mingled. I wanted to be in a place that was too inconvenient for Cal's parents to drop by and check on us every time they heard a wreck reported on their police scanner. I wanted to be in a place where anyone who wanted to see me had to hike up a mountain. A place that couldn't get torn down as the yellow Victorian house beside Hardee's had been, making way for a parking lot, a shopping center, more asphalt. The weedy garden razed and buried. The fencing and gate pushed over. The crepe myrtle swept down with a bulldozer. The house itself crumbled into a pile and hauled off as though it had never been.

7.

Every night as we ate our dinner at the vinyl-topped table, sitting on the chairs that went *pffft*, there would be a knock on the door. Cal would get up to answer it. From the kitchen I'd hear him say, "Hey, man. Come on in. I'm just finishing up dinner. I'll be right out." And then I'd hear the first boy of the evening reply. He would be followed by a second and a third and a fourth. We had become the house without parental supervision, the go-to pad, and we had a stream of young boys visiting us nightly.

For someone who had always wanted the magic of boys surrounding her, I now had it. Only they weren't so magical anymore. They were predictable. As Cal finished his dinner of whatever bland, brown food I'd put in front of him, the boys answered the door for each other.

"Hey, man. Come on in." As if they lived here.

Then the jokes started up. The same jokes every night, followed by guffaws.

I knew their voices. Some of these boys I liked, some I didn't. Some saw me and thought I was worth interacting with, some didn't. Cal would eat and then push his chair back and join them. Not a kiss. Not a *thank you for dinner.* Certainly not a *let me help you clean up.*

Each night after washing the dishes, I retreated to the bedroom to get stoned and watch TV alone. One show in particular spoke to me. *The Waltons*, created by a man named Earl Hamner.

At the heart of every story was John-Boy Walton, who wanted to be a writer. I had a little crush on John-Boy. There he was sitting beneath a tree scribbling into a notebook just as I liked to do. Or he was reading and looking out the window of his room, the only Walton child with a room of his own. I could see him puzzling over the right word, chewing on his pencil. He looked pretty good in overalls riding his mule too. The folksy voice of Earl Hamner opened every episode, speaking as though he was John-Boy Walton. And clearly, he was John-Boy at one time. He had once been a boy who wanted to write, and he'd done it. He'd created *The Waltons*. He'd also written *Spencer's Mountain*, which was turned into a movie my mother and I had watched on TV one night. I'd liked that movie. So had she.

I hadn't lost hope yet that I would become a writer, even though I no longer had creative writing classes or a teacher or any guidance whatsoever. All the same, I submitted a poem responding to an ad in the back of a magazine. The poem was accepted, but even I knew not to send money for the anthology I'd be published in. It was a scam, a vanity press, a place I could get published again and again, if I was willing to pay the price of the book.

Beyond the writing itself, I didn't know how to "become a writer." I didn't know how to get published. So, I just kept writing. Putting things on paper still fed me. The page still held my inner life. Paper and ink were still my best friends.

Every night I had a visitor in the bedroom while I watched TV. Trip would knock on the door, then come in and sit on the side of the bed and offer me a joint. I'd reluctantly turn the volume down on the TV. We'd smoke. "You know," he said every night, "TV is an escape from reality." I shrugged. So what? Wasn't the joint we shared also an escape from reality?

I didn't really welcome Trip's visits. I wanted to watch TV. I wanted to be alone. The only place I felt comfortable, besides work, was alone.

Work was a relief. My job at Chain Store #1 was fun, largely because I was good at it, and because a friend from high school had recently joined me there. Jackie and I were both stock clerks. We split the store in half for the work of maintaining and ordering products, and we took turns covering the cash register when the cashier needed a bathroom break or went to lunch. Our boss lusted after the big-boobed cashier and draped himself over the pharmacy counter above her, so he had a good view of her breasts, which left Jackie and me alone to do our work.

Every Monday Jackie and I combed through the store with clipboards in hand, ordering what had been sold over the week. When the truck came in on Wednesday, we unpacked the boxes and stocked the shelves. Jackie and I were both hard workers. We kept that store in shape. If a product was sold down, we moved the rest of it to the edge of the shelf to make it easier for the customer to see, reach, and buy. We cleaned constantly, which meant taking all the product off the shelf, spraying with a blue liquid, and wiping the surface with a rag. If a product was completely sold out, we moved the items on either side to fill in the gap.

The job might have been boring except for the fact that Jackie and I took turns bringing a joint to work. One of us would smoke half in the employee bathroom with the fan on and then leave what was left for the other in the unused fem-hy disposal. After we'd both gotten sufficiently stoned, we'd glide out onto the floor in a mellow haze, wiping the shelves down or rotating the products or fronting the products. High on pot, neither of us minded the work, and the store's appearance didn't suffer for it. It might have even been enhanced.

Working with Jackie at Chain Store #1 was an extension of how I'd felt in high school with two exceptions. One—I couldn't leave. I couldn't wander across campus or climb trees or waste time, as Becky and I had done. And two—in Chain Store #1, I felt smart, competent, and capable. I never felt that in school.

Given my complete lack of academic prowess, it might seem odd that I wanted to grow up to write historical novels, especially since I hated the subject of history in school, where all that was expected of me was memorization of dates and battles and treaties. But even though history was never taught in the form of stories, I knew from the novels I'd read that all these events had affected people. History was stories, and I loved stories. Stories were my friends. Stories had always been my friends. I wanted to write stories. I wanted to write stories more than the poems I scribbled.

I didn't read much anymore. I didn't have money for paperbacks, and the library wasn't close enough to walk to, so television became my story field. And Chain Store #1 became the place where I felt smart and appreciated.

After my shift, I went home and cooked a bland, brown dinner for Cal, cleaned up, and turned the volume on the TV up in the bedroom so I didn't have to hear the laughter and jabber in the living room just beyond the wall.

Sometimes I didn't go home right away. Sometimes Jackie suggested we hang out after our shift, and she'd give me a ride home later. I'd call Cal and tell him. "Alllll riiiiight," he'd say, in that mud-dragging voice that told me it wasn't all right at all. But I didn't care. I'd even miss *The Waltons* for a chance not to go home.

With Jackie giving me a ride, I could spend my return bus fare on a Coke, but that was about it. Sometimes Jackie would buy French fries from the hamburger stand across the street and we'd split them sitting on the same rock wall I'd sat on during my first date with Cal.

"Your turn to bring the joint tomorrow," Jackie said when she dropped me off at home.

And tomorrow we'd be back at it. Cleaning the shelves, stocking the shelves, fronting the product, ordering the product, leaving half the joint for the other in the fem-hy disposal in the bathroom.

But then Jackie got fired.

I can't remember the infraction. I think she mouthed off to the boss. I remember him saying, "Hang up your smock and get out of here. You're fired." And I remember Jackie angrily taking her blue smock off and leaving, and I remember thinking, *no, no, no.* I remember the temptation in my body to follow her. It was as though my arms were already pulling my blue smock off and angrily hurling it to the floor, as though my legs were already walking out with Jackie in solidarity. I remember talking myself out of it. I remember thinking, *What would Cal say if I left my job?* Instead, I stood there, tears quivering in my eyes.

We'd been married a year now. First anniversary gifts are meant to be made of paper. I bought Cal a card from the rack at Chain Store #1. It said something sweet and mawkish. Whatever it said, I didn't mean it.

He was perhaps more honest as he bought me nothing,

but his sister gave us something to mark the occasion: a pine plaque on which she'd decoupaged our wedding invitation. I hung it in the hallway, beside the phone. I passed by it every time I went anywhere in that house. As if I needed reminding.

8.

Jackie got a job in the sewing and crafts section at Rose's, which had moved from Franklin Street to the mall close to our house. I started applying for work at different stores there. I needed to be close to Jackie. She was like medicine to me, a life-giving force. In Chain Store #1 she had been a daily drip of joy keeping me alive. Even the fact that Cal worked in the mall didn't deter me from trying to find a job there.

Besides, Cal went to work early. He had to clean the mall before the stores opened. Any shift I worked in any retail store would only overlap his by four hours. How much would I see him anyway?

Given my experience in Chain Store #1, I soon landed a job at Chain Store #2, just across from Rose's. Whenever I subbed for the cashier at the mall-side register, I could look across the hallway and see Jackie unfolding a bolt of fabric. It wasn't the same as it had been in Chain Store #1. We weren't together. We didn't have the daily shared jokes about our boss. We didn't even have the same boss. But our lunch breaks synced, and we worked out a new ritual. We each had thirty minutes, just enough time to walk across the parking lot to the woods behind the Baptist church, where we shared sandwiches and a joint.

The mall was close to our house, and I no longer had to ride the bus to work. I could walk or ride my bike. I relished both. Walking took twenty minutes, and biking took ten. If it was raining, I biked. It got me there faster and less wet. And the store manager let me stash my bike in the stock room. I liked walking best of all though.

Walking slowed me down so I could notice the wild-flowers, which I took pains to identify in a book my father had given me years earlier. Red lobelia. Butterfly weed. Milk-weed. Aster. Chicory. I liked seeing things close like this, and I got to know the little crannies around our house. The pond where the ducks lived. The little ditch where the frogs lived. The woods with the stream where the watercress grew.

Things were the same as ever with Cal. The same bland food at the puffy-topped table. The same friends coming over every night. My devotion to television. Usually, I went to bed without Cal. I lay there and drifted off to the sounds and laughter and music coming through the walls of our "lit-tle love nest," as my mother had called this boxy yellow house when we first saw it.

There was a photograph of my parents' first house, their "love nest," in the drawer full of photographs in the creden-za in the dining room in my childhood home. I used to sit on the floor and plow through these pictures. Here was the picture of my mother with her first car, purchased with her own money earned from her job as a social worker. She'd looked proudly and directly into the camera with a lipstick smile, her arms outstretched across the rounded car top. Here was my mother sitting on the steps of a walkway some-where, holding an apple in her lap, again the lipstick smile. Here was their wedding, kissing passionately, my father in his US Navy uniform and my mother in a smart wool suit.

And here was their first house, a small white cottage with a curved front door. She'd told me she wanted to keep working after they were married, but my father insisted she didn't. I suppose it was a point of pride with him. He was the man. He would support her. Sometimes I wish I'd let her stories in. Sometimes I think she wanted to be seen as much as I wanted to be seen.

"There was a stream behind the house," my mother told me. "I used to go fishing there, with a string and a hook I made from a safety pin."

Even then I could feel her boredom at not being allowed to work, at having her growth and interactions with others cut off at the point of marriage. I looked at the house in the picture. It seemed so far away from the moment I was in, sitting on the dining room floor plowing through a drawer of photographs. I dropped the picture back into the drawer and moved on to more familiar ones. Easter Sundays and Christmases and Halloweens. Pictures that included me.

Although I'd rolled my eyes at my mother's phrase, "love nest," I wanted such a place, a place where I would have cuddles and snuggles and time alone with whatever spouse I had chosen. But I had chosen Cal, and he was about as romantic as a potato. Still, I tried to express myself, beginning with my request that we have some time alone every now and then. I was tired of the boys coming over to our house every night. Maybe left alone with me, Cal might notice I was there. Thank me for dinner. Talk to me. Kiss me on the neck as I washed the dishes. I had no illusions that he would help with the dishes.

"Can't you tell them it's not a good night?" I said to Cal, referring to the relentless stream of visitors. "Can't you tell them to not come over so much?"

Cal looked at me horrified. "I can't hurt anyone's feelings," he said.

"What about my feelings?" I asked.

"I can't hurt anyone's feelings," he repeated, as though it should have been obvious to me what a sensitive guy he was. The question about my feelings hung in the air, unanswered.

At some point each night, I woke to the sounds of people leaving. Car doors slamming. More laughter. Calls to each other. See you 'round, they said. I heard Cal lock the front door and turn off the living room lights. From beneath the bedroom door, I saw the hall light come on, and the bathroom light. I heard him pee and flush, and then I saw the lights go out, heard the door to the bedroom open. And then the overhead light trumpeted on above me.

Cal could have undressed in the bathroom. Or he could have undressed in the dark. He didn't have to turn the overhead light on, but he did. After being asleep for hours, I blinked against its brightness as he undressed. He turned the light out and climbed in bed. And I didn't complain. I didn't ask that he do anything differently. I'd tried that when I asked him to tell the boys not to come over so often. It was useless to talk to him. My needs fossilized somewhere inside me. They were prehistoric. Something evolution had left behind.

Each morning when the alarm went off, Cal moaned and hit the snooze button and then hit it again and again and again. Because he had to be at work before I did, every snooze was torture for me. I would lie there silently chanting, *Get up. Get up. Get up.* My body tensed, energetically pushing his body off the bed. Alarm. Snooze. Alarm. Snooze. Alarm. Snooze. *Get up. Get up. Get up.* The chant boiled inside me like an incantation.

Once the alarm was finally silenced, once Cal threw off the covers and got out of bed, the overhead light went on. I expected it and had a pillow over my head.

He didn't turn the light off when he left the bedroom. I had to ask. "Alllll riiiiight," he said, begrudgingly hitting the switch.

But his assault on me wasn't over yet. In the bathroom and the living room he slammed around as noisily as possible. Even though the light was off now, I kept the pillow over my head to block the sounds. Finally, I heard the front door slam and the car starting up. Finally, I felt my breath, held tight in my chest, release itself. I pulled the pillow off. He'd left all the other lights in the house on, including the hall light, but it didn't matter. I had four blessed hours without him before I walked to my job at the drugstore. Time enough to sleep again, and to wake up peacefully, to make tea, to clean the living room, to empty the cut glass coasters of their ashes and cigarette butts. There was always work to be done, but I got it done quickly, and then, if I had a book, I read.

Quietly and alone.

Or I wrote in my journal.

Quietly and alone.

And then I walked to work.

Quietly and alone.

My work at Chain Store #2 was much the same as it had been at Chain Store #1. I was a stock clerk. I cleaned anything that needed cleaning, stocked whatever needed stocking, and covered for cashiers during breaks and lunch. This store was larger than my previous place of employment, and there were three cashier stations, each one in a different department: a sports department, an electronics and gifts department, and a makeup department. When I worked the register located at the interior of the mall, I'd not only sometimes see Jackie working her department in Rose's, but I'd also see Cal miserably pushing a big broom down the hallway. Sometimes he'd lift his hand in a half-hearted wave.

There was a task in Chain Store #2 that I'd never done at Chain Store #1. It was called "price changing," and it was tedious, involving peeling old price tags off products and replacing them with new, higher price tags. The price-change list was generated by someone in upper management and sent to each store. The list was kept on a clipboard that hung in the pharmacy and new price changes were added as they came in. It was understood that whenever I had some extra time, I would chip away at the price changes.

This involved looking at the list, getting all the old product off the shelf, putting it in a cart, wheeling it to the back, peeling the old sticker off with a fingernail, and replacing it with the new sticker using the price gun.

Prying the old sticker off was difficult and took a long time, but Chain Store #2 would not have us putting new stickers on top of the old ones. This would clue the customer to the fact that a lower price lurked beneath the higher one. It could also result in a stack of stickers, one on top of another.

Price-change work was never done. I'd finish one sheet of price changes, and two more would appear on the clipboard. It was a constant, monotonous task, and one that I really didn't mind. It kept me back in the stockroom, usually alone, which I liked.

But then I started having a visitor, a pharmacy student named Don, who began to find time to hang around and talk to me. In the stockroom he leaned against a two-by-four that held up shelves close to the table where I worked. When I had to cover for a cashier, he leaned against the counter next to the register.

Cal occasionally visited me at the cash register beside the mall entrance to the store, and Don knew I was married. I'd introduced them once when they'd both ended up at the mall-side cash register, but apparently a visible husband was not a deterrent to Don. It may have even been a plus. It may have been a thrill. He may have read a hungry-for-attention look in my eyes. There are men who can read such things. I didn't know that then, and I'm not sure it would have even mattered. I was hungry for attention.

I justified what I was about to do in clinical terms. I reasoned to myself that, sexually, I'd only been with Cal, and it wasn't that exciting. What was everyone singing about? I needed more data. I used that very word with myself. Data. There must be more to it than what I was feeling, but how would I know if I didn't collect more data?

It was remarkably easy. All I had to do was suggest to Don that we get together away from Chain Store #2. I told Cal a lie about where I'd be that night. I made up a friend. Jackie told me not to use her name in a lie, so I just made up a new friend. I was going to be with her this night. We were going out for a little while. She was picking me up when I got off work. Cal was always home when I got off work. He wouldn't see someone picking me up at work.

"Alllll riiiiight." Cal was easy to lie to. And I knew that when I came home, he'd be smoking dope and drinking and laughing with the boys. The boys whose feelings he could not hurt.

At the end of my shift at the drugstore, I walked through the mall to the back entrance, where Don was waiting for me in his blue Gremlin. He drove us to his apartment in a complex in Carrboro, a few blocks from Cal's childhood home, where I'd gotten carpet burns during sex on the floor in front of the TV in the den. The apartment complex was oddly named Yum-Yum, although there was nothing yum-yum about it. Not about the apartment complex or what was about to happen.

Don shared this one-bedroom apartment with another pharmacy student. They had twin beds next to each other. Whenever one of them had a girl over, he camped out with her on the living room floor. I was that girl. Back to carpet burns. I carefully constructed a lie to tell Cal.

"Oh that? I'm such a klutz. I scraped my back on one of the upper shelves while cleaning the lower one at work."

I knew that he might be more willing to skip over the logistics of scraping my back on a shelf if I berated myself as a bumbling fool.

I got away with it, but the data I collected was inconclusive, except for one thing: I felt something new and wonderful. It wasn't sexual satisfaction. It was the power of being able to say, "I'm free tonight," and have Don say, "I'll pick you up after work." I enjoyed the summoning, and the response to the summoning.

I was lucky to have grown up with my father's love. He was a good man, and I falsely believed that almost all men were good. I didn't realize that part my father's charm was only seeing him at nights and on weekends. Part of it was the mysterious world he went off to and returned from every day. I didn't realize that I was kept out of my father's world, and I didn't realize that my mother took care of his biological needs just as much as she took care of her children's.

It was a shock to be married. I'd stepped away from a family with a gentle man into being Cal's wife. He wasn't violent, but he wasn't loving, and he clearly wasn't the man I needed. I needed a good man. A man who was willing to try something new for dinner. A man who wasn't so intent on never hurting his friends' feelings while bulldozing those of his wife. I needed a man who could pluck me out of the vast ocean of being female, the place where I floated and floated and floated without a raft, a place where my entire life was suspended until I was chosen. A good man would choose me over all the other floating female bodies available to him. He would give me mouth-to-mouth resuscitation, like the kiss Snow White received from the prince.

I knew the story of Snow White was a fairy tale, but I didn't know how much the fairy tale permeated my whole being. I was nursed on that shit. I waited to be awakened from my slumber with a kiss. Cal could not wake me from my slumber with a kiss, but he could wake me from my slumber with the overhead light, which he did nightly.

How was it that, even married, even with a ring on my finger, I felt unchosen? I felt unsaved. I still floated and float-ed, like an embryo waiting to be born.

The man I needed was out there. I needed to collect more data.

I don't remember how I met Dale. He was tall. I liked him better than Don. He seemed very handsome to me, and he had a space between his two front teeth that I found at-tractive and wrote a poem about. He lived in a funky house on Wave Road, so named for its dipping and climbing hills.

More lies to Cal. Sex in Dale's bed tucked against the wall of his A-frame. At some point I decided that I loved him. I decided this because I could not keep on doing what I was doing and call it data-collecting. What I was doing was bad and damnable, and God, that bloviating dude in the sky whom I had not yet kicked out of the cathedral of my mind, hated me for it. I felt ashamed of it, but I could not stop. So, I had better make up a good reason for it, and the reason was the poisonous little word I'd been told held all the magic. I had to tell Dale I loved him.

We lay on his bed after sex. It wasn't much better with Dale than with Don or with Cal. I didn't know how to relax. I was so concerned about being wanted that I couldn't let myself be wanted. It was frightening. Was I doing it right? Was I making the right noises? Was I moving my hips the right way? All I knew was that if I told Dale I loved him, he might say he loved me too and then I'd have a good reason to leave Cal and a place to go besides my parents' house. One man for another was a reasonable progression.

When I said the words, Dale moaned and slapped his forehead and said, "Let's not go there."

The worst possible response. I was embarrassed. I didn't say anything more because I'd said too much already. I dressed, and he took me home and dropped me off a few houses away from our house. I never saw Dale again.

Walking to Chain Store #2 the next day, I decided I didn't need any more data. I'd collected enough, and it was getting me nowhere. It was stupid. I was stupid. I wasn't going to have any more affairs. I wasn't going to see Don or Dale again, or any other man. I may as well just be married. I said to myself, *You made your bed. Now lie in it.*

Lie in it, I would, but I wasn't about to tell anyone what I'd done. I certainly wasn't going to confess to Cal. I would simply hold the secrets of these affairs inside me, just as I held everything else inside me.

It had now been three years since I'd stood on my parents' back porch and said, "I do," to this man. I could have left him. I could have gone home to my parents' house. I could have faced my mother's tears. I would have eventually found my way to a new life. But I couldn't face the shame I felt. I couldn't end it. To leave would be to invite my mother and Cal's mother into our relationship. Here they would come, to the rescue, intent on saving our marriage. I could hear their opinions, handed out freely, like bandages for our brokenness.

It's only been three years.
Have you really given it enough time?
Every marriage has its difficulties.
I'm sure if you go home and apologize, he'll take you back.

9.

I worked hard at Chain Store #2. I stocked the shelves, faced the shelves, placed orders for different sections, filled in at the cash registers, worked on the never-ending price changes whenever there was time, and helped unload the delivery truck, which involved catching boxes in a train of employees, of which I was the only female.

I relished discovering my physical strength in that job. It was the only strength I had. Sometimes the boys I worked with told me I was going to hurt myself, and that a woman was too weak to do the work I was clearly doing. But the manager, Mr. Greene, never said this to me. Mr. Greene valued me. We both knew I was a good worker. I didn't shirk. I tackled difficult jobs. I was punctual. I was honest. He didn't need to know that I got stoned during my lunch break.

One day the owner of all the Chain Store #2s paid a visit. Mr. Greene called me to the pharmacy over the intercom. He wanted Mr. Chain Store #2 to meet me. "Our best stock clerk ever," Mr. Greene said, resting his hand on my shoulder proudly.

"Pleased to meet you," I said and held out my hand, which Mr. Chain Store #2 shook, saying nothing.

I returned to my work. One of the cashiers was out sick, so I would be at the cash register close to the interior of the mall all day. There were no customers in my section that morning when Mr. Chain Store #2 came wandering up. He poked around the displays, examining things, and I thought I had better look busy rather than leaning uselessly on the counter watching him. After all, he was paying my salary, and I liked being busy better than being idle anyway. So, I cleaned the shelves behind the counter. I took the cigarette cartons down and sprayed and wiped the metal shelves. I did the same with the radios and the Zippo lighters and the minia-ture TV sets. I was spraying down a glass shelf in the display case of electric razors when Mr. Chain Store #2 walked over to the counter. I stood up. Greeted him. Smiled. He reached into his pocket and dumped a small pile of trinkets on the counter and said, "I just stole all this, and you didn't see me." Then he walked away.

I stood there bludgeoned. What the fuck? I mean, what the ever-loving fuck? What could I have said, even if he'd given me the chance? Why would I watch the owner of the store for shoplifting? And if I saw him shoplift, what would I have done? Accuse him? Either he did not remember meet-ing me or he was determined to take me down a notch. If it was the former, he would have taken his stolen trinkets to Mr. Greene to make a case for firing me, so I assumed it was the latter.

I never told Mr. Greene about this incident. He would have stood up for me; I know he would have, but he was re-tiring in a few months, and I would lose his protection when he left. There was nothing I could do.

I missed Mr. Greene terribly after he left. He'd seen some-thing in me that the new younger manager, Joe, did not see or value. Joe was a yes-man, eager to get ahead in the company. He walked fast, moved fast, and acted as though everything was an emergency that only he could fix. Mr. Greene may have been like that when he was younger, but I doubted it. He'd been with the company a long time, and he'd established himself during an era when fast-walking and fast-talking did not necessarily denote managerial skills. Mr. Greene had not been a showy man. He was slow and steady with nothing to prove. Joe, on the other hand, seemed to have everything to prove. I worked as hard for him as I had for Mr. Greene.

One day after filling out my weekly order form, I impulsively wrote Wonder Woman where my name should have gone at the top.

It seemed harmless enough. A little playfulness never hurt anyone. The order form went out as written, and the next week, I did it again. No one told me not to do it. No one crossed it out and wrote in my name. The order sheet went to the warehouse, and the stock came in just as it always had. I heard though, from the pharmacy student who'd replaced Don, that the employees in the warehouse were openly wondering who Wonder Woman was.

I used her moniker, but I was certainly not Wonder Woman. Wonder Woman could surely drive a car, and I couldn't. Had I been able to, trips to the laundromat and the grocery store would have fallen solely on me. In retrospect, that wouldn't have been so bad. Instead, Cal and I did these tasks together.

Six months after I'd ended my collection of data via sleeping with two men, I walked behind Cal as he rapidly wheeled the grocery cart past the entire produce department. I longingly eyed what we skipped. Lettuce, apples, oranges, broccoli. Cal did not eat these things, and therefore we did not buy them. I didn't know how much I loved fruit and vegetables until there were none.

Apples. My god, I remembered apples.

Crisp iceberg lettuce with sliced red onions and green goddess dressing.

Strawberries. Tangerines. Peaches.

Artichokes like the ones my father brought home in a large paper bag.

A trip to the grocery store was a trip through everything missing from my life. In the freezer aisle I eyed the coffee ice cream. In the dairy aisle I eyed the Swiss cheese. In the grocery aisles I eyed the ketchup and mustard and pickles.

Had I been able to drive, had Cal given me money for groceries, I might have treated myself to a jar of pickles. To a head of lettuce. To an apple.

Instead, I trailed behind him as he pushed the cart, then I saw a wooden spoon wrapped in plastic hanging as an impulse buy next to the cake mixes. It cost eighty-nine cents. I clipped it off the display and placed it in the cart.

"Do we need that?" Cal asked, always watching the money when it came to something I wanted.

"I need it," I said, and I walked away. It was the same tactic I'd used with my mother. I didn't ask permission. I didn't plead. I just put the wooden spoon in the cart and walked away. If I wasn't going to have crummy sex with strange men, I was at least going to have a wooden spoon. In the kitchen, I freed the spoon from its plastic wrapper and put it in a drawer.

There was a lot of buzz at work about a pending visit from the district manager. We all worked hard to make sure the store was clean and functioning smoothly. The day the district manager arrived, dressed in a suit and carrying a briefcase, was a delivery day. When the truck from the ware-house backed up to the double doors that opened to an alley, one of my coworkers called over the intercom for all stock clerks to come to the stockroom.

I loved unloading the truck. I loved being a part of the human chain we formed, with the driver tossing a box from the back of the truck down to one person, who tossed it to the next person in line, and him to the next and so on until the boxes were stacked neatly in the stockroom. I was good at this. And on this day the district manager was here to witness the efficiency with which we performed this task, the teamwork of which I was a part, the skill which every one of us showed. He leaned against the table where I did price changes, and watched, appreciatively I assumed, be-cause how could anyone not admire this productive, choreo-graphed dance?

After the truck was unloaded, we spread out to stock the shelves. I finished my section early and took the price-change clipboard off the wall, read what needed to be done, and cart-ed the products back into the stockroom.

I'd been chipping away diligently on the price changes for some time now, working on them daily, and it looked to me like I might finish that day. And if I did, it would be the first time in my two years of working at Chain Store #2 that all the price changes would be caught up. I knew that the empty clipboard would not last; there would be another sheet of price changes tomorrow. But still, it was a milestone. And the district manager was here, and I'd be able to say that all the price changes were completed. If only he'd hang out long enough for me to finish.

I sat in the stockroom, peeling the stickers off with my fingernails and applying new stickers, then restocking the shelves, checking my list, and gathering and carting more items to the back. I worked hard and steady. Back and forth. Back and forth.

Joe and the district manager were in the office, a room up a short flight of stairs next to the pharmacy, with a wall of glass that overlooked the entire store. When I finished the price changes, I hung the empty clipboard in its place. I knocked lightly on the door of the office and stepped inside.

The two of them were bent over a sheaf of papers on the desk. Joe looked at me, clearly uncomfortable. Nervous, I thought, because of the regional manager being there. He was always trying to make an impression. I was trying to help him.

"I just want you to know the price changes have all been done," I said. "I'm going to clean the stockroom now unless you have something more pressing."

"Okay, go clean the stockroom," Joe said quickly.

The regional manager did not look at me. I felt nothing from the back of his suit as he stayed bent over the papers. I got it. I was nothing to him, but it didn't matter. I'd accomplished a big task, and I'd made Joe look good by being one of his hard workers. If the price changes were completed, then Joe clearly had things under control.

I left and did as I said I would, sweeping up the accumulated debris in the stockroom, organizing the shelves, breaking down empty boxes, and hauling them out to the dumpster. The stockroom looked spic and span. Top-notch. The best it had ever looked. The clipboard that had held the price changes was empty. My section was stocked, and the shelves were clean and fronted.

Perhaps it was foolish to take so much pride in a menial job at a chain drug store, but work was the only thing I'd ever found to be proud of. At work, I was somebody. Mr. Greene had said so. My coworkers said so. And while Joe was no Mr. Greene, he never criticized the job I did. People depended on me at work, and I was there. I was never late. I knew what to do. I knew where everything was. Nail clippers? Aisle 7, against the wall. Dental floss? Aisle 5. First aid? Aspirin? Thermometers? Douche bags? I could tell you instantly where to find anything you asked for.

At the end of my workday as I collected my bicycle from the corner of the stockroom where I kept it stored, Joe popped in and said, "Nancy, I'd like to see you before you leave."

"Sure," I said. I leaned the bike against the wall and followed him to the office. The district manager had left, and Joe and I were alone in that glass-walled castle. He picked up a pink piece of paper from the desk and handed it to me and said, "As of today you're no longer with us."

"What?"

"You no longer work here."

"Why?" I asked. The pink slip was held between my fingers, flaccidly bowing toward the floor while Joe repeated his point: "You no longer work here. Your paycheck will be waiting for you next week. Clock out and leave."

"I'm already clocked out," I said, numbly.

"Then get your bike and leave."

I was furious. On my way out I smacked my hand against a display cage filled with paper towels, doing nothing to upset it. It held firm.

As I wheeled my bike out the automatic doors in front, it began to dawn on me that this had everything to do with the district manager's visit, with his suited back leaning over the table when I'd knocked on the office door. It began to dawn on me that Joe's discomfort had been because he was being told to give me the axe, and he wasn't going to argue about it. He was a yes-man. He was going to go against his own best interest, because someone higher up than him had told him to.

My anger grew as I mounted my bike and rode out of the parking lot for the last time. I couldn't figure the reason for it. I kept on thinking about those price changes, that nice empty clipboard, and the stockroom so clean and well organized.

I wasn't so arrogant to think they couldn't get along without me. Joe would hire another stock clerk. There'd be a learning curve, but he or she would be fine at the job. Chain Store #2 would survive without me. Chain Store #2 was monolithic, just like Chain Store #1 had been.

Going home from the drugstore involved a stretch of highway that I did not feel safe riding my bike on, so I always walked it. Slowing down gave me time to think, to mull over what had just happened. The only infraction I could think of, the only bold thing I'd done that might have put me on the district manager's radar was writing Wonder Woman on the order sheets.

Along the way I anticipated Cal's anger. He would blame me for this. How stupid could I have been to fuck around with the order sheets like that? How dumb. He would see my firing as inevitable. It would all be my fault. He would gnash his teeth and worry about money.

Cal and I'd had some epic fights in the beginning, back when I was willing to express a need or desire. During these fights, Cal usually left, slamming the door behind him, getting in the car, and driving away, leaving me behind alone.

I hated it when Cal walked out on me. I hated his dismissal of me, and my inconvenient needs. I hated his return.

He would come back and slam the door again, put on a record, turn the volume up, and angrily pick his guitar.

"Where did you go?" I asked the first time.

"Driving around."

There was no further talk about the subject that had caused the argument, and nothing ever changed. The problems were mine, and mine alone. I held the air of that fight in my hands like a small bird fallen out of its nest, its heart beating rapidly against my palm. There was nothing I could do for it. It would die in my hand.

Once after Cal left during a fight, I decided to not be home when he returned. I walked away. I went down to the end of the road where there was a field and a tree to sit under. I sat there until I saw him drive by, and then I walked home.

As I approached this field on my bike, I saw Cal walking along the road toward me. This was unprecedented, but I didn't think why he might be there. I pedaled up to him, dismounted, and said, crying now, "Oh Cal, I've been fired."

"It's just as well," he said quickly. "I've been thinking we should call it quits anyway."

I dropped the bike in the grass. I managed a small squeak. "What?"

"I was getting a pen off your desk," he said. "And I knocked your journal off and read some. I couldn't help it. I know about Don."

He was lying, and we both knew it. He'd not accidentally knocked my journal off my desk. He'd not accidentally read it. He'd deliberately read it. He'd invaded my privacy. But what could I do with that considering the lies I'd told? Standing there, facing the man I'd married, facing a man who was lying to me now, I wondered how much he knew. How far had he read?

"And Dale," Cal said.

So, he knew it all. It was the perfect intersection of events, being fired from my job the same day my husband found out I'd been cheating on him. The door showing me the way out of this marriage swung wide open. I could have walked through, but a movie played in my mind. I saw Cal dropping me off at my parents' house at the top of the hill. I saw myself carrying a small sack of clothes, walking down the long drive-way, stepping onto the front porch, and opening the door to my childhood home. My parents would be eating dinner. Walter Cronkite would be on. News about the Watergate investigation, Richard Nixon's involvement unveiling itself.

My mother would exclaim gladly to see me.

"Hey, honey," my father would say.

They would offer me dinner, my mother already in the kitchen getting a plate.

But when I told them my marriage was over, she would put the plate down. She would clasp one hand to her mouth, as she did when the nurses were murdered, as she did when my sister ran away, as she did when my sister separated from her husband.

My mother would cry.

She would cry and cry and cry. She would cry every day until I found another job and figured a way to get out of there again.

And when she found out why my marriage was over, that I'd slept around with other guys, that I'd committed such an egregious offence against God, not just against Cal, not just against her, not just against the marriage vows I'd taken, but against GOD, I imagined her frenzied hysteria.

How could you? How could you? How could you? I imagined.

I taught you better than that, I imagined.

Hell would be trotted out again. And again. And again.

And then the whole scene would repeat itself, until I crawled into my childhood bed.

The next morning, over breakfast, my mother would cry … And me with nowhere to go… No place to escape to… No place to smoke a joint… No television show to watch without my mother sniffling beside me on the couch they'd purchased to replace the scratchy brown one.

All this galloped through my mind like a pack of wild dogs. And so, I did the only thing I knew to do. I fell to my knees in the grass and begged Cal to stay.

Cal didn't seem to mind the begging. He didn't seem embarrassed when cars went by while I supplicated myself before him. I was dimly aware how we must have looked, my purple bicycle laying on its side, a young man with scruffy, unkempt hair wearing jeans standing beside it, a young girl with long brown hair also wearing jeans on her knees, crying, clutching at his cuffs. Cars went by. People saw this. And Cal never said to me, "Get up. You're embarrassing yourself."

"Please stay," I begged, crying. "I'm sorry. Please stay. Don't leave me. I love you."

After a time, Cal said, "We might work something out."

And I rose from my knees, wiped my face on my sleeve, and picked up my bicycle.

We walked home together, me wheeling my bike beside me, steadying it with one hand while keeping the other on Cal's shoulder, as if to say, once again, "I'm sure. I'm sure it's you I love. I'll never do that again. Let me prove it to you."

I fixed dinner. There was a knock on the door. The first of our boy visitors. Cal let him in.

After cleaning up the kitchen I went to the living room

instead of the bedroom. Life was too precarious now to take time away from my husband. I sat beside him. I laughed numbly at the jokes. I smoked the weed. I am sure Cal felt as strange as I did. After everyone left, we went to bed. We may have had sex. I don't remember, but I know if he expressed the desire, I said yes. I would say yes for years to come. To whatever Cal wanted. Yes would be my penance.

10.

When the alarm went off the next morning, Cal hit the snooze button. When he finally got up, he turned the overhead light on. When he left the room, I didn't ask him to turn it off. I lay in the blaring light. I didn't even put a pillow over my head. I didn't deserve the comfort. I listened to him bang things around, open and close the refrigerator, cuss, and finally slam the front door and lock it. The car started up. After I heard him back out of the driveway, I didn't get up to turn the overhead light off. I didn't fall back asleep. Instead, I got out of bed and went to the kitchen. I retrieved a grocery bag from the stack wedged between the refrigerator and the wall, and I went to my desk.

The journal Cal had read lay there, exactly where he had left it, which was exactly where I had left it. I picked it up. I pulled more journals off the bookshelf. I would start with these. I would begin, of course, with the most recent one, the one that had spilled my secrets, but it all had to go. Everything I'd ever written had to be destroyed, including my poems and stories. Including the novel I'd written in high school. The whole damn lot of it. Fuck this shit. Fuck keeping writing in the house, just waiting for Cal to read what was never meant for him, what he'd never taken any interest in before.

Fuck that! Fuck that! Fuck that! As far as I was concerned, writing could go to hell. I was done with it.

I would no longer put words on paper. Nowhere would my words be read again. It was safer that way. This was how I would save my marriage. This was how I would avoid going home to my mother's tears and my father's disappointment.

Words were dangerous. Words were traceable. Better to never stare into fallen leaves in a puddle and write a poem. Better to never look at bare winter trees against the sky and create a description in my mind—black lace, I remembered thinking. They look like torn black lace against the sky.

Well, fuck that! Just as soon as the memory surfaced, I ripped it out of my head.

In the bedroom I dumped my stack of notebooks on the floor. I sat on the edge of the bed. I opened the grocery bag and set it at my feet. And then I began.

I tore out six pages from the journal Cal had read. I ripped these pages in half, and then in half again, and then once more until the stack of papers became too thick to tear. Then I separated the pages and ripped half of them in half. Again. And again. And again. Fuming. Raging. I tore at my writing. I tore at myself.

But my writing still wasn't small enough yet. I wasn't small enough yet. I kept dividing and tearing at my journal until I'd reduced these first six pages to quarter-sized pieces, which I dropped into the grocery bag at my feet.

I reached in and gave the pieces a stir. I filtered the clumps through my fingers. I broke them apart. I had to make it impossible for anyone to figure out how the pieces might fit together, how the words might fit into sentences, the sentences into paragraphs or stanzas, and the paragraphs or stanzas into meaning.

By six, I hadn't come close to tearing it all up, but I had to stop. I returned the untorn journals to the shelf beside my desk. In the bedroom, I folded the top of the grocery bag over and stapled it shut. I had to go into town to look for work. There was no way I was applying for jobs at the mall. Cal worked there, and I'd been fired from one of the stores there, and Jackie was gone anyway, off to Florida to visit a new boyfriend.

At the bus stop each morning. I sat on the covered bench with the other commuters, my grocery bag of ripped-up self in my lap. No one asked what was in it. They acted as though it was typical to carry a large, stapled grocery bag every day, to sit with it on one's lap as though it were lunch.

They were all normal people, and I pretended I was normal too. We talked casually. We talked about TV shows and shared tips about sales on hamburger. Some of the women traded coupons and swapped recipes. Some of the men talked about sports. But, as I sat waiting for the bus, pretending to be normal, I could feel the vibrations of my stories and poems and journal entries pulsing through the paper grocery bag into my legs. Things I'd never called myself spoke up now.

Dirty. Filthy. Unclean. Shameful. Whore. Slut. Bitch. Adulteress.

That's what my writing said, and it was right. I was all these things. What had begun as a gathering of data, a sexual curiosity, a desperate need to be wanted had become these words. They stomped around inside of me now, threw their weight around, jumped on me like bullies. I couldn't wait to get rid of them.

Every morning when I disembarked from the bus on Franklin Street, before looking for work, I walked to the service street behind the stores. There, I chose a dumpster and tossed my paper bag into it. The next day, after tearing up more writing, I chose a different dumpster. As I tossed each bag in and heard it land with a small whump among the cardboard boxes and food waste, I thought of the "Humpty Dumpty" nursery rhyme.

Humpty Dumpty sat on a wall
Humpty Dumpty had a great fall
And all the king's horses, and all the king's men
Couldn't put Humpty together again.

I never wanted to be put back together again. Even my little red five-year diary from my childhood got torn up and dropped in a grocery bag and deposited in a dumpster. My childhood self. My frustrations over sharing a room with my grandmother. My bewilderment over the man following me in the library. The beery breath of the neighbor boy knocking on my window. The false enthusiasm I'd written before my wedding. My dreams of becoming a writer. Gone.

If Cal noticed the journals and notebooks disappearing from the shelf beside my desk, he didn't say anything. If he saw that I no longer sat on the heating grate in the hallway scribbling into a notebook, he was either delighted or didn't care. I suspect the former. I suspect he took some satisfaction in seeing that I'd truncated myself, that the thing I'd held onto as sacred and holy and exclusively mine no longer competed with him. On the other hand, he was hurting, and I knew that. And I knew I was to blame for everything.

Cal needed constant reassurance from me, and I needed to appease my guilt. This intersection of needs worked out well in Cal's favor. Sex whenever and wherever he wanted it.

Compliments from me to him. All the right kinds of food. Longing looks in public from me to him. Pride shown in him. Joy when he came home. Strokes to his ego.

I played it. And I knew I was playing it.

All around me the women's liberation movement rose and surged, and I became as small and insignificant and undemanding as I could. I asked for nothing. I joined his friends in the living room, and I looked adoringly at Cal, and I made sure everyone saw it. If he expressed doubt to them about my love for him, they assured him that judging from the way I looked at him when he was playing guitar, my love was genuine. Cal reported what his friends said, just as he'd reported Earl Johnson's comment that I would become shrill and horrible after we were married.

Writing this now, one can feel sorry for Cal. The way I lied. The way I manipulated. The way I was ungenuine. I'm not proud of these things, but Cal was open to every maneuver I could perform. He has nothing to be proud of either.

Every day for two weeks I tore up my writing and applied for jobs. I applied for jobs everywhere along the bus route. I applied at hardware stores and gift shops and drugstores, citing my experience in retail. I had an exhausting two-hour interview with the head of housekeeping at The Carolina Inn. I applied at movie theaters and the head shop and clothing stores, and I finally landed employment in a privately owned drugstore with a lunch counter.

The craggy-faced pharmacist came in every day from the post office carrying an apple left in the P.O. box by the postal clerk who had a crush on him. The man who cleaned the floors would never say excuse me in the narrow aisle behind the counter, and I only had to feel him behind me once, grinding his crotch against my ass, before I learned to keep an eye out and give him wide berth. Another clerk at another counter was a tall, thin, creepy man, who said to a pregnant woman once while wagging his finger, "I know what you've been doing." He was best friends with the craggy-faced pharmacist. It was a misogynistic, horrible place to work, and I couldn't complain. I wasn't about to share with Cal the nature of the environment I now worked in. He might accuse me of inviting the janitor to rub up against my ass.

Not long after starting my new job, we received a phone call from our landlady's daughter. Her parents had signed the deed of our house over to her. She intended to live in the house and was calling to evict us.

We found a rental in Durham. To help us move, we lined up friends who drove trucks, and while Cal and the other boys moved furniture and boxes, I stayed behind to clean the house. I swept and mopped my way through the bedrooms, the living room, and the hallway. I cleaned the bathroom and mopped. And then I faced the kitchen. We had lived in this house a little over three years, and I had never defrosted the freezer. It was an old refrigerator with the freezer closed off from the main compartment by an aluminum door, ice bulging behind it.

I remembered my mother defrosting the freezer. I remembered her spreading the floor with newspaper and chipping away at the ice with an ice pick, grunting, sighing, and tossing chunks of ice into the sink. I had no ice pick, but I did have a kitchen knife I'd held back from packing, and newspapers I'd gleaned from customers leaving them behind at the lunch counter. I turned off the refrigerator and unplugged it. I spread the newspaper on the floor and began.

As I chipped away at that solid span of white freezer ice, I grunted and sighed just as my mother had. As the ice melted,

I pried my knife into spaces, occasionally pinging loose a large chunk, which I tossed in the sink. Cold water spread across the newspapers as the ice melted. My jeans and sneakers got wet with dripping cold water as I hewed my way through the freezer compartment.

I uncovered hamburger. Was it still good? It didn't seem like it. I tossed it in the trash. Ice trays. I turned them upside down in the sink to melt. Ice cream filled with crystals. I ran hot water on it to melt it and threw the carton in the trash.

Hot dogs. Into the trash.

Popsicles. I took each from its cellophane sheath and left them in the sink to melt.

In the back, I saw one more thing held in the freezer's frosty white grip. It seemed to be wrapped in tinfoil. I slid my knife under it and tried to pry it loose. Damn it. I had better be done by the time Cal came to pick me up.

He would be mad if he had to wait for me. Even though I'd been working steadily, with no breaks, I'd feel as though I was being accused of being slack while he slaved away at the new house. Although in truth, I knew he and the boys were setting up the stereo and getting stoned while I was alone chipping at the freezer. And I still had the sink and counter and stove to clean, not to mention the floor.

I hacked my knife all around the thing, whatever it was. I stabbed and stabbed and stabbed, like Norman Bates in the shower scene in *Psycho*. I pulled at the thing, and a piece of tinfoil shredded loose in my hands, revealing the frosted edge of our wedding cake, which we were supposed to thaw and eat on our first anniversary.

Well, fuck that, I thought.

When it finally came loose, I tossed it in the trash.

I wiped the inside of the freezer dry. I ran hot water on

the mess in the sink and cleaned it and the counter and the stove. I dried the ice trays and put them in the freezer. I wadded the wet newspaper and put it in the trash.

Cal had instructed me to leave the refrigerator unplugged and the door open. As I draped the cord in the door to keep it from closing, I noticed the poem I had written in high school and taped to the refrigerator. It had escaped the destruction of my writing and become such a fixture on the refrigerator door that I hadn't noticed it, just as I no longer noticed the rust spots dotting the enamel. But there it was now, taunting me.

> *Could've and should've*
> *Are words we don't use.*
> *They only depress us*
> *And give us the blues.*

I ripped it off the door and shoved it into the trash.

11.

In the move, we got rid of the scratchy brown couch, the green puffy-topped table, and its chairs, as well as my desk, desk chair, and bookcase. We had no seating in our living room except a rocking chair I'd inherited from my grandmother and a straight-back chair Cal sat in to play his guitar.

Our new home was nearly empty, but we decided not to furnish it. There was no need to make it comfortable. We hated it there. Next door to us a kid noisily circled his go-cart around the homemade racetrack in his backyard. A sheriff's car came and went out of their driveway. Due to the sheriff's car, the endless stream of visitors we'd had at our previous house dried up. Not even a trickle.

Without the nightly hoard of boys to get high with, Cal had no distraction from my infidelities and his fury. After work and on weekends, to the background of the neighbor boy going around and around and around on his go cart, Cal erupted again and again in near violent anger at me. He yelled at me. His face contorted. His fists clenched.

"I don't know what I would do if I thought you were sleeping with someone again."

I sat in my rocking chair with my head down, looking at my shoes, a punished child. I would not look up except to squeak out, "I'm sorry. It will never happen again. I love you."

Again and again and again. I love you. I'm sorry. I'm sorry. I love you.

Around and around and around, like the go-cart next door.

We hated the go-cart, and we hated the landlord.

The landlord was—how do I say this delicately?—a shitty fuckwad who complained about our calling him whenever something broke.

Our landlord owned rental property all over Chapel Hill and Durham and was building even more. We'd never had anything malfunction in our previous house, but in this one the well pump was always breaking. Several times within our first months there, we came home, and I turned the water on in the kitchen to cook something, and nothing came out.

No water to cook with, no water to clean up with, no water to shower with, and no water to flush the toilet with. The first time I called the landlord about the pump he grumbled and drove out to fix it. When it broke again, and I called, he got angry with me, but he drove out to fix it. The third time he told me that he had more important things to do than constantly drive out to fix our well pump.

I stayed quiet on the line. I never knew how to deal with him. It seemed obvious that the broken pump was inconvenient for us, too, and that we'd stop calling him if he'd just fix it right or replace it. It seemed equally obvious that it was his responsibility. Finally, I heard him sigh, and say, "I'll be right there."

"Thank you," I said. "I'm sorry," I added unnecessarily.

"What a bastard," I said to Cal when I hung up the phone.

"What'd he say?"

I told him.

"That shitty fuckwad."

"Yeah. Can you believe it?"

"What a shithead."

"I know."

Our communal hatred felt good to me, like it was something we could build on, something we could heal with. Next door, the noise of our neighbor-kid's go-cart shrieked around their yard. The boy drove around and around and around the track. Before school. After school. All day Saturday with a short break for lunch. After church on Sundays. The sound of the go-cart pervaded everything. We could hear it in every room.

Neither of us was about to go over there, introduce ourselves to the sheriff, and ask him that their kid be more considerate. As it was, we smoked our dope in the front room with the drapes closed, as far from the neighbor's yard as possible. We hadn't attracted attention to ourselves yet and weren't looking to do so.

We had to escape that house on weekends. We had to get out.

Without the boys constantly visiting and with the forced togetherness of exile, Cal and I found a place to be together, and that place was in the car. Cal drove and I rode, of course. We passed a joint back and forth held low, out of view of other drivers.

In the car, there were ceasefires between skirmishes, space where Cal wasn't yelling at me, which he filled with long-winded, digressive stories. I found Cal's conversational style to be one of two things—either uh-uh-uh or these long, meandering stories. I reasoned that I owed him my attention. It was hard to give though. The point of one of Cal's stories became murky, and I could not help but drift away from his voice, my attention pulled out the window. I had to make myself return to his story again and again, and I found that I hadn't missed much when I did.

It seemed we would stay together. It seemed we would see another anniversary. It seemed I would not have to go live with my parents. I would not have to confess my sins to them. I would not have to face their disappointment in me, or my mother's wailing. I chose instead Cal's disappointment and Cal's emotions. If there was pot, I could endure it.

In the car, as Cal's voice droned on, the wind would be in my hair, the countryside slipping by, and the pot made it all pleasant. I made him laugh sometimes. Often, in fact. He liked my imitations of people. He liked my jokes. Amid all the pain I had caused him, he came up with a term of endearment for me. He called me Bear, after the bear I'd kept from my childhood, the one that got tossed on the floor when we cleared the bed for sex.

One day, on one of our weekend drives, we stopped at an old, abandoned house, just to investigate. The yard was weedy, with tree saplings growing right up to the house and crowding the gutter. We waded into the weeds and came upon a well house, and on it sat a tiny owl. The owl turned its head to watch us approach. I was amazed to see an owl during the day, and to see it so calmly sitting on a well house.

"That's got to mean something," I said. "Something magic."

Cal glared at me. It was hard to interpret Cal's many glares, and the interpretation was always left to me. I took this one to mean that there was no magic. Magic was for children. Don't mention magic. Magic annoyed him.

Cal moved on toward the house, but I still stood facing the owl. I smiled at it and bowed a little, as though it could receive my awe. It seemed important to acknowledge its regalness before moving on to follow my husband. The owl watched me move with its large eyes, swiveling its head as it did so.

"It's so small," I said, catching up to Cal's back. "I wonder what kind it is."

"I don't know," Cal said, as if I had ever believed he would know.

Cal didn't wonder, so neither should I. But I did wonder. I couldn't help but wonder, and I vowed to look the owl up in my bird book.

At the back of the house, we tested our weight on the porch steps and then the floorboards, and finding them safe, we crossed the porch and tried the door. It creaked open and we entered a kitchen with dishes in the sink, the crusted remains of a meal still visible on a plate. A dry-rotted towel hung sloppily on the handle of the oven. An ashtray sat on the table with a half-smoked cigarette stubbed out in it, the chair cocked at an angle, as though someone had just pushed away and stood up suddenly.

Our shoes left prints on the dust-covered floor as we walked to another doorway and peered into a living room. A couch eaten by mice, stuffing trailing out. A chair to one side of a fireplace. A shoe turned on its side on a rug.

The people who'd once lived here had vanished. Lives, it seemed, had been cut short by some event. I took a step deeper into the living room, intending to go into the hallway and the bedrooms that were surely on the other side of it.

"Let's go," Cal said.

I couldn't believe he would not want to explore more. I

couldn't believe that he was eager to leave, that he wanted to turn away from the haunting that was drawing me in. Yes, it was spooky, which is why we needed to go further into the house, into the lives of the lost, into the story of what had happened here. But Cal didn't like stories that weren't his own. He called, and I followed. I turned and left.

But the story in this house felt like a spell as I closed the door. It reached its fingers out to me as I walked across the porch. I felt story like an enchantment as we passed the owl still sitting on the well house. It watched me walk by, watched me open the car door and get in, and watched me leave.

We were both silent for a long time. Finally, no longer able to contain myself, I said, "What do you think might have happened?"

"I don't know," Cal snapped, his annoyance with me clear and loud, as though even speculation was against his religion, against his sense of right and wrong.

But the owl and the house and its contents had taken possession of me and overrode his obvious displeasure. "It's like everyone just walked away one day. I mean there were dishes in the sink. If we'd opened the cabinets, I bet there'd have been cans of soup."

He turned and glared at me.

"Maybe someone died," I said, still spinning a story to explain the sudden vacating of the house.

I might no longer be writing on paper to leave behind for someone to read, but I could still speculate on a story, and that house had a good one to tell. "Maybe someone died, and the spouse couldn't stand to come back to the house."

"I don't know," he snapped. "Can we just leave it alone?"

"Yeah, sure," I said meekly.

And I shut up. The message was clear. Let's not talk about this. Let's not imagine anything. Let's not engage in the world of make-believe.

We continued to take long drives on weekends. We continued to smoke joints held low between us. We continued to buy Cokes and packs of Nabs at country stores. We continued to visit abandoned houses. Somewhere along the way we started looking at these abandoned houses as possible places to live.

Some of our friends were living in previously abandoned houses. Wild places where they'd swept floors and mopped and sponged mouse droppings out of the sink. They'd added posters to the walls and built fires in the old fireplaces and dragged in couches purchased at thrift shops. Some of these houses had no running water, outhouses in the backyard, muddy ponds to swim in, porch swings rehung. Some of these houses rented for as little as fifty dollars a month.

We could have a place like that. With the pump going out constantly, we barely had running water anyway. We could find a house and ask around who owned it and move into it. We searched farther and farther afield. It did not matter that I didn't drive and that Cal's new job with UNC housekeeping already required that he get up even earlier than before. It did not matter that we already had a complicated system of transportation, with Cal dropping me off at my parents' house in the early morning before I had to be at work and picking me up again from my job after he'd been home for several hours. None of that mattered. What mattered was finding a place we didn't have to flee every weekend, a place we could enjoy, a place to call home, a place without a sheriff and his go-carting kid as neighbors.

Our visit to every empty house we found was some

version of the first. Rickety steps. Check the porch to see if it held our weight. Try the door. Sometimes it opened, and if it did, it often opened to a room full of stuff. Rugs—sometimes spread, sometimes rolled. Shoes—moldy—pairs and singles. Jars on shelves, sometimes full, sometimes empty. Old mattresses. Bedsteads and benches. The stories of these places spun in my mind.

At first, I could never resist saying out loud, "I wonder what happened here."

To which Cal replied gruffly, "I don't know. Let's go."

And so, after a time, I ceased saying anything. I moved through the houses as quietly as if I was the ghost. I just wanted to stay a little longer. I just wanted to listen to my own imagination. I just wanted to listen to the spirit of the house.

I have always believed that houses have spirits. Not just the spirits of the people who once lived there, but that they have their own spirits. Houses are living breathing things that take notice. I could feel the houses that Cal and I entered taking notice of me, if not Cal, as we opened their doors, walked on their floors, looked at their accumulated and abandoned things. Whatever haunting I felt, I held inside of me. Poems and stories might have been born from these abandoned places, but I didn't write anymore. So they lived in my heart, in my bowels, in my gut, like specters.

Cal had always wanted me to take LSD with him, and I never would. I was scared of it, but after he discovered my affairs and I began my journey of atonement, agreeing to anything he asked of me, I took a hit to please him. We did it in that awful house, one Saturday night after the go-cart next door had been put to bed, in the fall before the weather turned cold. Cal was cautious in how big a hit he gave me.

He didn't overdose me. He took a little more than I did, but he didn't insist I go the distance with him. The result was a very mellow and wonderful trip.

Even though I hated our house, I didn't hate it for being itself. I only hated the go-cart next door and the grumpy old landlord and the problems with the pump. Tripping that night, I could feel how much the house wanted to be loved. I admired the windowsill in the kitchen that looked out over a deep backyard. I admired my rocking chair sitting on my braided rug. I admired the blue bathtub and the spigots and the shower curtain. It was all so beautiful. Even Cal was beautiful. We laughed together and listened to music and smoked joints to take the edge off the acid.

When we started coming down, Cal went to bed to sleep it off, but I stepped outside to our little front yard and watched the sunrise. It was not long before the go-cart started up, and the boy next door started going around and around and around. Cal slept through it, but I couldn't, so I cleaned the house. I needed physical labor to purge the chemical feeling from my body. As I scrubbed, I told the house that I couldn't stay. You're a fine house, I told it, but a bad location for us. I wiped the windowsill and apologized to the wood. When I dusted the books, I remembered the little owl we'd seen months earlier. I'd never looked it up, but now I did. Screech owl. "Our only small eastern owl with ear tufts," the book said. I didn't mention it to Cal when he woke up. I held the name of that owl in my mouth, like a tiny pebble.

Screech owl.

I reshelved the book and took down *Handmade Houses: A Guide to the Woodbutcher's Art*. When Cal woke up, he found me sitting on the floor looking at wooden houses, stained glass, the art of domestic hippies.

Later that day we took a ride out in the country and continued our search for a place to live. I'd not slept for over twenty-four hours, but I wasn't tired. I watched the houses slide by outside the window. One of them was ours. I just didn't know which one. Or maybe I hadn't even seen it yet.

I wonder now what exactly we were looking for. Did we really plan to move into an abandoned farmhouse, or were we just killing time? We were earnest about leaving the house in Durham, but was this really the way to go about it? Shouldn't we be checking the classifieds? We weren't logical in our search. We weren't rational. As the weather grew colder, we grew bolder in our ventures. The ground froze, and Cal drove up previously impassable driveways. With snakes and ticks no longer an issue, we waded through deep weeds to houses that were clearly uninhabitable, roofs collapsed on floors, shattered glass from windows glittering in the dead, dry grass.

One day in December Cal said, "I might know of a place." He took a turn, and then another, and another, and then he turned onto a dirt road. "I think this is it," Cal said.

"There's a house." I pointed to a dilapidated house way off the road to the right.

"That's not what I'm looking for," he said.

He didn't say what he was looking for. He didn't say that he'd heard about some little houses, and he thought they were down this road. He didn't say that this place was called Wildwood. He didn't say that this was one of the most magical places I'd ever know. He didn't say that I would find strength here. He didn't say that I would learn to drive here. He didn't say that bit by bit, this place would give me independence from him, and him freedom from me. He didn't tell me that this would be the place where I would cease my atonement for my affairs, the place where I would write again, the place that I would return to again and again because I could not leave that magic behind.

He didn't say any of that, because he didn't know it, and magic was a word Cal would never use.

But magic it was.

The dirt road dipped down into a curve with swamp on either side before rising up a hill. On the right, at the top of the hill, was a field filled with short, scruffy pine trees and, across from it, a trailer, clearly unlived in. The road curved again. The first house I saw was a tiny wooden cottage; roughhewn, with a small, screened-in porch to one side, a stovepipe puffing smoke on the opposite side, and ivy growing up one end.

It was a house out of a fairy tale. The witch's cottage in the woods. It was a mystical, enchanted mojo of a house, and my breath stopped at the sight of it. "Look at that little house," I exclaimed. And then the most amazing thing. I turned to see Cal smile in a way I'd not seen before, as though he was pleased with himself for pleasing me.

We slid by a thick stand of woods, and then another house came into view, a larger roughhewn wooden house also with a stovepipe on one end, puffing smoke.

"There's another one!" I said.

And before I could take it in, I saw the next one—a log cabin with a huge front porch, columns made of thick peeled cedar trunks. "And another one!"

All the little cabins and shacks were on the right-hand side of the dirt road. The left was woods. Soon there was a fourth little house, and a fifth, an unfinished cabin, and a sixth, a finished cabin with a deep screened-in front porch.

"Are they for rent?" I asked.

"I think so," Cal said.

"How do we find out about them?"

"I don't know."

Eleven little hand-built houses in all, each made of rough-hewn wood, each with a different architectural style. Some with porches. Some without. Each one was a bohemian, nonconformist, dropout of a house, and each one, except for the unfinished cabin, had a stovepipe spewing woodsmoke into the fairy-tale air.

Something stirred deep inside of me. Something primal. An animal awakened and stretched her bones and looked out of my eyes at the little houses.

The road ended abruptly. A span of woods stood in front of us. Cal executed a three-point turn between the ditches on either side and drove slowly back toward the blacktop. I leaned forward and looked around his profile so I could see the little houses again.

At one, the door opened, and a man stepped outside. Long hair pulled back into a ponytail, bearded, wearing jeans and a red knit Henley shirt. He held the door propped open with one moccasined foot while leaning over to pick up firewood, loading it into his arms. And then we were past his house, and I was looking at the next one, and the next one, and the next one until we'd passed the first one I'd seen on the way in.

Once past the houses, Cal sped up, and the field with the scruffy pines appeared on our left, the empty trailer on our right, and soon we were going through the big curve with the swamp on either side. At the end of the road Cal stopped and turned to me and said, "Don't get your hopes up, Bear."

I nodded and smiled. *Fuck you*, I thought. *I will get my hopes up. I will dream about these little houses all I want to. I won't share my dreams with you, but I will dream.*

I started the dreaming immediately. As Cal droned on with a story, I spread my braided rug across a wooden floor I had not stepped on. I put my rocking chair beside a woodstove we did not own. I put a spool table we did not have on a porch that was not ours. I washed dishes looking out a window at a view I'd never seen.

Curtains. Sunrises. Tea and joints and hash pipes and biscuits. Pots of soup Cal would never eat. I filled vases with flowers and listened to birds and looked out at trees and imagined a tire swing.

Maybe Cal was dreaming too. Maybe our combined dreams, held separately, manifested a power neither of us could conjure on our own. I needed that place, and I think Cal did too.

Just after Christmas, Cal picked me up from work and told me there was a notice on the bulletin board at his job. A cabin for rent, the notice said. Take over the lease. He'd written the number down and, at home, pulled it from his jeans pocket. As he dialed the phone, he said, "I think it's down that little dirt road, Bear."

I knew what little dirt road he was talking about. I stood beside him, mute and still and frozen with hope, listening to Cal's end of the conversation. "Uh huh… uh huh… uh huh…okay." He hung up the phone. "It is on that road, Bear. We're going to look at it on Saturday. It's Number Six. One twenty-five per month. Half what we're paying now."

12.

As Cal turned the car onto the dirt road, I looked out the window, watching for the first house, and when I saw it, it was no less enchanting than before. Smoke puffed out of the stovepipe, ivy climbed up its siding, the little porch waited patiently for summer. I imagined how cozy it must be inside.

Passing by the next house, a wooden house with no porch, Cal said, "That one's kind of a shack, isn't it?"

Then we passed the log cabin with the deep porches.

"That's Number Four," I said. "Number Five," I said, as we passed by the unfinished cabin. "Number Six." Cal pulled into the driveway of the small log cabin with the screened-in front porch.

A burly blond man wearing jeans and clogs stepped out of the house and greeted us. His name was Tom. His girl-friend Karen joined him. She was small and friendly. They led us through the deep front porch and into the cabin. I took it in quickly. One room, with a sleeping loft above and a kitchen and bathroom tacked on the back. There were three outside walls in the main room, and in each was a set of three long, mullioned windows hinged to open out, with no screens. Leading to the loft, a narrow wooden spiral staircase built around a trunk of unpeeled cedar was tucked in one

113

corner. Beside it sat a large potbellied woodstove with brass trim.

I'd never been in the presence of a woodstove before, but I could feel its radiating heat, and I walked over and held my hands out above it.

"Take a look around," Tom said.

"Watch your head going upstairs," Karen added.

I headed straight for the loft while Cal stayed downstairs and talked with Tom and Karen.

I had to contort my body as the staircase twisted closer to the slanted ceiling. At the top I crawled across an ugly brown carpet to reach the only place I could stand up, the center where the roof peaked. I could see a view of the living room and the tops of Cal's and our hosts' heads. Directly across from me, above the living room, was one window high in the wall that looked out over the porch roof. Outside I saw a large black bird coasting in the sky. And then another joined it. And another.

Vultures. I admired the way they wheeled in the sky, each one effortlessly riding an air current, tilting its wings to one side or another to turn. There was joy in that ride. I could see it, and what I'd always heard about vultures, that they portend death, flew out of me, and joined the big black birds in the sky. From this moment on, I would love vultures.

I heard Cal climbing the staircase to the loft. He crawled across the floor toward me, then straightened, and stood next to me in the peak of the roof. We looked at each other. His eyes said it all. He wanted to live here too. We descended the staircase and continued our tour, moving toward the kitchen.

A rough wooden counter divided the living room from the kitchen, as did a step down. The doors between the kitchen and the bathroom were slatted half doors that swung in and out, like the doors I'd seen in saloons on TV Westerns. Orange Formica covered the only kitchen counter. The same orange Formica covered the walls surrounding the tub. Green Astroturf covered the kitchen floor. The color combination of green and orange was garish. That's ugly, I thought, but I can live with it.

I went and stood at the sink in the back of the kitchen. The window there was long and had a wide sill, perfect for rocks and turtle shells and feathers and plants, all of which I mentally placed there. It overlooked a bare-dirt backyard sloping down to a stand of woods, not a house in sight in this direction.

Behind me I heard Tom say, "You have to buy your own stove and refrigerator. We're taking the refrigerator, but we'd consider selling the stove and leaving it here."

My heart caved. There was no way we could afford both a stove and a refrigerator. I turned away from the window overlooking the yard and the woods and faced the room again. Cal and Tom were standing in the kitchen, in the narrow space between the appliances in question.

"How much for the stove?" Cal asked without hesitation.

Tom shrugged. "Ten dollars."

"We might be able to get a used refrigerator," Cal said to me. "Use a cooler until we can find one."

I nodded, happy. We were on board again. We'd live here.

"And a woodstove," Tom added. "You'll have to get a woodstove. We're taking that one with us."

And my heart collapsed again. Purchasing a refrigerator and a woodstove was out of the question.

"When are you leaving?" Cal asked.

"End of the month. You can move in in February."

Cal turned to me. "That's almost spring," he said, although it wasn't even close. "Just a few months. It starts warming up some in February. We could get the woodstove next fall. Just tough it out until then. We have an electric heater."

I nodded. "Okay," I said, my voice barely finding the air it needed to be heard.

"It gets pretty cold," Karen said.

Tom intervened, clearly wanting to get out of the lease. "Well, that's their business, honey."

He needn't have worried. Nothing could sway us from taking this cabin, although it might seem like Karen was trying.

"The Bakers own the place," Tom said.

"They come around the first of the month. Five o'clock on weekdays, anytime on weekend. After church if it's Sunday," Karen said. "Don't think you can dodge them by not being home, because they'll come back until they get it."

"Honey," Tom said, gently.

"And if you don't come home that day, they'll be here first thing in the morning."

"Honey," Tom said again.

"You can't count on them for anything. They're cheap," Karen said, warming up to the topic of the dreaded landowners.

"But you can do whatever you want to the place," Tom interjected.

At this Karen poked her foot at the green Astroturf on the kitchen floor and said, "We thought about taking this up."

"Would that be okay?" I asked.

"Sure," Karen said. "They don't care. It's just plywood under there. Not very pretty."

Prettier than fake grass, I thought.

"It probably helps keep it warm," Tom said.

To hell with warm, I thought. That fake grass has got to go.

"The carpet in the loft," Karen said. "It's wearing out and leaks dust downstairs."

It's out of here, I thought.

Karen pointed to the floor in the main cabin, covered with a square of blue carpet that I thought looked terribly out of place. "The floor is uneven. You'll need carpet."

"I didn't feel it slanting," I said, remembering my grandmother's house in Alabama, with its tilted hallway.

"Oh no, the foundation's fine, as far as I know." We walked into the main room. "Nothing's sinking. It's just that the boards are different thicknesses, so one is higher than the one next to it." Karen knelt and pulled one corner of the carpet back to show me the uneven floorboards. "You have to be careful not to stub your toe. It helps to put a rug down." She replaced the edge of carpet and stood. "It'll wear it out though." She nodded to a straight line worn into the carpet by an edge of flooring. "I don't know why, but every house here has this uneven flooring."

"I have a braided rug," I said. "It would look nice here."

Karen continued, advising us not to sign a lease. "The lease is terrible. It'll have you fixing everything."

"We signed it," Tom said. "Which is why we're doing the looking-for-a-tenant thing, just hoping to get our deposit back. But there are people here who've never signed a lease and never given a deposit. If Mrs. Baker gives you a lease, just take it and never give it back. If you're here with the rent every month that's all she cares about.

"And if she asks for a deposit, just tell her you're short this month. Give her the rent. Eventually, if you're paying the rent she won't ask anymore."

"So, you want it?" Tom asked.

We nodded in unison, probably the only thing Cal and I had ever done in unison.

"You want to buy the stove?" Tom asked.

"Uh, uh, uh, yeah," Cal said, and he reached for his wallet and pulled out a ten-dollar bill.

"We're leaving the end of the month. We can get out on Friday so you can move in on Saturday if you like. The first is Sunday. The Bakers will come by right after church on Sunday. About noon. Just be here with the rent."

"Okay," we said.

We got a little more information. The phone number, which at that time stayed with the house, the number for the electric company, a bit of information about the well.

"There are only a few wells for all the houses. It's not enough water for everybody. You can't flush the toilet too often."

"Okay," we said.

"And there's a brick in the tank, so it uses less per flush. We'll just leave it in there."

"Okay," we said.

"I'll leave the key under the rock next to the steps," Tom said.

"Okay," we said again.

On the way back to our house in Durham, I stared out the window at the scenery I'd be passing by every day. The fields and woods. The old farmhouse with stained glass in the front door, next to the country store. The bigger farmhouse off the road, with the wrap-around porch. The one on the hill in the big curve, hidden by a row of cedars. The cows grazing in front of the barn at the end of Mt. Carmel Church Road.

"Didn't James Taylor live around here?" I asked.

"I think so," Cal said.

I loved his song "Carolina in My Mind." I liked that it had put North Carolina on the map and made it seem almost as cool as California. I hummed a few bars, and Cal turned to me and grinned. He might have even reached across and squeezed my thigh.

<h1 style="text-align:center">13.</h1>

We gave notice to the landlord. We called our friends and arranged for trucks and boys to help us move. We told our parents and mentioned that we'd need to buy a refrigerator and eventually a woodstove. My parents offered their refrigerator, a hulking side-by-side thing I'd grown up with. They were thinking of replacing it anyway.

"Wood heat is so hard," my mother said.

"We can do it," I blithely replied, never thinking that she might have some experience in this area.

When moving day came, I was left behind again to clean the old place. Cal and the boys who'd come to help us took several loads over. I was anxious to be in the cabin, but this was a team effort, and my job was cleaning. I'll be there soon, I reminded myself as I scrubbed the bathroom and the toilet and mopped the floor. I'll be there soon.

I felt bitter that I'd been left at the house to clean alone again while Cal was smoking dope and listening to music in our new cabin. Not driving meant that I had no right to complain, though. If I chose to drive and had my own car, I could have gotten the house cleaned in an hour and taken myself to the cabin. And not driving was a choice; I knew that. I feared driving. I feared failing my test again. I was scared of everything, and because of the limitations I placed on myself, I'd married Cal. And now, instead of so many things that could have been, I waited in the empty, clean house and listened to the kid next door drive his go-cart around and around and around.

It was the end of the day when Cal finally drove up to get me. I was waiting on the stoop with my mop and bucket and rags and a can of Comet sitting next to me. We loaded the stuff into the car and left.

I should be able to remember more about that first night in the cabin. I wish I could recall the phase of the moon and whether or not it shined in the mullioned windows. I do remember that there was tremendous darkness outside those windows. I thought I knew woods, but this little neighborhood of cabins and shacks was surrounded by six-hundred acres of game land reserved for hunters.

These were not like the woods behind the house I had grown up in. Suburban houses ringed those woods, but they were as close to wild as I could get. In the center, there was a small creek and a rope swing my father had made for me. Those woods were my refuge. I had favorite trees I leaned against while I wrote in my journal. I had favorite rocks that I lay across. And I had the rope swing. The woods were where I went when I needed to be alone.

But even during our first night in Wildwood, without having yet ventured into the woods behind our cabin, I understood that I'd stepped into a place without the hard defined edges of yards and known cut-throughs to friends' houses. A soft porousness suffused Wildwood, but it denoted a hard natural reality. I could easily get lost in those woods.

I felt something invisible reach for me. There was a spirit here who had been waiting for me, a spirit who would not condemn me to hell, a spirit whom I was not afraid of, a spirit who wanted to help me. Maybe there was a god, and maybe, just maybe, it wasn't my mother's God, it wasn't the hand-me-down God given to her by her preacher father, it wasn't the punitive, mean-spirited God I'd grown up with. Maybe it was a god, or spirit, who believed in me, no matter how much I believed in it.

Cal rolled a joint and lit it. We pulled our chairs close to the electric heater and smoked. He cradled his guitar and idly picked. The cold wrapped around the cabin and crept in through the windows. Cal had stuffed a towel in the clay thimble in the wall where Tom and Karen's stovepipe had gone through. He got up and rearranged it, pushing it to fill the hole better and prevent streams of icy air flowing in. Even so, the cabin got colder and colder as the night went on. We draped ourselves in coats and scarves and plunked knit caps on our heads, pulled them low over our ears. I got up and putzed about the house, as I tended to do when I smoked good pot. I unpacked a few boxes, put a few things away, and then returned to the electric heater.

Eventually we turned the heater off and climbed the little staircase to the loft. We crawled across the brown carpet to bed.

The next morning, Sunday, we tested the temperature with our breath, puffing clouds of steam into the cold air. Our clothes were jumbled on the floor. Cal reached over and dragged them into bed with us. The icy denim of our jeans cut against my bare skin. My shirt warmed up first, wadded into the hollow of my stomach. Eventually we got out of bed and dressed. We crawled across the floor and turned around to back down the spiral staircase. We turned on the electric heater and huddled around it.

The heater did little to warm the cabin. Mostly it just warmed us, and mostly it just warmed one side of us, and mostly it just warmed parts of one side, our legs and feet if they were stretched out to meet its glowing coils. Eventually I would feel the burn through my socks. My jeans heated up and scorched against my skin, signaling that it was time to turn and warm up my backside.

Cal and I had no morning rituals on weekends except to smoke pot, but we couldn't smoke pot now. The Bakers would be showing up after church to collect the rent, and we needed to stay straight for that.

We heard them before we saw them. A rattling engine pulling into the driveways up the dirt road from us, one house after another. A voice. Old. Grizzled. Southern. Loud. They drove into our driveway in a dented blue pickup truck. We stepped outside, and met them.

"Now, are you the new people?" Mrs. Baker said, getting out of the truck while her husband sat in the driver's seat with the engine sputtering, his arm propped in the open window despite the cold.

"Yes ma'am," Cal answered.

"And what's your names?"

"I'm Calvin Powell, and this is Nancy."

I nodded to her but stayed quiet.

"And you're moved in now?"

"Yes ma'am." Cal pulled a wad of bills from his pocket. "A hundred and twenty-five dollars. Right?"

She reached for it. She wore a printed burgundy dress covered by a dark brown coat. Her hands were gnarly and veined. Working hands. They sifted through the money Cal had handed over, counting. After satisfying herself that it was the correct amount, Mrs. Baker folded the wad and shoved it into the pocket of her coat. She pulled a few folded pieces of paper from the same pocket. The dreaded lease.

"Calvin, you say?"

"Yes ma'am, but folks call me Cal."

"And Nancy?" She turned to me.

"Yes ma'am," I said. "We love the house," I added.

"Well, that's good. That's real good. I think you'll be real happy here. And are you … married?" She hesitated in the asking.

"Yes ma'am," we said, knowing it would help put us on the good side of this church-going lady.

She was clearly pleased and relieved. "Well, that's good. That's real good. Some of these folks here aren't married, you know," almost whispering it, as if it was too shameful to even say out loud.

"Yes ma'am," Cal said.

She looked at the papers in her hand "Now the fellow that left here," she said. "He told you now, you'll have to get your own refrigerator and stove?"

"Yes ma'am. We bought his stove, and Nancy's folks are giving us a refrigerator."

"Good. Good. Now, that's real good. And you know rent's due first of the month and we come around for it?"

"Yes ma'am."

"And you'll have to get a woodstove and your own wood too, you understand?"

"Yes ma'am."

She looked at the place in the cabin wall where the stovepipe would be and wasn't.

"We're not going to be able to do that right away," Cal said.

"Well now, how are you going to heat?"

"An electric heater for now."

"Well now." She paused, considering. "It's February. It can get mighty cold still. Don't leave it on if you're not here. It could be dangerous, you hear?"

"No ma'am, we won't."

"Or while you're sleeping," she warned.

"No ma'am."

We'd already thought of this. Every year there was a story on the news of a house that burned down from a fire started by an electric heater, sometimes trapping someone inside.

"You'll need a stove by next year. I don't think we'll have weather that'd make the pipes freeze again this year, but you'll need a stove by next year."

"Yes ma'am," Cal said, though I don't think either of us had ever heard of pipes freezing.

"What's your last name again?" Mrs. Baker asked.

"Powell," Cal answered.

"Powell. Would that be the Powells up in Knightdale?"

"I have an aunt living in Knightdale," Cal said.

"Velma?"

"Yes ma'am."

"Well now, I believe we're kin. She never married, did she? Velma is..." She strung out a complicated web of names and relations that proved she and Cal had shared blood somewhere way back. Having worked that out, she turned to her husband still sitting in the truck with the window down and hollered to him, "I believe this is Chester and Fairly Mae's son. Is that right?" she asked, turning back to Cal.

"Yes ma'am."

In acknowledgment, Mr. Baker lifted a hand.

"Well now." Mrs. Baker folded the papers and shoved them back into her pocket. She retracted the bills Cal had just handed her. "You paid in cash so that's…" She considered the situation. "… five dollars back to you." She peeled off a five and handed it to Cal.

"Thank you." Cal slid the bill into his pocket.

"I don't think there's any need for you to sign a lease. Or put down a deposit. Is there?" She tilted her head as if to judge our honesty.

"No ma'am," Cal said. "We'll be here with the rent the first of each month."

"Well now, that's good. That's real good. Now, you're going to be pretty cold without a woodstove and without any underpinning." She nodded to the cabin. There was nothing between the base of the cabin and the ground except foundation columns. "We might be able to get some underpinning done before next winter. Don't believe we can do it this season. We'll have to collect the rocks and all. But that'd help you out considerable. What do you think, Mr. Baker?" she hollered to the truck. "Think we could get these young folks some underpinning for the cabin?"

"That'd be fine," he hollered back, lifting his hand out the window again.

She nodded and smiled and reached out her hand. Cal shook it. She shook my hand, too, and said my name to make sure she got it right. "Nancy?"

"Yes ma'am."

"And how long you been married now?"

"Almost four years," I answered.

"Well now, that's fine. That's real fine. They're married," she hollered back to the truck.

"Good," Mr. Baker acknowledged, his hand automatically raising again.

Mrs. Baker went back to the truck and climbed in. Mr.

Baker waved his arm out the window one more time and backed up. He drove a short distance down the road and pulled into the next driveway.

Tom and Karen had filled us in on the history of Wildwood as they knew it. Just up the road the Army Corps of Engineers was building a massive lake. The Bakers had lived on a farm, land that had been in his family for generations, but the Army Corps of Engineers said they, and many others, whole communities, had to leave. The Bakers were especially angry, Tom said, and before leaving, while the land still belonged to them, they had every single outbuilding taken down, as well as the trees. They had the trees milled into lumber, and they purchased this land, as well as their new place in Bear Creek, thirty miles away from Wildwood and the church they still attended. Their son had graded Wildwood's dead-end dirt road. The Bakers dug wells and cleared lots, and they gave the lumber and the logs to a bunch of hippies and told them to build houses in exchange for a year's worth of free rent. The hippies went at it, and the result was eleven funky little houses collectively called Wildwood. The cabin we moved into was made of old logs that might have once been a tobacco barn.

I can't vouch for the truth of this story, except that there was Wildwood, and up the road the Army Corps of Engineers was clearing land for a lake.

Years earlier, my brother had read about this lake. He'd read that people were being evicted from their homes, the houses left empty. "It's a ghost town," he said. "Want to take a bike ride out there?"

I was game. He mapped out the route we'd take. We loaded some packs with bottles of water and sandwiches. It was a long bike ride, and we didn't find a ghost town. The houses had already been auctioned off and moved, leaving a snake of dirt roads running from Mt. Carmel Church Road to Highway 64.

The community had been called Seaforth. Eventually, I would learn to drive on those empty dirt roads. Cal would teach me. Later, after I left him, after the lake was finally flooded, I would sometimes drive across it, and if there was a drought, the roads would be visible, as if they'd risen from the water like a lost city.

14.

On our second morning in the cabin, we woke at 3:30. It was freezing. Our breath puffed in front of our faces as we pulled on our clothes. Our clothes were no comfort until our body heat warmed them. We rushed out to the car. Cal started it and backed out while I shivered in the passenger seat.

The plan was as it had been in the house in Durham. Cal would drive me to my parents' house. I'd sleep a little there and catch the bus into town for work. At the end of the day, he would pick me up. This had never been easy on him, and now from the cabin, far out in the country, it would be an extra burden. He would have to drive past his place of employment, and then, after depositing me at my parents' house, drive back to it. At the end of the day, once he got home, he'd only have a few hours there before he had to return to Chapel Hill to pick me up. This arrangement added two hours driving time to his workdays. All because of me.

I didn't acknowledge how difficult this arrangement made his life. I blithely told myself that if he really loved me, he'd be happy to do this, the man/woman fairy tale still alive in my mind, still running my thoughts. And instead of complaining directly about it, Cal found ways to take it out on me, things I wouldn't directly complain about either or even mention.

On our first weekday morning of commuting from the cabin, Cal started a tradition. He pulled into the parking lot of Farrell and Son's, the local gas station just up the road from Wildwood, the tires crunching the gravel and then stopping in front of the bright red vending machine. "I need a Coke," he said. He pulled out a handful of change and handed it to me.

Given that I had slept with other people and then begged Cal to stay, there was no question that I owed him this. I got out of the just-now-warming-up car and stepped into the cold, brittle air. I had to take my mitten off to get the coins in the vending machine slot. It was so cold that I dropped a quarter and leaned down to pick it up and slide it in. I punched the buttons, and a can of ice-cold Coke dropped into the bin below. I put my mitten back on and pushed the plastic door and reached inside to get it, but I couldn't get a grip on it. I had to take my mitten off again and grab it bare-handed.

When I handed it to Cal, he opened it, took a swig, and handed it back to me.

"I can't hold it and drive too," he said, although I knew he could. I'd seen him do it.

I had both my mittens back on now, but the can of Coke sweated through, and my fingers were wet and cold.

Cal put on the radio. I stared out the window and passed the Coke to him whenever he held out his hand for it.

Staring out windows has always been one of my best things. On this morning I noticed the things that I would come to always look for during our early-morning commutes, beacons and markers that I came to love.

In the window of a house near an intersection was a nightlight shaped like the Cape Hatteras lighthouse.

Up on the hill of the Nature Trail Mobile Home Park so many porch and deck lights glittered through the trees and vegetation that I imagined them as a distant medieval village.

In one farmhouse after another, a lone light could be seen in one window, with a woman moving about in her bathrobe, fixing coffee and breakfast, I assumed.

At the end of the road, where we turned onto the highway, I smiled at the ghostly white faces of the cows in the field in front of the barn.

The rest of the trip was streetlights and occasional headlights. A turn past the mall where Cal and I had both worked. A turn into my parents' neighborhood. A drive up the steep hill I used to sled down on snowy days and slog up after school. Cal dropped me off at the top of the hill above my parents' house. I stepped out into the night. He pulled away, leaving me to make my way down the drive to the brick walkway my father had built, down its many steps to the porch where my parents had left a light on. That light wasn't enough to illuminate my way, but Cal didn't care, and I didn't dare complain. I slipped through the unlocked front door and went to bed in my old room. My mother woke me in time to have breakfast with them and then catch the bus into town for work.

At the end of my workday, I scurried up the sidewalk to meet Cal at the corner. He was grumpy if I wasn't there when he drove up. It pissed him off if he had to circle the block or wait for me. I did everything I could to keep him even keeled, to please him, to appreciate him, to avoid his glares. I did everything but learn to drive.

Even though we lived in the cabin now, even though we'd bonded over the search for this home and moving into it, Cal was still Cal. The move to the cabin had taken some of the heat off me, it had given us a mutual goal, but now we'd landed here, and we were facing each other once again in day-to-day life. I cooked, I cleaned, I acquiesced in every way I was capable of. He drove and played his guitar and told his long-winded stories.

Each night we huddled around the electric heater. It was colder than I could have imagined. I turned my body one way and then another to face the electric heater. Trips to the bathroom were preceded by the fog of my breath. The toilet seat was another thing. It absorbed the cold and transferred it to my bottom every time I peed. This is penis envy, I thought, as I returned to the heater and backed up to it, trying to warm my ass.

We discovered we had mice. At night we heard them stir in the eaves above our bed and scuttle about in the kitchen. In the afternoon, when Cal returned me to the cabin, I swept their droppings off the counter and the stovetop. I started bringing home large glass jars from the lunch counter at the drugstore where I worked, boxes of them that I schlepped up the sidewalk to the corner where I met Cal. Once home, I put all the food mice might find interesting into the jars.

We learned a few tricks for dealing with the cold. It was Cal's idea that we fold our clothes for the next day and put them in bed with us to keep them warm. Now every morning when the alarm went off, Cal cut the lamp on, and after testing the temperature with our breath, we started pulling our clothes up from the foot of the bed and wrestling into them while still under the covers. We bumped elbows and knees worming our legs into long johns and our arms into knit shirts. Finally, one of us got enough clothes on to get out of bed and finish dressing in the narrow channel of floor where one could stand up straight beneath the peak of the ceiling.

There was no breakfast and no warm beverage. We dressed and rushed out to the car. I fumbled the coins Cal gave me into the bright red Coke machine in the parking lot of Farrell and Son's. I held the can of Coke and passed it to him whenever he held out his hand. Cal turned on the radio. We did not talk. I looked out the window for the first beacon of my ride into town, the nightlight shaped like the Cape Hatteras lighthouse, sitting on a windowsill.

I'd climbed that lighthouse many times during our family vacations. One week I climbed it every day until I'd done it so often I could scamper up the 257 steps to the top, scurrying past the grownups panting in the windowsills. At the top I stood close to the rail and looked out over the sea with its waves churning repeatedly and rhythmically and endlessly and reliably.

I loved the ocean. I loved the week we got to spend there every year. When I was very young my father carried me out into the water and held me, my legs and arms clasped around him, as he jumped waves. One time we went under, and I remember having my eyes open and seeing his feet against the sandy bottom, the sand shifting around, his toes digging in, my hair floating in front of me. When we popped up again, he looked at me, concerned, and asked, "Are you okay?" I nodded, mute and happy.

Passing the lighthouse nightlight every morning, I smiled to myself at these memories. I churned them up.

My siblings found cans and cans of C rations along the beach one year, washed up from some ship. They gathered them in a plastic sand bucket and carried them back to the cottage. My father opened one labeled peaches and, eating them, he said, "This takes me back."

I didn't ask what it took him back to. I thought I knew.

World War II. He'd gone to officer's school. He'd been some-thing, but I didn't know what. He'd been somewhere, but I didn't know where.

The pictures I saw from WWII were black and white and strange. How could that have happened? How could Anne Frank have had to hide away in an attic for years, hoping to avoid the horror of a concentration camp? We'd read her diary in eighth-grade English class, but even sitting on the porch of our rented cottage at Cape Hatteras while my father ate a can of C rations, I didn't ask about WWII, what it was like, how they managed the uncertainty. I asked instead for a taste of the peaches, and my father lifted the fork to my mouth, the yellow syrup dripping onto my bathing suit.

Now Cal lifted his hand for the can of Coke, and I passed it to him. He took a swig, draining it and passing the empty can back to me. I held it until we reached my parents' house, where I threw it away in their kitchen trash and then crawled into my childhood bed.

One Saturday Cal and I knelt in the kitchen together, our breath puffing in the cold air and the green Astroturf carpet grinding into our knees as we sliced at it with retractable knives. Bit by bit we cut at it and peeled it off the floor. Our butts bumped into each other as we worked. We paused to smoke a joint and eat some potato chips while huddled around the electric heater, then returned to the work. When finished, we had a wooden floor made of plywood. Cal hauled the old Astroturf to the car while I vacuumed up the shiny green plastic shards it had shed. Together we drove the carpet to a roadside dumpster and tossed it in.

Back at the cabin, I fixed dinner. Potatoes or sliced ham or fried corned beef hash out of a can. The plywood floor may have looked slightly better than the fake-grass carpet, but it was colder on my feet. I could feel the cold creeping through the soles of my sneakers and up my legs. I hurried to get back to the electric heater, where we would eat with plates balanced on our knees, the breath puffing in front of our faces a constant companion.

Cal's rage over my affairs still boiled up. I don't know how it was that we were both standing in the living room, and not huddled in front of the heater, and I don't know what triggered him this time, but his face contorted with anger, and he clamped his fists at his side, and he stalked toward me. I instinctively knew that I was about to be hurt, and I backed away from him.

"I just can't stand the thought of you with someone else." His teeth were clenched, and the words came out like bayonets. He advanced, and I stepped back again.

"I'm sorry. It won't happen again."

"I don't know what I'd do …" He advanced again.

"I'm sorry."

"It just makes me so mad."

He kept advancing, and I kept apologizing, backing away from him, back and back and back until I was pressed against the front door with nowhere else to go. His foot came out. As his leg lifted, I anticipated that foot landing on my shin. Or in my gut. But his foot kicked the door next to me. I'd not seen his hand come up. It landed across my face, giving me a black eye.

"I'm sorry," I bleated.

Cal turned and stalked away.

I made up a story to tell at work, about a walk in the woods, Cal in front of me, letting a branch loose that hit me in the eye. It was plausible. I laughed about it. Made light of it.

Because our house was so cold, we only had a few visitors here and there, but one of the boys who'd helped us move dropped by while I still sported the bruise around my eye. When he commented on my shiner, I told him my walking-in-the-woods lie.

"It popped you a good one," he said, passing the joint back to me.

There was no doubt in my mind that he believed me. He pulled his jacket closer to his chest and stood, rotating his body to the glowing coils of the electric heater.

When he'd gone Cal gently touched my face and shook his head. "I'm sorry," he said.

The bruise around my eye faded from purple to blue to yellow, and Cal's rage began to dissipate. He never hit me again. He never threatened to hit me again. His violent eruptions, his yelling at me, became less frequent. The affairs weren't brought up as often. But my guilt did not go away and neither did his sourness.

It was hard to tell what exactly Cal was sour about. My affairs? My inability to drive? Any pleasure I eked out of life that didn't involve him? Cal's sourness was a sauce that covered everything. I walked in it. I lifted my feet from its sticky goo. He was grumpy if I got excited over seeing a hawk land in a tree. He was grumpy if I mentioned a book I'd read and enjoyed when I was younger. He was grumpy if I did not pay rapt attention to him 100 percent of the time, except when he was distracted by a visitor, and there were fewer of those this winter.

I leaned on him. I leaned on him heavily to get me to and from work. The price I paid for not driving was staying. The sacrifice I'd made to stay married was writing. I had no creative outlet anymore. Nothing to do while he cradled and picked his guitar after dinner by the buzz of the electric heater. Alone, without the boys visiting and distracting us, I was thrown into the privacy I'd always wanted with him. There was space now for me to sit in the presence of Cal's personality, and in particular his stories, none of which I remember because Cal had zero story-telling ability. He had no feel for a narrative arc. Each story he told branched off into digression, and each digression branched off and branched off and branched off some more.

The tributaries wound around themselves until they choked off their own beginnings. I lost the original entry point. I couldn't keep the pieces together. Digression upon digression tangled like seaweed, pulling me down and trapping me underwater. To breathe, I fell into my own mind as Cal talked. His monologue became background noise, lulling me into my thoughts, thoughts I could no longer write down because I'd given that up.

So it was that my own mind digressed and digressed. Without paper and pen, nothing much made sense. There was no point to ever arrive at. No poem to create from something I'd seen or heard. No story to tell myself. No journal to sort it all out in. No narrative arc in my mind and certainly none in Cal's story.

I was aware that Cal was talking and that I needed to give the appearance of attentiveness, so I nodded and said uh-huh, until finally it dawned on me that I was no longer hearing the drone of his voice.

I looked up to find him glaring, his eyes narrowed, mad again.

I tried to cover for myself by repeating the last thing I remembered him saying, but it was no use. I was busted. He glared some more, but rather than give up telling the story, he returned to it. I paid attention for as long as I could, but the story had been lost long ago for me, and I had no idea how the last thing I remembered him saying fit in with all the rest. But I tried. I really did try. I tried to engage with him on what little I could retain, to prove how much I cared.

Once the story was finished, Cal would pick his guitar some more, satisfied that he'd snatched my attention back to him. We'd have a few more tokes. I was mostly silent and idle. With nothing to do to occupy me, nothing in my hands, nothing to read, no book to open, no pen to hold, my thoughts tramped around in my head like the homeless vagabonds they were.

And then Cal would begin another story, and I'd try to listen. I was going to pay attention this time. I was going to listen to every part of his story to see how all the pieces fit together, because he would reach the end of it eventually.

It's amazing to me that Cal never got lost in his stories. He never lost his train of thought. His digressions were never digressions to him. He never said, "I can't remember where I was going with all this." He always had a view of the original river; he just couldn't tell a story that would keep the river in anyone else's view.

One Saturday our friend Joel came by and found us as we usually were, cold and layered in clothes and stoned, huddled around the electric heater, getting up every now and then to brave the bathroom or get a snack from the kitchen.

"I might have a woodstove you can use," Joel said. "It's got a crack in it, but I think I can patch it."

The next weekend Joel brought over a box stove with a piece of metal bolted and stove-cemented to the side. He brought stovepipe too, and together he and Cal, with Joel giving instructions, installed the box stove. He showed us the damper, instructed Cal on building a fire, and told us a little about the wood we should burn. "Stay away from pine. Pine burns easy, but the fire doesn't last, and it builds up creosote."

There was a little bit of wood left in the woodshed built onto one side of the cabin, and we went out to inspect it. "This is good wood," Joel said. He unloaded a little more from the back of his truck, cut to size and split. "It won't last you long," he added. "You'll have to get more."

We thanked him, paid for the stovepipe he'd bought, and gave him some pot after burning a joint together.

Cal and I drove up to the end of the road, to the mailbox where the free weekly advertising paper was delivered. There was always a wad of newspaper left behind, and we grabbed some and drove back home. I walked the woods picking up sticks for kindling while Cal hauled in firewood by the armful and dumped it on our rough, uneven floor. He knelt before the stove and built our first fire. We stood around it, turning this way and that, warming our bodies to the radiant heat.

Gradually the main room of the cabin warmed, and the loft warmed. The kitchen and bathroom didn't warm. We could still see our breath in those places. We moved the electric heater to one corner of the kitchen.

The stove wouldn't hold a fire overnight, but it was toasty in the loft when we went to bed. Not so in the mornings when we woke up. We did not kindle a fire before leaving the cabin. It would have been a waste of wood.

In the evenings, once we were both home, Cal built the fire, and gradually the cabin became warm and comfortable. With his guitar cradled more comfortably than his thick coat had allowed, with warm fingers to pick with, Cal paid more attention to his music, and his stories slowed.

I loved sitting stoned by the woodstove with Cal picking his guitar. The pot burned sweetly as the music washed over me. The woodstove crackled and popped, and while I continued to keep myself small, I felt a comforting largeness around me.

Every day I stepped outside and looked up. Vultures wheeling in the sky. Hawks. A murder of crows filling the branches of a tree cawed and cawed and cawed, then lifted off in a cloud of black wings.

Every night while I held the flashlight for Cal as he gathered firewood from the shed, I looked up at the stars. Before the need to gather firewood, I'd not stepped outside at night in Wildwood. I'd never seen the night sky without city lights. I'd never seen stars like this, sparkling and winking and million-filling the sky, and then filling it some more. I loved those stars. I loved them so much. They nearly cracked me in two.

One night while holding the flashlight for Cal and looking up, I saw a meteor. My first.

"I just saw a falling star," I blurted.

"Great," Cal snapped. "Could I get some light here?"

I stopped looking at the sky. I focused on the beam from the flashlight. I didn't think it had wandered from its target of firewood while I watched the sky, but Cal's message was clear as always. *Don't enjoy yourself if I'm not enjoying myself.*

I wanted to help with the daily fire tasks. I wanted to do more than just passively hold the flashlight or stand to the side as Cal knelt on the uneven planks of our floor, crumpling paper, and adding kindling to the woodstove. "Teach me to build a fire," I said.

"Later," Cal grumbled.

I'd ask again later, and "later" was the answer.

I even asked on weekends, when he wasn't trying to get the house warm after a long day of work.

"Later" was always the answer.

Later, later, later, like my mother's promise that my grandmother wouldn't stay in my room the next year. Later. Not now. Later. The message? *You're inconvenient. You're an annoyance.* Cal would never teach me to build a fire.

I had good reason to want to know how to build a fire. I'd changed jobs again, leaving the drugstore with the janitor who looked for opportunities to grind his crotch into my behind, to working in a hardware store up the street. In my new job I had to work one Saturday a month, which meant I had a weekday off once a month, a cold weekday, with Cal gone to work and no fire in the cabin. A day in which I drank multiple cups of tea while huddled in front of the electric heater in my coat and hat.

15.

On the days I didn't have to work, and Cal did, the alarm went off and the snooze button got hit and hit and hit and hit and hit and hit. Then the lamp beside the bed went on. I didn't resent the lamp. I understood that in the cabin, Cal actually did need light by which to dress and navigate the twisty staircase.

But Cal never made any effort to dress quietly and slip out. He engaged me in every part of his miserable, unfair, persecuted morning when he had to go to work, and I didn't. First up, the clothes he'd stashed under the covers. "God-damn it, where's my other sock. I can't find my sock. God-damn it." And on and on until I helped him find his fucking sock, which was right there at his feet next to the other one.

When he finally got out of bed and completely dressed, he made his way downstairs and the overhead light came on, the one that was way up high, in the peak of the cabin's ceiling, eye level to anyone standing in the loft. It was a bare bulb, high-wattage, and neither of us ever used it any other time, preferring to use the light mounted directly under the loft's floor. That light shouted into my eyes as I lay in bed, just as Cal had known it would. I turned off the lamp in the loft, and I pulled a pillow over my head to block the light out.

But Cal was not done with me. Not even close. A plethora of questions started up.

"Do we have any Coke?"

"No, we don't have any Coke."

"Fuck."

I'd hear the refrigerator door slam shut. The sound of Cal putting his shoes on, shrugging into his coat. More cussing.

"Where are the goddamn car keys?"

"Have you checked your pockets?"

"They're not there."

"Coat pocket?"

I'd hear the rustling and the jingle of keys. "Alllll riiiiight. I found them. Fuck. Now I can't find my wallet."

I kept my voice even. It was all so absurdly predictable, the pattern blatant and unmissable. Cal's role was to demand my attention, to bring to light his suffering and the unjust situation of me having a day off while he had to go to work. And my role was to endure while sounding concerned and helpful about every bullshit obstacle to leaving the house that he could invent.

"Have you checked the counter?"

"It's not there."

"Is it on the TV?"

"Noooo."

"On the dresser?"

"Noooo."

Jesus, I thought, the cabin is not that fucking big. And the wallet is never lost on the mornings I am riding with him.

"I'll check the car," he'd say, and he'd go out, the door slamming and shaking in its frame. I'd hear the engine start up.

Is he leaving? I thought hopefully.

But no. He'd come inside again, the door slamming, Cal

stomping his feet. "Damn it's cold. May as well let the car warm up."

Yeah, anything to delay your departure. You never warm the car when I'm riding with you.

"Did you find your wallet?" I asked, making sure he knew I was still participating in his theater, as if I didn't know it was theater.

"Yeahhhh," the word strung out in his mud trail of sourness.

"Okay," he'd say. "Well, I guess I'll go."

"Okay," I'd say from the loft.

I knew better than to wish him a nice day. That would have been an offense to Cal. Hadn't I noticed that he had to go to work and that a nice day was out of the question? Was I rubbing it in that I got to stay home while he had to work?

I made a different mistake the first time I had a day off without him, the first time we went through this drama. I asked him to turn the overhead light off on his way out the door.

"Alllll riiiiight." Gruffly, begrudgingly, he hit the switch. I listened for the tires on the driveway as he backed out. But he came back. He made an excuse. He'd forgotten something. He had to find it. The overhead went on again, and this time, I didn't ask him to turn it off. It was easier and more effective to accept that I'd have to crawl downstairs and do it myself.

It was hard though to be sure he'd really gone. He'd often return after I'd heard his tires on the gravel. He wanted a joint. Or he needed some cash. Or he'd forgotten the much-looked-for wallet.

So, I pulled the covers over my head and waited. I listened for his tires rubbering down the dirt road, back to the cabin. I waited a beat, two beats, three beats, to make sure he was really gone. Then I turned the lamp on, climbed out of bed, crawled across the loft and down the little staircase, turned the overhead light off, climbed back into the loft, back across the floor and into bed. I turned the lamp off and slept. When I woke, I had a blessed day alone ahead of me.

A whole day. A cold day, for sure, but all the same, a day to myself stretched out before me. A huge span of time alone, satin sheets of time and solitude, the kind I'd not experienced since high school when I showed up for homeroom and skipped the rest of my classes.

I had plans for these days. I had a mental list of things to do, and at the top of that list was take a walk in the woods behind the cabin. Cal would call me midday. His use of the phone was as weaponized as the overhead light. Ostensibly he called to make sure I was okay. We both knew better. Cal called to make sure I was home and alone and not enjoying myself, and to remind me that, while I was home, he was at work and he was miserable.

I knew what would happen if I wasn't home for such a call. I'd have to tell him I was out in the woods without him, that I'd dared to take pleasure in something while he had to work. He might even rev up some suspicion that I was with another man, and then we'd have to rock that boat again.

But I could be as cagey as he believed himself to be. I took my walks in the morning, giving myself plenty of time to wander and get lost and still make it home by the time he called.

There was a small creek behind the cabin, and I headed in that direction, going downhill toward it. There were no paths, so I wound around this tree or that one, never arriving in the same place twice. But if I was going downhill, I knew I was heading toward the stream. Once I found it, I could recognize where I was and whether I needed to head upstream or downstream to find the small rent in the forest that told me an old homestead was close by.

When I found that opening in the trees, I jumped the stream and went up the hill where the woods gave way to a field. There was an old house here, the walls collapsed long ago, so that the roof sat almost directly on the ground. I knew what was under that roof, as far as I could see anyway, but even though I knew I always knelt on the ground and looked as an homage to the woman who'd once lived here. There was her shoe, and a black purse. A blue-and-white-speckled kettle turned on its side. Behind a shed, not far away, was a pile of empty liquor bottles, and on the wall of the shed hung a belt on a nail.

It didn't take much for me to speculate that hard lives had been lived here. I felt heartbreak here. I felt stories waiting to be teased out, waiting to be written. I reached under the fallen-down roof and laid my hand on the woman's shoe, as if it might tell me what I wanted to know, as if her story might flow into me.

And what would I have done if it had? I no longer aspired to be a writer. That was over.

A faint road led away from the farmhouse, and I followed it. It took me around the dead end of Wildwood's dirt road and delivered me to a junkyard, an acre or more of ancient cars with rounded tops and fenders and steering wheels the size of tires, cars like the one I'd seen my mother leaning against in the photograph, her arms spread out along its top, a huge lipstick smile on her face, looking seductively into the camera.

I gingerly opened the door to one of the cars. I sat on the dusty, cracked seat. I placed my hands on the steering wheel. It felt huge and monstrous, like something that could easily get away from me, were I to try and drive it. I eased the glove box open and found a woman's lace glove, a receipt for cotton sold, a prayer card from a church, and a worn leather coin purse with nothing in it. After handling these remnants from other lives, I gently replaced them and closed the glove box and the car door.

From the junkyard, I headed east, or if it was a cloudy day and I could not see the sun, what I hoped was east. East would deliver me somewhere along the dirt road of Wildwood on the other side from the little houses, but I often inadvertently veered south and ended up along the blacktop road, which required a little more walking to get home.

I had my old Cinderella watch I'd received for Christmas years ago strapped to my wrist. I checked to make sure I'd be home for Cal's phone call.

One morning on a day off without Cal, instead of taking a walk, I chopped all the firewood we'd dragged up from the woods over the weekend. The wood was dogwood. Dead dogwoods are easy to kick over, but hard wood to chop. We only had a hatchet that first winter and I flailed away with it. I chopped and chopped and chopped. My arm ached. I took short breaks and then went back to chopping some more. I threw each stove-sized piece in a pile, and hours later, after I'd finally gotten the job done, I carried the logs to the woodshed and stacked them.

I was having a cup of tea when Cal called. "What have you been up to?" he asked. This question from him always felt like an interrogation. I answered that I'd chopped the wood. He seemed neither surprised nor pleased, but that evening when he came home, he announced, "I'm taking you out to dinner. *Anywhere you want to go.*"

An unexpected dinner out? My choice of restaurant? Cal never took me out to dinner.

"Anywhere you want to go," he repeated.

"Papagayo's," I answered instantly. I'd never eaten at the popular Mexican restaurant in Chapel Hill. What little I knew of it came only from casual mentions by one or two of the boys who had visited us in our first house and had taken dates there.

Sometimes I walked by Papagayo's large plate glass window as I took a lunch break stroll from my job. I gazed longingly at its gathering of tables spread with crisp white cloths. I envied the people sitting there, a waiter or waitress standing at the ready, memorizing their orders, taking the huge menus out of the customers' hands, delivering drinks and then plates of food.

Table service. That's all I wanted. Someone to come take my order. Someone to serve me a plate of food and refill my Coca-Cola and take away the dishes and offer dessert.

"Nah," Cal said. "Too expensive. How about Golden Corral?"

I should have known. Anywhere you want to go. Why had he even said it? Why had he given me, for that one tiny moment, the hope of eating in a place that did not have pictures of steaks and potatoes backlit behind a display of chilling salads and desserts. I never understood Golden Corral. Why did we get plastic trays to push along a railing like I'd done in the school cafeteria? Why did we pick up empty red plastic cups to have them filled with iced tea at the table? Why did we need trays to carry napkins and utensils and empty cups to the table? Was it table service, or was it a cafeteria? It seemed to be both, and neither.

"Okay," I agreed, hiding my feelings, not pointing out the

offer of choosing any restaurant I wanted, not making a fight out of it.

We got in the car. Before we'd reached the end of our dirt road, Cal told me that when he was leaving work one of his coworkers asked if he had to go home and chop wood, and he'd said, "Naw, my wife did it." And she said, "You better take that woman out to dinner, son."

Of course, I thought. It wasn't even his idea. I wished he'd kept that information to himself.

Spring arrived at last, and along with the warm weather came whippoorwills, dogs, and a pedal steel guitar.

The whippoorwills were relentless. I'd never heard one before, and I've never heard such a cacophony of them as I did that year. If there was one, there must have been fifty. As dusk came on, they started up.

Datada-datada-datada-datada

Whippoorwill-whippoorwill-whippoorwill-whippoorwill

They were magic. They were charms, they were blessings, they were incantations, they were my mojo. I was in love with the whippoorwills, and I looked them up in my bird book. *Small brown birds, rarely seen, nesting at the edges of fields and woods.* Like me, I thought. I nest at the edge of fields and woods.

The fields and woods I nested near were perfect dumping places for unwanted pets. This is how we acquired dogs. They came to us singly, pushed out of cars and abandoned along our dead-end dirt road, or wandering the parking lot of Farrell and Son's where we went to buy gas and Cokes and bags of chips and candy bars. We ended up with three. We fed them. Let them inside at night and let them run wild during the day.

Before we went to bed, we called for them. Sometimes

they stayed out all night, or one or two would come home. As each arrived, panting and happy, we gave him a large Milk-Bone.

One night one of our dogs didn't come home, so we turned off the lights, locked the door, and went to bed. But once in bed, I remembered that we'd left his Milk-Bone on the counter. "Shit. The Milk-Bone. The mice."

"You can go get it if you want to," Cal said.

Cal slept on the outside of the bed. Without question or discussion, I'd automatically given him the easier side to get up from. My side of the bed was snugged up beneath the eaves with only a foot of space between my head and the slanting ceiling. To go get that Milk-Bone meant climbing over Cal, hunching my body so my head didn't hit the ceiling until I could stand, then hunching my body again, sitting down on the edge of the loft, searching out the first step of the spiral staircase with my foot, and turning around to go down backwards. And clearly, Cal wasn't going to offer to do it.

"Fuck it," I said. "The worse they'll do is nibble on it."

"Yeah, probably." Cal reached over and turned off the lamp.

In the middle of the night, I woke to a dragging sound just above my head in the eaves. Cal woke too. "Is that…?"

I finished for him. "The Milk-Bone?"

"Nah," he said. "It couldn't be."

The sound continued and then stopped. We fell back asleep. The next morning at 3:30 when we got up to go to town, the missing dog was asleep on the porch, and the Milk-Bone was gone from the kitchen counter. The mice had managed to move it all the way up into the eaves. They ate on it for a week, dragging it around in the ceiling above our heads every night.

The third thing that spring brought us was the pedal steel guitar. When Cal said he wanted one, I asked what it was, and he explained, "You know the twang in country music?"

"Yeah."

"That's a pedal steel."

I suppose I'd seen them. I'd watched *The Porter Wagoner Show* and *Hee Haw*, but I had no remembrance of such a thing. Cal found a used one, and we scraped up the money for it. When he brought it home, I watched him open the case, screw the legs on, and pick it up, turning it upright. I marveled at this thing. The strings were horizontal. It sat on the floor like a small piano. Cal attached rods to pedals that raised certain strings. He sat down in front of it with a heavy metal slide cupped in his fingers.

Cal taught himself to play the pedal steel, just as he'd taught himself to play guitar.

He put a record on and then tried to emulate the sound. He was infinitely patient with himself in the process of learning anything musical. He never got frustrated. He never thought ill of himself for not getting it right immediately. He never gave up on himself. I don't think he ever had a formal music lesson in his life, and he was good.

After dinner each night, after cleaning up, I stepped out on the porch to hear the whippoorwills. The dogs were sometimes in the yard, their tails a swirl of fur and canine joy. From inside the house, I heard Cal practicing his pedal steel guitar.

The spirits of Wildwood were all around me now, holding my hand as I walked the woods. I knew those woods. I knew the woman's shoe under the roof of the old homestead. I knew the paths and the stream and the junkyard cars.

These were places I never shared with Cal. He and I some-times took walks in the woods, but never as deep and far as I went alone.

16.

The heat of summer came on. We opened the screenless windows, let the air and bugs in, turned on the fans to stir things up, moved our bed downstairs, and started sitting outside a lot.

Warmer weather also brought visitors, not just our own visitors coming to see us in the cabin, but strangers. Both the sheriff and sightseers, wanting to gape at the hippies, drove down Wildwood's dead-end dirt road and back again.

The sheriff came randomly, all days of the week. We could tell it was him by the slow crawl of the patrol car's tires grinding along the gravel road, taking the curve in the swamp, slowing even more once he started passing by the houses. We scurried the pipes and joints and ourselves inside the cabin and waited until he'd passed, turned around at the dead end, and passed again.

The sightseers were more amusing. They showed up on Sundays, after church let out. Sitting outside, hearing a big car creeping along the road, not quite as slow as the sheriff drove, one of us said, "Sightseers," and we stashed the bong or the pipe or joint inside the cabin again, but we didn't go inside and stay there. Instead, we resumed our places outside in our chairs and waited. It was a game to make sure that these families, come to Wildwood to see the hippies, got what they wanted.

The storyteller inside me imagined that a drive into Wildwood was always the father's idea, but I knew better than to wonder out loud to Cal. Speculation was still taboo. A story that wasn't his and factual, a story coming from me, still made him cross. But it was always the father behind the wheel, and it wasn't hard to see his bubble-haired wife's disapproval as she sat beside him, resolutely staring straight ahead, refusing to glance one way or another. In the backseat, the children pressed their faces to the window. As the car glided by, they stared at us, their eyes big with fear. Cal often lifted his hand and gave it a slight shake, barely a wave, which inevitably caused the children to dive down into the seat and hide. But they would be pressed against the window again on the way back, and the father would have an amused expression on his face, while his wife continued to stare straight ahead, refusing to look.

That could have been me with the bubble hair staring straight ahead. That was the life my parents had planned for me. That was the life I'd seen on TV. That was the life I'd rejected, but not fully purged myself of. I imagined the wife going home and fixing the midday meal. I would be doing the same thing shortly, the difference being clothing and hair, the members of the family, and the house and kitchen. I doubted she would be standing barefoot on a plywood floor. I pictured her slipping out of her high heels and into her bedroom slippers, just as my mother had done after church. Tying an apron around her waist, bustling about in the kitchen pulling out leftovers from the refrigerator and putting together a meal for her brood. My brood was Cal, and he didn't help with kitchen or housework.

He was served, just as I imagined the sightseer father was served.

As fall came on, we moved the bed back upstairs and started collecting firewood from the future site of Jordan Lake. We had a crosscut saw now and a truck, and we drove out on Saturday mornings looking for piles of debris pushed by a bulldozer close to the road. When we found one, Cal parked the truck, and we pulled wood out of the pile and cut it on site, with Cal on one end of the crosscut saw and me on the other.

Something happened to me out there on the edges of what would become Jordan Lake, matching rhythm with Cal as we sawed a piece of wood. Something happened to me as we gathered the resulting logs and tossed them into the back of the truck. Something happened to me as we drove home, sharing a joint, and then once home, unloaded the wood into the woodshed and stacked it. What happened was that I came to love Cal. Or perhaps I was merely transferring my love of Wildwood to the man I shared it with.

Whatever it was, my feelings for Cal were not earth shattering, not made up of fireworks or passion. But things changed for me, gathering firewood, unloading the firewood, passing it to Cal as he stacked it in the woodshed, using my body and muscles for something besides cooking and cleaning. I felt cradled, cradled by my life, cradled by Wildwood. Never cradled by Cal, but he was a part of it all, and this was what I wanted. The country. A rough cabin. Entertaining dogs and mice. Good pot and music, and Wildwood continuously revealing herself to me, continuing to show me a new sky every day.

Cal answered an ad he found on a bulletin board at work, the same place he found the ad for the cabin. A band was looking for a pedal steel player. He got together with them and showed them his chops and soon joined the band. He played the pedal steel and his acoustic and sometimes lead on his electric guitar.

The band often practiced at the cabin, setting up in the living room, smoking joints, and carrying on. There was a female lead singer, so it wasn't all boys, which I liked. When they played out in public, I enjoyed sitting at a table with the other girlfriends and wives, being separate from Cal but connected to him too. He was up on stage, and I was proud of him, but as Cal's creative life expanded, I could feel my own abandoned creativity tugging at me. There was something inside of me that wanted out, something pawing at my vow to never write again, something opening its sharp claws and tearing into that vow, just as I'd torn into my writing years earlier.

I still gave Cal my money after cashing my paycheck, but I'd learned long ago to hold out five bucks to use throughout the week for Cokes and the occasional hotdog. One day on my lunch break I walked to the drug store where I used to work, and I bought a very small notebook for twenty-five cents. I still had the large fringed leather purse I'd carried in high school, although I hadn't used it in a while. At home, I unearthed it from Cal's childhood trunk next to the bed in the loft. I moved my dailies into it, along with the little notebook. I would write again, but I made new vows around it. I vowed to keep writing small and safe by carrying it with me everywhere. I vowed not to write in anything so obvious as a journal. I vowed to never let Cal see me writing. I vowed to never tempt him to invade my privacy as he'd done before.

During my lunch hours, I sought out a small stand of woods close to my work at the hardware store. It was solidly winter now, and I would bundle in my coat and sit beside a semi-dry streambed and write. Not ideal conditions for writing, plus I was rusty. It had been over two years since I'd quit. Poems did not pour out of me as they had before.

I persevered. I wrote pretty descriptions of what I saw in front of me, just for the sake of translating the world into words. I stared out the window while Cal drove me home from work and composed poems in my head and then scribbled them down in my little notebook, often in the bathroom so I wouldn't be seen or quickly while Cal was building a fire and I was supposed to be fixing dinner.

My notebook was the size of my palm. It was never meant for anything more than shopping lists or jotting down phone numbers. Like those little entry blocks marked by faint gold lines in the five-year diary my mother had given me, it wasn't large enough to receive me. But it was something. It was a place where pen met paper.

Cal picked me up from work one day and said, "I've got a surprise."

"What?" I asked.

"You'll see when we get home. I didn't do it," he added, "but you'll be pleased. You'll see."

What I saw when Cal turned into the driveway was that the Bakers had kept their promise to underpin our cabin. In one day, while we worked, the two of them had hauled in the necessary rocks and cemented them in place. On one side they'd framed an opening and hinged an access door.

We got out of the truck and walked all around the cabin. There was no trace of the Bakers' labor except the resulting underpinning. No dropped blobs of cement, no stray rocks, no forgotten tools. Just the underpinning with the cords of cement between the stones still drying.

"Damn," I said. "They did all this in one day?"

"I came home, and it was done. They were gone. I'm going to call them and thank them."

"That's a good idea."

"It's amazing, isn't it? It's going to be a lot warmer."

It was amazing. How many truckloads of rocks had it taken? Where had they gathered them from? How long had they been collecting them? I started dinner. Cal called the Bakers to thank them.

"Yes ma'am," I heard him say. "We're very pleased. Thank you."

The cabin was definitely warmer without the wind whistling under it, but it was still cold in the kitchen and cold in the morning, and the woodstove required constant feeding.

And I still made my appeal: Teach me to build a fire.

And Cal still said: Later.

During the night, as we sat around the woodstove, I refined my request, asking him to at least teach me how to stoke the fire.

"Later," he said, as he performed the task.

After a time, I stopped asking and simply watched, and then one night, as the fire dwindled and the cold crept around the edges of my body and Cal stayed absorbed in picking his guitar, I stood and opened the damper as I'd seen Cal do. Then I opened the door to the stove, slowly so there was no back puff of smoke. I raked the remaining coals, and I selected a few logs from the pile on the floor. I laid them on the coals with enough air around them. I closed the door slightly, creating a draft, and once I was satisfied that they'd caught well, I closed the stove door and shut the damper partway. I sat back down in my rocking chair.

Cal looked at me, nodded, and said, "Pretty good."

A few weeks later I had Monday off. After Cal had finally left with the usual dramatics ("Do we have any Coke? Where are my keys? Fuck, it's cold. I'm going to let the truck warm up. I forgot something." On and on.), after I was sure he was gone and I had climbed downstairs to turn the overhead light off, after I'd returned to sleep and woken up again, I backed down the twisty staircase and looked at the box stove, my breath puffing in front of me. A stack of newspaper lay piled close to the basket of kindling, next to logs stacked inside the door. I knew what I wanted to do.

I had ingredients for baking bread. I had it all planned out. I would build a fire, bake some bread, and when Cal called, I wouldn't mention any of it. He'd come home to a warm cabin and freshly baked bread. If that wouldn't please a man, then I didn't know what would.

I gathered materials for the fire. I opened the damper and knelt in front of the stove. I cleaned out some of the ashes, but not all. I crumpled the newspaper and made a pile inside the stove. I covered it with kindling. I chose small pieces of wood to get the fire going before adding larger pieces. And I lit it with a wooden match.

Slowly the cabin air warmed. I went into the kitchen and boiled water for tea. While the tea brewed, I stepped outside for more wood and looked up at the stovepipe, at its satisfying stream of smoke pouring out. I went back inside and dropped my armful of wood into the pile by the door. I got my tea and sat in my rocking chair pulled close to the stove. I tended that fire all day long.

As planned, when Cal called that afternoon, I did not mention the fire or the bread dough rising in a bowl behind the stove. I gave him a litany of tasks completed. Cabin cleaned. Woodstove cleaned. I gathered more kindling.

I still thought it better not to let Cal know I was enjoying his absence. Better not to remind him I was free on a day he was not. Better not to mention that I was burning wood for warmth he wasn't enjoying. This wasn't so much for his benefit as it was for mine. Any maneuver I could make to avoid his bleating was worth it.

And it worked. When he got home, he was happy to not have to build a fire. Happy to not have to haul in the night's wood. Happy to have a slice of warm bread with butter, while his wife fixed dinner.

Now I enjoyed my days alone in the cabin more than I had before. I was warm and cozy with a crackling fire. I rolled a joint and got stoned. I went on walks. I baked bread. I read. I sat and watched the dust motes drift in columns of light. I watched the way the sun tracked across my braided rug. Sometimes I stepped outside and looked up. Sometimes I pulled out my tiny notebook and recorded a tiny thought, all my own.

17

On my days off without Cal, I learned a lot about fire. I learned how to coax a fussy fire into a good fire. I learned to feel, from the temperature of my skin, when it needed stoking. I learned the subtleties of the damper. I learned that dead dogwood is a good dry wood that easily catches. I was good at working with the fire. It was Wildwood and fire that gave me confidence enough to think about driving.

Cal's eyes lit up when I asked him to teach me. He didn't say "later" to this request, as he had with the fire. Maybe seeing me learn the woodstove made him believe I could learn to drive. Or maybe he'd been wanting this for a long time. Maybe he'd never intended, when he asked me out, to become my chauffeur.

"We can drive at Seaforth," Cal said, referring to the maze of dirt roads that had once been a community, the roads my brother and I had biked on believing we'd find a ghost town, the roads that would eventually be under the waters of Jordan Lake.

"We'll start this weekend," he added.

"Okay." I took a deep breath. I was still scared of driving, but I was committed to this. I wasn't going to fail this time. And I didn't have to learn with a group of other kids, during a specific amount of time. Plus, I could learn on empty roads where no one else was at risk.

For all my nervousness, Cal was remarkably calm. On Saturday, he drove us to the entrance of Seaforth. Once on the dirt road, he cut the engine of our Datsun truck, and we got out and switched places. He explained the clutch to me. Before starting the truck, Cal had me press it in with my left foot and go through the gears. "You'll brake and accelerate with your right foot," he said. "Left foot is clutch only. Even in an automatic, let your right foot do the work. Always start in first gear. I'll tell you when to switch to second and so on. Clutch always in when you want to shift." He told me that if I didn't have the rhythm of working the clutch and the acceleration together, letting one off while applying the other, the truck would either stall out or lurch forward. "You'll get the hang of it," he said.

I started the truck, eased my foot off the clutch as Cal instructed. We rolled forward. "Give it some gas," he said. "Not too much." I did as I was told. The truck did not stall or lurch.

We rolled along a little faster. "Shift into second," he said. I did. The truck lurched a little, but not enough to stall out. A little more gas, and I went up to third, then fourth. And at the end of Seaforth, where the dirt road met Highway 64, Cal talked me through a three-point road turn, and I drove back again.

We did this for hours. I was more impressed with how patient Cal was, and with what good, clear instructions he gave me, than I was with myself for driving. This was not a Cal I'd seen before. I suppose he was motivated and determined not to scare me off from learning by overreacting. As for my part, I listened to his instructions, and I understood them and did what he said. I drove back and forth along the roads of Seaforth, steering and shifting and watching the road for other vehicles.

Usually there were none, but occasionally I would round a curve and encounter a truck spattered with mud, filled with young reckless boys inside the cab and the bed. They reeled around the curve confidently and happily waved while I closely stayed on my side of the road, both hands on the wheel. But I did not stop. I did not freeze. Cal waved to them as they went by. "Good job," he said.

He told me to listen to the engine and feel it to know when to shift gears. And after a time, he stopped telling me when to shift, because I knew, left foot pressing the clutch, right hand on the gearshift knob. Third gear. Fourth gear. I drove and drove and drove that first day, and Cal sat beside me and said again, "Good job." "Excellent." "Well done." Had I not been focused on driving I might have cried for hearing these words. I'd longed for them all my life, not just from him, but in school, from my family, from my mother.

After a time, Cal and I got hungry and decided to call it a day. I drove to the entrance of Seaforth where we'd started from, where the dirt road ended and the pavement began. "Leave it running," Cal said. "Put it in neutral, and pull the brake." I did so, and we switched places.

That night as Cal practiced his pedal steel guitar, I sat out on the porch bundled against the cold and remembered something. Coming home from a family vacation, sitting in the backseat, I'd watched two young women with curlers in their hair passing us in an open Jeep. They were laughing and talking. I saw the driver effortlessly shift into gear using a stick on the floor of the vehicle. I didn't know what shifting was, but I took note of the ease she had, and the freedom they exuded. Not a man in sight. Nothing but laughter and talk between them. I wanted that, but I was younger then. My lack of confidence hadn't been nursed and fed and fattened yet. But then it was, and by the time I was a teenager, I was trapped between wanting out of my parents' house and fear of taking care of myself.

The next day, Sunday, we went out again. And the weekend after. And the next weekend too. And every weekend throughout the winter. When we weren't getting firewood or getting high, we were engaged in driving lessons on the dirt roads of Seaforth.

It snowed one Monday but was mostly cleared and melted by the weekend, and we decided to go ahead with driving lessons. Cal drove us to Seaforth, and we switched seats at the entrance. I drove a few passes back and forth, avoiding a solid strip of ice on a hill by steering the truck to the sunny side of the road where the ice had melted. But on the return, coming down that hill, I came around a curve to meet a joy-riding truck full of boys coming the other way. I was on the shady side of the road, and there was no way to avoid driving on the ice. Cal said, "Gently pump the brakes. Don't hit them hard. If you spin out, always turn into the spin instead of against it."

I had no intention of spinning out. That was key. Stay out of trouble. I did just as Cal had instructed. I gently pumped the brakes, slowing the truck down just a little so that we glided over the ice without incident. When the boys waved to us as we passed, I even dared to lift a hand off the steering wheel to wave back.

That night lying in bed, Cal suddenly said into the dark, "You did a good job on that ice."

I remember this vividly because it wasn't just praise. It was praise delivered hours after the fact. Cal had been thinking about it. He'd been thinking about me. I rolled over and wrapped my arms around him. "Thank you," I said.

The next morning, we woke up early, blew our breath into the air, and dressed under the covers. At the gas station Cal handed me a few coins, and I got out and stood in the shivering cold dropping them into the vending machine. On the way to my parents' house, I held his can of Coke, passed it to him when asked, and looked for my landmarks along the drive. The lighthouse nightlight, the mobile home village, the farmhouses with the women in their kitchens. I would miss these landmarks once I got my license and we got another vehicle, once I started driving myself to work. I watched for them tenderly and appreciatively.

In spring, I got my learner's permit. The dirt roads of Seaforth were still where I did most of my driving, but I could now be on all roads with a licensed driver in the seat beside me. I drove us to and from Seaforth's entrance. As the weather warmed and dried, we took to going up driveways in Seaforth, to the empty yards, the land scarred bare where a house had once stood. Almost always there was a huge oak tree and a smattering of blooming daffodils. I imagined the tree shading a porch where rockers had sat. I imagined barns and outbuildings and chickens and gardens. Of course, I said none of this to Cal.

We smoked dope sitting under the trees. At first, I protested. I was nervous about driving stoned. "Eh," Cal said, "You're going to have to learn sometime. Better to do it out here." He had a point, and I reached for the lit joint.

In the summer, I got my driver's license. I started doing the laundry and grocery shopping all by myself. These became my jobs, and I was fine with it. For one thing, I owed Cal some time without ferrying me about, but more than that, I enjoyed the chores without him. I enjoyed lingering over the produce in the grocery store instead of speeding by it as we'd done when Cal was pushing the cart.

I had never lingered over produce before. When shopping with my mother as a child, she'd bought what was ripe and in season, and I'd paid it no mind. But after years with Cal, I was starved for the sensation of produce, and now the grocery stores carried things I'd never heard of: kiwis, papaya, star fruit, mangoes. I touched these things, but knowing nothing of them, I chose an orange.

At home I put it in the refrigerator. The next day I was home alone while Cal was at work, and I took my orange to the front steps and sat down. The sunlight filtered through the trees. A few vultures spun in the sky. The cicadas had come up from their many years underground, and their calls in the trees sounded alien, like something not of this world. I loved them as I loved all of Wildwood's wildness. The orange was cold in my hands. I slowly peeled it. It had been a long time since I'd peeled an orange. I set the peels down on the step next to me and admired the way they cupped into each other. I sectioned off a piece of orange and ate it, reveling in the sweet juice bursting into my mouth and running down my chin and arms.

It wasn't long before we got another truck, and I inherited the little orange Datsun. I began driving myself to work and home. Cal quit his job with UNC housekeeping and started working for a Christian music company run by two gay men. No more rising early in the mornings. No more passive-aggressive theater. No more lost keys, lost wallet, overhead light thrown on while I buried my face in a pillow in the loft. Now we rose and left the cabin in our separate trucks at the same time.

Cal was in a new band, and they often practiced at the cabin. I did the laundry those nights. As they got high and practiced riffs and drank beer and made jokes, I sat in a brightly lit laundromat, warm from the dryers and other people, watching our clothes spin, peacefully identifying Cal's plaid shirts as they swirled in the dryer, the pink corduroy pants I'd found at the thrift shop on one of my solo excursions to town, the gold towels we used with the fleur-de-lis on them. I pulled everything out and folded it and drove home.

I was becoming used to driving now, but I still felt nervous. For the longest time I said a prayer every time I got behind the wheel. Please God, don't let me hurt anyone, although the whole notion of God was still confusing to me. Wildwood had given me a deep connection to something beyond myself, something spiritual, but this wasn't my mother's God. Still, for lack of a replacement, I used the name when I prayed. One night, some sort of grace or divinity prevented me from hitting and killing an owl.

We heard them occasionally in the woods, but the woods were thick, six hundred acres of wildlife preserve, snugged next to huge tracts of undeveloped land. The wildlife had plenty of habitat in those days, so we didn't see much except for birds and snakes, squirrels, mice and spiders. Deer, raccoons, possums didn't come close to the houses. The same was true for owls. They were like falling stars, their calls an occasional treat.

On this night, as I drove into the curve that went down through the swamp, something small scurried across the road in front of me, and following it flew an owl ready to seize its dinner. I braked hard to avoid hitting it, but the owl came so close to colliding with my windshield that I let go of the steering wheel and instinctively covered my face with my arms crossed in front. Even as I did so, I kept my eyes open, and I saw its eyes. I saw its talons spread taut. I saw its wings spread wide. I saw the feathers on its legs rippling. It veered up and was gone, but I saw its majesty, and its majesty went into me.

I drove home to the cabin. The band was packing up their gear, passing a joint around.

"Here you go," one said, handing me the joint held in a carved stone holder shaped like a fish. "Go suck a whale's ass."

I took a toke and told no one of the owl. But that night, lying in bed in the loft next to Cal, I closed my eyes and brought it back to me. Its eyes. Its talons. Its wings. The rippling feathers on its legs. The next day, in the parking lot behind the hardware store, I pulled my little notebook from my big bag and wrote about it.

I still kept my writing hidden from Cal. I wouldn't put words on paper in front of him, and I wouldn't deny him anything he said he wanted. When he said he wanted a Redbone coonhound puppy with papers, I asked what a Redbone coonhound was, and then said okay, as I always did.

I don't know how Cal became aware of Redbone coonhounds. These were not the days of the internet, where you could get on the Web and find things to want that you didn't know you wanted. Out of the blue, Cal wanted a pure, pedigreed Redbone coonhound, even though our dogs had always been mutts that we found at gas stations or that someone dumped along the road.

We'd had as many as three dogs at a time, but we shouldn't have had even one dog. We did nothing to train them or keep them home. Over the years, our dogs had undoubtedly killed chickens and been shot at. Sometimes they came when we called, and sometimes they didn't. If the dog wasn't at the cabin the next day after we got home from work, we drove around calling its name and looking, but the dog was certainly dead somewhere, hit by a car or killed by an angry farmer.

We were down to one dog, a dog we'd named Grendel, when Cal got the notion of wanting a Redbone coonhound. Maybe Cal wanted Grendel to have some company. In any case, he found a breeder, called the guy, and *uh-uh-uh*ed his way through setting up a meeting. On Saturday we drove a long way out into another county. The litter of Redbone coonhound puppies ran around a fenced-in backyard, flopping and tumbling all over each other and tripping over their own ears. Cute as hell.

The man asked us some questions, and while he may have disapproved of the fact that we weren't going to hunt with the dog, he agreed to sell us one anyway. We paid forty dollars and picked one out. She was tiny, and she shivered with fear as I held her in my lap, and Cal started the truck. Before we'd reached the end of the road, she'd crawled between the small of my back and the seat to hide. We named her Scarlett for her reddish color and never bothered to register her, although Cal had insisted that she have papers.

Once home, Grendel sniffed at this shivering little thing and then put himself in the *let's play* position. It was not long before Scarlett stopped shivering and started romping with Grendel around the cabin floor. At first, Grendel had the sense not to lead her off in the woods on one of his long sojourns to trouble farmers and chickens. Scarlett was too young for that, and Grendel kept her close to home, going no farther than the stream in the woods behind the cabin.

Despite our recklessness and lack of responsibility with dogs, we fully intended to get Scarlett spayed. There was plenty of time. She was just a baby. A puppy. A joyous, en-thusiastic presence who liked to stick her nose into the water bowl and blow bubbles. Scarlett made me laugh.

It was a good summer, and it ended with a viewing of the Perseid meteor shower while tripping. I'd heard a story about the Perseids on the radio while driving alone to get grocer-ies. Always occurring in August, the Perseid meteor shower took place close to our anniversary. Our fifth this year.

Less in celebration of that and more in celebration of the fact that there was good acid in town, we decided to watch. I cleaned the cabin, as I always did before tripping, and set a Coke bottle of wildflowers on the cold woodstove. We took our hits, timing our peak to coincide with the peak of the meteor shower. As we started getting off, we dragged a blan-ket out in the driveway and lay down on it.

I'd only seen one falling star in my life, the one I'd seen while holding the flashlight for Cal as he gathered firewood. Now I saw hundreds. The meteors zipped across the sky. All different colors. Blue, red, green, yellow, energetic dots of light leaving quivering trails in their wake.

"Look."

"Look."

"Look at that one."

"Did you see that one?"

We pointed and pointed and pointed.

Cal went inside to call our neighbor, who we knew was tripping on the same acid we were. "Go outside and look at the meteors."

We heard his door slam. "Which direction?" he yelled.

"All over," I hollered back. How could he not see them?

A few weeks later we took acid again, and as we were coming down, we lay in bed together and had a slight dispute about the lamp. Cal wanted it off, and I wanted it on. I wanted it on because he had a big hairy beard now, and in the dark he looked like a gorilla. I didn't tell him this. I was afraid he'd make gorilla jokes and scare me further. Instead, I acquiesced to the light being off, and I lay there chanting silently to myself, *This is Cal. This is not a gorilla. This is Cal. This is not a gorilla.*

Cal and I had always been ritualistic about acid, although he would never use that word, and might have even been offended by it, but it was true, nonetheless. While I cleaned the cabin and picked wildflowers, Cal plowed through records and stacked up a soundtrack for the experience. We made sure we'd eaten and digested enough. We had Cokes stocked in the refrigerator. We always took the phone off the hook before placing the tabs in our mouths.

Every time I tripped, I had a good experience, often walking around the cabin and admiring the beauty we'd created. Looking deep into the orange flowers of butterfly weed, gazing at our dogs' fur vibrating and juddering to the music. Once I went outside and gazed at the bark of a tree. It was so alive, and I could feel the tree looking at me and even loving me. Acid helped me shed my human blinders to the real world pulsing beneath our consciousness. Maybe this was God.

But the trip in which Cal looked like a gorilla was my last one. It had required a lot to convince myself Cal was not a gorilla. I'd been able to soothe myself, but what if I'd not been able to do that? I knew of people I'd gone to school with, and hippies in town, who'd never returned from a trip, whose brains could no longer deal with the world we all have to navigate. The world of rules and money and work no longer made sense to them, and I could relate to that, but

I needed to hang on to being able to pilot through without freaking out. I decided not to trip anymore. Cal did. But I didn't. Still, when he was about to take acid, I cleaned the cabin, and I gathered wildflowers.

Wildwood gave me seasons. They'd always been there of course, but they'd been measured by the beginning of school and holidays, and now they were measured by the natural world. Soon enough fall was snapping the air, and we began preparing for winter again, driving out to the site of the future lake, gathering wood. We had a chainsaw now, and while I missed the rhythm of the crosscut saw, gathering wood was a lot easier. We could now glean two truckloads in a weekend, which we stacked in the woodshed. We also cleaned the stovepipe, and I gathered two bushel baskets full of kindling.

A small portion of our outside cabin wall remained unchinked, meaning that the cement between the logs had never been applied. The interior walls had all been completed, but whoever built the place had apparently run out of steam. It was not as though you could see through the cabin to the outside from the inside, or vice versa, but it might keep us a little warmer if we finished the job. All we needed was cement, trowels, scaffolding, and a wheelbarrow, all of which Joel brought over one Saturday.

Joel mixed the cement and showed us how to dip it onto our trowels, slap it between the logs, and smooth it out. We went to work, each with a bucketful.

I enjoyed the work. I liked scampering up and down the scaffolding. I liked walking along the boards Joel had placed on top. I liked smacking the cement into the spaces between the logs and smoothing it. I liked physical work, and physical work, except for childbearing and housekeeping, wasn't acceptable for women to do. Because of this and other "norms,"

I'd not grown up knowing my capabilities. In Wildwood, it was physical work, the work of gathering wood and tending a fire, that gave me to myself.

Below the corner of the cabin where I stood on the scaffolding, smacking trowels of cement between the logs and smoothing it, was a large log turned on end. During the winter one of us would set a smaller log that needed splitting on this chopping block and swing the maul down into it. At first the person doing this work had always been Cal. My job had been to gather the fallen wood and stack it in the woodshed, but one day, while Cal was gone, I maneuvered a log onto the upturned stump, picked up the maul, and drove it down. I was not prepared for the power I felt when the log blew apart. I did that? I split another one, and another, and another, reveling in my potency.

We had much better tools now than we'd had the day I'd hacked at the dogwood with a hatchet and been rewarded with dinner out at the Golden Corral. We had the chainsaw and the maul now, and two trucks. We did a lot of hard work together. The gathering of wood, hauling it inside, heating with it, keeping the fire going. I was no longer the passive partner holding the flashlight and being snapped at for letting the beam wander as I gazed at the night sky. I'd go outside alone now, at night, and gather the wood while Cal stayed inside picking his guitar. I liked gathering wood at night. I liked filling my arms with a load. I liked pausing and looking at the sky before stepping back inside.

When we'd finished chinking the cabin, Joel and Cal took the scaffolding down and loaded it into Joel's truck while I went inside and rolled a doobie. We sat outside on the porch smoking it. "You should scratch your names in the chinking," Joel said when we'd smoked the joint down to a tiny nub.

I pulled a stick from the basket of kindling sitting on the porch, and Cal and I went to the front corner of the cabin. He wrote his name: Calvin Powell. And I wrote mine: Nancy Powell. I didn't want "Calvin and Nancy Powell" written in the chinking of our cabin. I wanted my name to be separate from my husband's, even if half of that name was his.

"Put that roach in there too," Cal said, referring to the nub of joint I still held in my fingers. I jabbed it into the wet chinking and smoothed the cement over it. Cal pulled a penny out of his pocket and embedded it into the cement beside our names. We smiled at each other. "As long as we live in this cabin, we'll never be out of dope or money," I said.

We'd not live in the cabin much longer.

18.

One night after band practice, after the guys had broken down all the equipment and returned our living room to normal, after we'd all smoked a joint together and they had left, Cal said, "It'd be nice to live in a larger house where we could leave the band stuff set up, and not have to break it down every week."

"That would be nice," I said. "I wouldn't want to leave Wildwood though."

"No, me neither."

A few more times in the coming months, typically after band practice, Cal brought it up again.

"Sure," I said each time. "That'd be nice. But I wouldn't want to leave Wildwood."

I was still in the habit of giving Cal whatever he wanted, still paying penance for my affairs. If he had pushed it, if he had started the process of looking for another house, the process of leaving Wildwood and our cabin, I'd have joined in. I'd have had to, because in my mind, I still owed him. In my mind, I still needed to stay small, to hide my writing, to cook to his tastes, and to eat my oranges alone.

But Cal didn't push the idea of a larger house. He only mentioned it occasionally.

I might have known that he felt as strongly about staying in Wildwood as I did, but there was no way to know that he would eventually create a battle with me for the right to live there, and that in this battle he would wage emotional warfare. He would run me down, criminalize me, vilify me, and make my life a living hell, all so he could force me out, all so he could stay in Wildwood, all so he could gain custody of the woods he rarely walked in, the paths I knew of that he didn't, the old homestead and the old cars and the spirits that patted their gentle, loving hands on my shoulders. He would take it all away from me, banish me from it, leave me to cry alone beneath a large pine tree in the woods behind a different house. He would care nothing about hurting me. He would take delight in my leaving.

But for now we were safely ensconced in the cabin with both our names separately scratched into the chinking at one corner.

In early summer, Mrs. Baker came by for the rent and told us that the tenants in Number Three hadn't paid their rent in five months. She was evicting them and asked if we knew anyone who might be interested in the house. Cal said, "We were thinking about a larger place."

"Well now, that would be fine," Mrs. Baker said. "That house is larger. Let me see..." She rubbed her chin, then shoved her hands into the pockets of her overalls. "It's got three bedrooms, if I remember right. One of them is real small. A larger kitchen than here. But I can't show it to you until they leave. You can look at it then. If you decide to take it, and know someone interested in your house, you let me know."

We nodded our agreement, and after the Bakers left, we went inside and smoked a joint, as always. Cal picked his guitar. I got up and started sweeping the kitchen. We didn't even talk about it. The possibility seemed distant, as distant as Wildwood had seemed when I first saw it.

But now, even though we didn't discuss it, I started looking at Number Three. Whenever Cal was driving and I was in the passenger seat, or when I walked by, I peeked through the small copse of trees that stood in front of it. The house was one story, and it lacked a porch. A sad stack of cinderblocks served as steps. The siding of the house was covered in shredded tarpaper. It was the same house Cal had called a shack the day we'd come to see the cabin for the first time.

I'd met most of the folks living in Wildwood while strolling by when they were outside, digging a garden, making a repair, or sitting on porches or in their yards, relaxing. It was easy to strike up a conversation under these circumstances, but I'd never seen the people living in Number Three outside at all. The yard was weedy and overgrown.

I noticed that the tenants of Number Three habitually parked their car right in front of the cinderblock steps and never to the side, which I took to mean they didn't sit on those steps looking out, never hearing the whippoorwills or the owls or noticing the moon.

The next time Mrs. Baker came by for the rent, she said, "They won't move. I've told them to move, and they won't. That's six months they haven't paid the rent. Do you think you want it?"

Cal shrugged. "We don't know."

"Well now, if you do want it and you know someone who might want your place, that'd help us out."

"Well, we might know someone who'd want our place," Cal said. "I'll ask him if we decide to move."

I knew that he was thinking of our friend Jim. Jim and his

wife were separating but still living under the same roof until he could find a place.

"That's good. That's real good." Mrs. Baker climbed in the passenger seat of the old blue truck. We waved to Mr. Baker sitting in the driver's seat. He waved back, dimly visible through the windshield, and they backed out.

When I stepped back into the cabin, I thought about leaving it. I loved it, but we'd reached our limits on how to make it better. We'd removed the nasty brown carpet from the loft. We'd chinked the exterior. We'd pulled the Astroturf up from the kitchen floor, although a small bit remained under the leaky hot water heater, tiny mushrooms occasionally appearing, white and starved, from beneath it. Above it was a rod with our clothes hanging on it.

A real closet inside would be nice. A hot water heater that didn't leak would be nice. Windows with screens would be nice.

I started taking more walks up the road, just for the purpose of studying the house. I liked the trees in front, the way they shielded the house from the road. Tear off the shredding tar paper, dismantle those cinderblock steps and put up a porch, and it'd be a nice place to sit in a summer evening. I noted that the stovepipe exited the wall on the right. This being a one-story house, it didn't have far to climb before clearing the roof. That would make it easier to clean than the cabin's stovepipe, and provide less opportunity for creosote to build up. There seemed to be good garden space on that side of the house, although it was a field of tall grass and weeds now. The windows were standard, not large and romantic and hinged outward as the cabin windows were, but I saw that the windows were open and had screens, a box fan sitting in one.

I had no idea what the interior was like, but I knew from my experience with the cabin, and from watching my neighbors make structural improvements on their houses, that things could change. It was part of the magic of Wildwood that anything was fine with the Bakers as long as you didn't take down a load-bearing wall.

The next month when Mrs. Baker came by to collect the rent, the couple was still living in the house. "They won't leave," Mrs. Baker said. "I hate to do it. Now I hate it. I hate it, but I'm going to have to get the sheriff involved. I'm going to have to do it official-like. I hate to do it, but I need to rent that house. Do you want it? It would help me out if I knew you were going to move in after them. They should be out within the month after the sheriff serves the papers on them. But I still can't show it to you, and I've lost so much rent already, and I know you'd take care of it."

Cal and I looked at each other. I shrugged. "I'd miss our porch," I said, wanting to advocate up front for the one thing I could see Number Three was lacking.

"Well now," Mrs. Baker said. "We can get you what you need for a porch. You'll have to build it, mind you, but we can get the materials to you."

Cal nodded and sight unseen, we agreed to rent the house.

We called Jim the next day. He said yes, he'd like our cabin. We called Mrs. Baker and let her know Jim would take the cabin. Everything was rented now. Mrs. Baker was pleased, and the three of us who were slated to move began preparations.

The first order of business for Cal and me was boxes, which I collected from my job in the hardware store, bringing home a stack in the back of my truck every day. We piled the boxes in one corner of the cabin and began packing. First, the things we could live without. The books, all mine, went into boxes. Our extra dishes, mugs, and towels. As the month marched on, we added to the boxes things we weren't likely to use in the next three weeks, then two weeks, then one.

But the couple in Number Three didn't move. Mrs. Baker came by to tell us.

Every week the sheriff served the eviction papers again. Sometimes when we drove by, we saw him standing outside, facing the couple who stood on the stacked cinderblock steps. He seemed to relish the official opportunity to drive into Wildwood. Every time he served the papers, he drove down to the end of the road and then drove back. Slowly. Arm out the window. Face and eyes swiveled toward the little houses and their occupants.

In a neighborhood of hippies living alternative lifestyles in cherished substandard housing, smoking dope, and sometimes lying outside naked, the couple who did not pay their rent to the Bakers were outcasts. No one along the road liked the fact that they were ripping off the Bakers and regularly bringing the sheriff into our lives.

The sheriff had never surprised anyone living in Wildwood with his random drive-throughs. We always recognized the sound of his car, but it was different now that we expected him once a week. We lived on edge, never truly relaxing until he'd served his papers for the week and driven in and then out of Wildwood.

The month came to an end and the next month began. Still the couple did not move. Mrs. Baker showed up for the rent on the cabin, which we handed over. After she'd shuffled through the money and said we got five dollars back for paying in cash, she stuck her hands in the pockets of her overalls and said, "I don't know what to do. They're supposed to be out by now."

We nodded and admitted it was inconvenient. But we didn't have to leave the cabin, and Jim could stay a little longer in the house he shared with his wife. No one was going to be homeless.

Fall came and winter followed. Months passed and still the people did not leave Wildwood. The woodstove in the cabin churned away. We sat close to it. Cal picked his guitar. I rocked in my rocker and stretched my legs out to the radiant heat from the crackling fire. The sheriff made his weekly visits to the couple being evicted. Mrs. Baker dropped by occasionally to keep us updated. She felt terrible that we'd committed to an unavailable house. She wrung her hands and said again and again that she didn't know what to do. They wouldn't move. Our boxes came unpacked, and then stacked empty on the porch. Every month we called Jim and gave him the news.

"All right," Jim said, his voice weary with limbo. "One more month."

"Yeah, one more month," I'd say. But I was beginning not to believe it.

It snowed several times that winter. The power went out. We learned that Wildwood would always be the last location in the county to have power restored to it and the last road that the snowplow would come down. If Wildwood was up and running, the world had been up and running for at least a week.

I loved the snow at Wildwood. I loved the beauty of it, the quiet of it, the darkness of a power outage. We took walks. All the neighbors except the people living in Number Three took walks. The road became churned with footprints, human and dog. Word had gotten around that we were waiting to move into Number Three.

"Oh," one neighbor said after we met her walking in the snow along the road, "the sheriff isn't taking it seriously, I bet. People around here don't like the Bakers for bringing a bunch of hippies in to live so close by."

"He does seem to enjoy cruising through every week," I said.

"Exactly."

Every time we drove by Number Three, we looked through the woods, hoping to see signs that the couple living there were moving out. Nothing. The door was closed. The cinderblock steps waited. Sometimes there was a long grey car pulled in front of them.

February came, along with daffodils. I drove into Seaforth and picked some out of the abandoned yards and put them in jars around the cabin. Mrs. Baker showed up weekly now. "Oh," she fretted. "I don't know what to do. I don't know what to do."

Neither did we. Neither did Jim. Months had passed since we'd agreed to move into Number Three. Months during which we'd packed and then unpacked. Months during which Jim waited under the pressure of his dissolving marriage to get out.

At least Jim had seen our cabin. At least he knew what he was moving into. He probably had ideas of how he'd arrange his furniture. What the place would look like once he occupied it. We had no ideas about Number Three, and this was one of the hardest parts for me. It was one thing to fantasize about how to fix up a house I only dreamed about seeing, as I had done when Cal first drove me into Wildwood. It was another to try and imagine a house you knew you were eventually moving into. What were the rooms like? What was the kitchen like? Was there a back door? I imagined one, but when I asked Mrs. Baker, she said no, she didn't believe there was one. "Well now, you can cut one in if you like."

The days became steadily warmer. Some sort of critter chewed on the boxes stored on our front porch, and still the sheriff crept his big car down our road every week, and the couple stood on the stoop and talked to him, and no one moved.

Jim dropped by one day. It was May. The last fire of the season had died; the stove had been cleaned, ashes shoveled out and tossed in the woods. My rocking chair sat out on the porch now, as did Cal's straight-back chair. We were smoking a joint, Cal cradling his guitar. I had bread dough rising in the kitchen.

We offered Jim the joint, and he took a hit. "I ran into the people in Number Three at Farrell's," he said after releasing the smoke from his lungs. "I overheard them talking to the sheriff, and after he left, I told them there were people waiting for them to move. Not just you, but me waiting to move into your house. They were holding things up for us, making it difficult. We were all packed and just waiting. They said they didn't know that."

The following week, when Cal and I drove by, I turned my head and looked through the copse of trees and saw a truck backed up to the front door, and two people wrestling a dresser into its bed.

"They're moving," I said. I couldn't believe it. After months of scoping out the house for any signs of movement, there finally was some. "They're actually moving, I think."

We went home and then walked up the road to see if it was true. There were a few more pieces of furniture in the truck bed now. An hour later, Mrs. Baker came by to officially give us the news. We hurriedly called the electric company to get the power switched to our names that afternoon, the order having been placed months ago, and delayed again and again and again.

By luck the next day was Saturday, a weekend when I didn't have to work at the hardware store. We called some friends for help with the labor. We called Jim and told him we'd be out at the end of the day; he could move on Sunday. We haphazardly packed our boxes again. Mrs. Baker brought us the keys at nine that night. We decided to save our first viewing until morning.

19.

Cal unlocked the door and eased it open. I peered over his shoulder, teetering on the cinderblock steps behind him, holding a broom and a dustpan I'd thought to bring with me. Dim light from the dirty windows illuminated thick columns of drifting dust motes. Cal reached in and flipped the light switch on. We stepped inside. It was filthy.

Someone had made a half-hearted attempt at sweeping, and piles of dirt lay in little islands across the uneven planked floor, weeping their contents. I walked over to a window and batted the broom at the bunting of thick cobwebs draped in one corner of the ceiling.

The ceiling was made of dark brown Masonite. The flue for the woodstove was in the far wall, as I knew it would be. The stove was gone, along with the stovepipe. No one had bothered to cover the flue. I could see through its round hole to the woods on the other side of the scruffy yard. Cal took his shirt off and stuffed it into the flue. "Good thing we don't have birds in here," he said.

"Or bats," I added.

I hoped we didn't have bats.

Across from the front door was the bathroom. Next to the bathroom was a small room with a rough built-in desk.

The room was closet-sized, the desk making it even smaller. A long hallway delivered us to two more rooms, one on the right and one on the left, neither as small as the first, but neither particularly large. The kitchen at the other end of the house was large, its walls covered in the same dark Masonite as the ceilings, some of it bowing out in places. The sink was a nice old cast-iron sink with a drain board, stained in places, and housed on top of a rusty metal cabinet.

I'd been in enough of the cabins and shacks in Wildwood to know that while some were completely charming, others were not. I'd always had an eye for how things could be improved. How to arrange furniture in a room, how to decorate, what ought to be left alone, and what ought to be revamped. There was quite a lot in Number Three that needed to be revamped, but it didn't scare me.

I walked to one of the windows in the living room and opened it.

"I'll bring the fan with the first load," Cal said.

"Okay. Thanks. Bring some Comet and sponges too."

"There's Trip," Cal said, seeing our friend dusting down the road in his truck. "I'll see you later."

After Cal left, I took another tour through the house. It wouldn't take much work to clean. The floor was filthy, and the cobwebs needed clearing, but the bathtub seemed reasonably clean, as did the sink and the kitchen. I didn't need the Comet and sponges after all.

By the time I returned to the cabin, Cal and Trip had one truck bed loaded and had started on another. I helped carry boxes out, my rocking chair, Cal's straight-back one. It took maybe two trips with the three small-sized trucks.

Finally, my braided rug was spread across the floor of the new living room, and our chairs were in place, along with a willow bench Trip lent us. Cal pulled his wadded shirt out of the flue and covered the hole with a sheet of aluminum foil.

It would be a while before we installed a stove. The old box stove with the patched side would not be coming with us. Joel and Cal would move it back to Joel's barn the next day.

We'd decided, as we waited for the tenants of Number Three to move, that we'd invest in a new woodstove come fall. We'd chosen, but not yet ordered, an Ashley that purportedly had a thermostat and held a fire for six hours.

Cal filled a pipe with some hash. We cracked tabs on cans of beers. The stereo had been set up first thing, and The Marshall Tucker Band sang "Heard It in a Love Song," a song about a rambling man who has to keep on moving.

It was not lost on me that so many of these songs I loved, and that Cal played with his band, were about a man leaving a woman behind and how he hated to do it, but that's just the way he was. He loved her, and she could count on him coming back some time, when he was ready. Inherent in the lyrics was the idea that she would welcome him back, that during his inevitable absence she would live her life suspended in space as he rambled about. She would not age during his absence. She had no needs he should concern himself with. She would be there, his ever-present love, always waiting for him, always welcoming him home, understanding that his coming and going was just a price she had to pay for loving him.

I didn't mind these songs. They fit right in with a fantasy of my own—a man who loved me but was gone more than eight hours at a time. I longed for large expanses of time to myself. Waking alone. Fixing a cup of tea alone. Sitting outside alone. No one to talk to. No one to respond to.

So far, I had this alone time only on my days off when Cal went to work, and some evenings when I chose to stay home while his band played a local gig.

But here in this house that I now sat in front of, crowded with Cal and Trip on the cinderblock steps, I would experience myself snuggled into those satin sheets of solitude that I craved so much. Cal's band would start taking gigs farther and farther away, overnights that would leave me by myself in this house for weekends, and sometimes three and four days at a stretch. I would keep a fire burning all by myself. I would play the music Cal hated—Donovan, Bob Dylan, Ian and Sylvia, my old flames The Monkees. I would feed myself with food that was not brown and bland. I would cook with onions while Cal was gone.

Trip, Cal, and I passed the pipe back and forth. The dogs, Grendel and Scarlett, romped in the yard in front of us, their tails and heads an excited, ridiculous swirl. Sufficiently high, I went back inside and vacuumed the screens and windowsills.

The Bakers delivered the materials they'd promised for our porch: planks of wood, some old tin for the roof, cedar trunks stripped of their bark to use as posts. It all appeared in our driveway one day while we were at work. Neither Cal nor I knew how to build a porch, so we enlisted two of our friends who worked as carpenters to help, and the next weekend we had a porch.

On my day off the following week, I knocked down a decrepit shed built onto the back of the house and ripped down all the shredding tarpaper that covered the siding. With the tarpaper gone and the porch added on, Number Three seemed to sit on its little hill a bit more proudly. I imagined a porch swing, and then, on my birthday, I came home to find one hanging there.

I walked up the steps and sat in it, creaked it into motion. Cal pushed the screen door open and stepped out. "Do you like it?" he asked.

"I love it."

He held up a joint and flicked a Bic lighter like a question mark. "Smoke?"

"Yeah."

Cal settled into the swing beside me. We kicked it into motion together. The chains squeaked.

"Thank you," I said. I ran my hands along the edge of the swing. "I've always wanted a porch swing."

"I know," Cal said.

20.

There wasn't much that could be done about the Masonite ceiling, but the Masonite that bowed out from the kitchen walls could be taken down. We did this and built shelving between the studs, on which I lined jars and mugs.

Soon after, I taped newspaper around the sink and along the floor to protect them while I spray-painted the ugly, rusting metal cabinet housing the sink. I chose blue, and I applied a decal to the front, just beneath the sink. An old-fashioned spray of flowers tied with a ribbon.

Cal and I threw ourselves into building things we wanted and removing things we didn't want. We knocked down the desk in the tiny room, and then we knocked down the wall between the tiny room and the next one to create one large room for the band to practice in. We shortened the hallway by building a closet at one end. We cut in a back door in the kitchen and built both a screen door and a regular door for it. We gathered pallets that had been discarded beside one of the roadside dumpsters and dismantled them. Using a stump we found in the woods as the base, bracing it with two-by-fours, we used the pallet wood to make a round kitchen table and stained it cherry.

I loved that table. I loved sitting there in the kitchen, running my fingers along its wavy edges because neither of us was great with a jigsaw, drinking tea, and looking out the open back door. After a rain one day, I stood at that door, water dripping off the tin roof into a puddle, watching a flock of small yellow birds joyously splash around. Goldfinch. I made sure to look them up.

We'd not gotten Scarlett spayed as planned, and now she showed signs of pregnancy, and we showed signs of denial. Cal had heard of something called a false pregnancy, and we told ourselves this was one. Surely Scarlett was too young to have puppies, but then one day, when I was home alone, she did. I called Cal at work. "You know how we thought Scarlett had a false pregnancy?"

"Yeah."

"Well, she just had five false puppies."

We were delighted, and Scarlett was a good mama. She nursed her puppies like she'd been doing it all her life. She herded them about as they grew. When the time came, we gave them all away except one. A beautiful large yellow pup whom we named Yella Fella. Soon after, we acquired another dog, Josh, a big black long-haired retriever our neighbor needed to find a home for. Now we had four dogs, and we got Scarlett spayed to make sure the number stayed at that.

As always, the dogs ran wild. All except Josh. Josh was a homebody. He wanted nothing more than to have you kick his basketball for him or, once he'd pressed enough air out of it, to carry it around in his big jaws.

Yella Fella grew. He was a solid little guy, but he was not full grown before a car hit him. After he didn't come home one night, we went looking for him the next morning. Cal drove while I scanned one side of the road, and him the other. Along Mt. Carmel Church Road, close to the pump-kin farm, Cal slowed the car. "I see something," he said. He turned the car around in a driveway.

"I hope it's not him," I said.

"I think it is, Bear." He pulled the car off the road, and we got out. I remember Cal hefting Yella Fella's body onto his shoulder. I remember walking to the truck and laying my hand on Cal's other shoulder. I remember pulling away from myself, seeing us as a passing driver might see us. A young hippie couple with their dead dog. This moment looked tender and heartbreaking. I could write an entire story about this couple based on this moment, and it would be wrong.

In the story I might have written, I would have included the man digging a hole in the yard of the unfinished cabin in Wildwood. I would have included his wife or girlfriend sitting on the ground crying, the body of a yellow dog lying in the grass beside her. I would not have included, and even after all my experiences with Cal, could not have guessed, that after three spades full of dirt he would turn to me, glare, and say, "Go home."

I got up off the ground and went home, as ordered. That fucker. Why couldn't I have an emotion? He had emotions. He'd cried when his father died, and I'd held him, and I'd never told him to stop crying. I would never do that, and now I was ordered to go home for feeling something. I lay in bed and looked out the window in the direction where Cal was working. I couldn't see him, but I could hear the shovel. I was too angry to cry now. When I saw Cal walking through the woods with the shovel, I got off the bed and went to the kitchen. I opened the back door and sat on the stoop. I didn't want to be in the same room as him.

I listened to him come inside. I heard him say, "Poor Scarlett." I knew he knelt in front of her. I knew he looked at her with concern. He hollered to wherever I was, "I think she's sad. Poor Scarlett," he said again.

I'm sad, too, I thought. But I'm a woman, not a dog, so you can't feel anything for me, you asshole.

I heard Cal move around the living room. I heard him tune his guitar and pick. He never came looking for me. He never said, "I'm sorry." He never asked if I was okay. He never comforted me.

I went to bed that night remembering Cal with Yella Fella's body slung across his shoulder, me laying my hand on his other shoulder. Sometimes it felt like I was in a play, each of us posing as a partner to the other, but with one of us always forgetting his lines. Forgetting his role. Not even bothering to pretend tenderness toward the woman playing the role of his wife.

The next day was Monday. Cal got up and scratched Scarlett behind her ears. "Poor Scarlett," he repeated, leaning his forehead against hers.

Scarlett and Grendel stayed around the house for a week after Yella Fella died. They lay around on the porch while Josh, the big black retriever, nosed his basketball across the yard, oblivious to the gloom. The next week Scarlett and Grendel were gone again, off romping in the woods and crossing roads they shouldn't have. And soon enough Cal moved on from his hurt, and I stuffed mine into the storage container of my heart, and we smoked dope and carried on.

I would be lying if I said there wasn't fun or joy. In Wildwood, for me, there was always the place itself. The dirt road. The curve where I saw the owl. The dip through the swamp. The puddles in the driveway I plowed the truck through when I came home. The scent of honeysuckle in the curve of our driveway. The walks I took in the woods. The moon to watch. The vultures spinning in the sky.

And there was the work Cal and I did together. We enjoyed our home improvements. We turned Number Three, the shack, into a fine abode, and I came to love it more than I'd loved the cabin. There was no twisty staircase to sleepily navigate in the middle of the night. No orange Formica in the kitchen. No windows without screens. The house held us perfectly. We smoked dope and sat outside on the porch swing. We listened to music. We ate at the round wavy-topped table in the kitchen with the back door open to the woods.

At the end of summer, we ordered our new woodstove. We built a hearth framed with two-by-fours, stained it with the leftover stain we'd used on our table built from pallets, and filled it with bricks. The Ashley woodstove was a pleasure, a dream come true, and a magnificent piece of engineering that really could hold a fire for six hours. No more waking up blowing clouds with our breath. No more coming home to a freezing house. No more huddling around the woodstove with only one side of our bodies warm.

I became the primary keeper of the fire. I stoked the stove before going to bed, I stoked it once in the middle of the night since I was up to pee anyway, and being the early riser in the house, I stoked it when I got up. I came to understand that stove. I came to commune with that stove. I came to commune with the sacredness of fire.

If you've ever heated solely with wood, then you know the altar-like qualities a hearth takes on. No wonder the pagan people worshiped as they did, at home, in the fields and the woods, beside rivers and lakes, and beside fires.

For lack of a better term, I still called something up there *God*, but this was not the God of the church I'd been forced to attend, not the God of rules, and fear, and scorekeeping. I felt divinity now. I especially felt it in the winter sitting by the fire in the early morning while Cal still slept and the house was quiet.

Slowly the day lightened. Slowly the birds started waking up, first one, then another, and another. The living room lightened. The woodstove radiated heat. The mug of tea I held warmed my hands.

I relished my moments alone in Number Three Wildwood. I became more and more brave. It was as though Wildwood had been giving me courage in layers, and Number Three was frosting on the cake. When Joel visited and said he was looking for a carpenter assistant, I asked if he'd take me on.

He did, and I left the hardware store to work on construction sites and learn about table saws, and sanders, and painting, and hauling lumber, and four-penny nails, and ten-penny nails, and sixteen-penny nails, which I learned I could hammer into two-by-fours with four swings of the sixteen-ounce hammer I bought.

I got muscles, a tool belt, the hammer, and a measuring tape. I trotted around construction sites and on roofs, did my work, and enjoyed flirting with the longhaired men who worked with me. They were helpful men. They were not condescending, and they understood that I was new to this work, that I didn't know everything there was to know. They taught me, but they didn't fawn over me, and they didn't patronize me.

They weren't the only men on site though. Other crews came in. One day I changed the blade on the table saw, and a large, burly guy whom I did not know said, "You got that blade on backwards."

I looked at it, checking to make sure the teeth curved in the correct direction. "No, I don't," I said.

He grinned. His friend guffawed. A big joke on the little lady who was in a man's domain. I hated men like that. But this was Chapel Hill, and there weren't many of them. Also, I wasn't the only woman working construction. There were others. Dump truck drivers, plumbers, carpenters, electricians.

The band left their equipment at our house now, in the room we'd created for that purpose. To improve acoustics, someone brought a green carpet, and we spread it on the floor. I became a band-wife. I entertained the women who sometimes came with the band members for practice. I especially liked Natalie and Ava, the only two women also married. I loved to sit with them at our wavy-edged kitchen table, sharing cups of tea. It was a chance for a little girl-talk while the menfolk did their thing in the other room. The band would eventually take a break, and the boys would pour into the kitchen, grabbing beers, and we'd pass joints around before they returned to practice. It was an easy party to be at. I was a part of a tribe again. I was the hostess of this tribe. Some of the boys sidled up to me at times and bumped my hip with theirs when passing me a joint. It was loose and uncomplicated, and after they'd packed up their instruments and left and I was home alone with Cal, I stoked the stove while Cal noodled his guitar, and we let the energy settle.

But after a time, Natalie and Ava came to practice less and less, and the bass player started bringing a string of women to my house and depositing them with me while he went off to play music. To the first one, I was friendly and welcoming.

To the second one, I was also friendly and welcoming. By the third, I began to grow weary. It became apparent that each woman was a one-off, and that she didn't know this. She felt hopeful about her relationship with the bass player. She was sure she'd see me again. I was sure I was being asked to participate in a charade.

Finally, I started leaving the house on band nights.

Jackie had left Florida, and now lived with the drummer for Cal's band in a trailer in a place called Morrisville, which was then a few old houses, a railroad track, and a country store. We started having what we called "business meetings," which amounted to a shared potluck dinner with just the two of us, followed by a joint and mild discussion of starting our own business. An antique store. A catering business. A photography booth at the state fair, where we provided props and costumes and made sepia-toned pictures that looked like they were from the 1800s. All of it was fantasy. The point was to play and visit and eat things Cal wouldn't eat.

To get to Jackie's, I had to drive across a newly constructed bridge, a bridge that would eventually span the water of Jordan Lake, but which currently spanned the land where I'd learned to drive, Seaforth and its neighboring forest. The forest was lumbered now, the trees cut down, and anything remaining was knocked over and bulldozed into piles. The piles of debris were set on fire to smolder and burn all night long.

Driving across the bridge at night, the fires were pinpricks of smoke and flame staggered across a barren, destroyed landscape. Every time I saw the scattered fires glowing in the distance, I thought of the Plains Indians. I couldn't understand why these fires triggered these thoughts, until I finally realized that the fires reminded me of movies I'd seen in which Indian villages were attacked. The piles of brush were like tipis burning.

Coming home one night, I slowed as my headlights fell across a deer standing in the parking lot of a church. He was huge, a barrel-chested buck with antlers towering off his head. Ten points? Twelve points? Fifteen points? Bucks shed their antlers every year and grow a new set with another prong to mark that year. A twelve-point buck has lived twelve years, a fifteen-point, fifteen years. This guy had been around.

He stood facing the land that had been scraped clean, its trees hauled away and what was left set to burn. I saw bewilderment in his eyes. I saw grief. And then my truck slid by him, and I went on, just another human, just another two-legged, like the ones who'd driven bulldozers into his home.

As the clearing for Jordan Lake continued, we saw more and more deer along the roads, both on the blacktop and on Wildwood's dirt road. Their land was being taken, just as the Bakers' land was taken. Wildwood was a result of all this destruction of habitat. My habitat had been born of it. Come spring, the deer would be hungry enough to walk into our yard and eat from my garden, and I would have to fence it.

The garden, of course, was of no interest to Cal. He still held that canned green beans were edible whereas fresh green beans were not. I'd been cooking to Cal's tastes for years, serving the bland brown food that he preferred, and I was tired of it. Here, in this house, in Number Three Wild-wood, I decided I was done paying penance for my affairs. I had pulled myself up by the roots and thrown myself on the compost pile. I had abandoned myself. I had abandoned my writing. I had abandoned my creative life. I had abandoned my tastes in food, and I was done with it. I learned that the best way to put a stake in the ground is to put a stake in the ground, and the first stake I drove down for myself was with food.

"What's for dinner?" Cal would ask.

"Chicken smothered in onions, a salad, and sliced tomatoes."

"Alllll riiiiight." Meaning of course that it wasn't all right.

"Broiled chicken, steamed green beans, and rice."

"Alllll riiiiight."

Egg salad.

Tomato sandwiches.

An omelet.

I tried my hand at a soufflé.

"Alllll riiiiight."

On these nights, and there were many of them, after Cal had mud-dragged his alllll riiiiight into the air, he would come into the kitchen. He would open a can of Campbell's Chunky Beef Soup, dump the contents into a pan, turn the burner on high, and leave the room. "Your soup's ready," I hollered when I heard it plopping bubbles of liquid onto the stovetop.

"Alllll riiiiight."

This scenario played out again and again. I ignored him. If he wanted to make a direct complaint, I'd deal with it, but I was tired of his subtext.

I was buying and growing and cooking food he wouldn't eat now. I took care of the fire. I split and hauled wood. I was driving wherever I wanted to and sometimes driving him home from a gig if he was too drunk.

I'd found independence from him. I thought this was what he wanted. To not have to drive me places. To not be so responsible for everything. To get some space from each other. We'd been through so much. We'd hurt each other a lot, but now we lived in a wonderful place. Cal played music, and I threw myself into homemaking and gardening and building things. We lived a creative life. We had friends, the boys in the band, their wives or girlfriends, hangers on. I liked being the social hub, and I liked driving away when I needed to.

I made peace with Cal's inability to comfort me when I needed it. I just wouldn't expect that. I wouldn't even hope for it. I'd comfort myself, as I'd been doing all my life anyway. I thought we'd both made peace with each other's shortcomings. I thought we'd live in Number Three Wildwood forever. I thought we'd keep on building our homestead, keep on eating our separate dinners, and keep on getting stoned afterwards and snarfing down the pan of brownies I made without nuts, because I acquiesced on the nuts. Cal wouldn't eat anything with nuts.

We were always at our best when stoned. Stoned, Cal picked his guitar, and I walked around the house admiring things. I admired the way my braided rug looked on the uneven plank floor. I admired the mugs Cal gave me for Christmas, sitting on the shelves between the studs in the kitchen. I admired my steel-toed work boots sitting inside the door and my tool belt hanging from a nail. From the looks of what I saw in the picture book of our life, I liked the people living here.

I still carried my little notebook with me, but I didn't write in it anymore. Now that I drove, I no longer had the idle mental time spent in the passenger seat beside Cal, so poems and descriptions didn't crop up in that space. Gone too were the solitary lunch breaks I'd spent writing in the woods behind town. I now ate lunch with a crew of carpenters and tradespeople, delighting in the banter and teasing.

Of course, I thought about writing, about taking up the pen again, about getting a larger notebook, but once again, writing became something I used to do. It just drifted away. This time it simply slipped out the door like a cat.

What I did was work on our house. I scrounged wood off the construction sites where I worked and closed the hole beneath the sink where a black snake got in. I mulched and weeded the garden. I built a planter for the end of the porch, planted Heavenly Blue morning glories in it, and trained them up strings to the roofline.

Cal gave his music to the home. He used the chainsaw to cut firewood from the pile of slab, the sides of trees taken off at a mill before the rest is cut into lumber, that we'd had delivered in the driveway. Sometimes we sat on our bed together and watched the sunset. We noticed that a fence lizard often sat on the pile of slab at the same time, seemingly also watching the sunset.

Once Cal and I created a piece of art together, a collage made of random pieces of wood I'd brought home from construction sites to use as kindling. We knelt on the floor, a piece of plywood in front of us, and a shared bottle of Elmer's glue. We picked up pieces of wood, and arranged them, and stood back to look, and arranged some more. Then we began gluing. When it was dry, we hung it on the porch, just outside our front door.

Our home was a mixture of Cal and Nancy. The squeak of the chain that held the porch-swing meant home. Cal noodling on his guitar meant home. A pan of brownies or a loaf of homemade bread. The blooms on the morning glories opening and closing daily. The fire. My rocking chair.

The braided rug. The big iron bed I'd inherited from my grandmother.

Home is where the heart is.

And then my father was diagnosed with leukemia.

21.

Cal went with me to see my father once in the hospital, and after that I never wanted him with me again. I could not tolerate standing next to Cal, my father prone on the adjustable bed, wearing his thin blue gown that flapped open at the back, saying hello to my husband, and asking him how he was, and Cal answering, *Uh-uh-uh, okay, I guess.*

I felt exposed. I didn't have Wildwood or our home to lean on. An undertow of feelings threatened to pull me down. In the hospital, my father lay on a path toward death. Standing beside me was the boy-child I'd only wanted to live with but had instead married. Married because of my parents. Because of Cal's parents. Because of the man I loved lying in the hospital bed before me. The least I could do was never ask Cal to go visit my father with me again. Never stand next to him beside my father's bed. Never ask for his support. Never even hope for pretended support. I would ask nothing of Cal during this time. It was safer that way.

My father went through chemotherapy. I watched him throw up. He'd always been a big man, and he wasted away to the old skin-and-bones cliché. There were trips in and out of the hospital. He'd be home and not home. Bedsores on his back. Dressing up in masks and gowns to visit him. My mother wringing her hands. My own inability to be present. I couldn't cry. I knew better than to feel my distress in front of Cal. I knew better than to show him pain, to show him grief.

I packed my sorrow into the secret place behind my eyes. I told my tears that I would let them out later, but not now. Now there was so much more to go through. Better for the tears to stay inside. Better for there to be no release, not yet. Better to stay strong. That's what I would be. Strong. I told my tears that I would release them when my father died. That time was coming. It was inevitable. I would not hold back when that day came.

One day I visited my father in the hospital after work. No one else was there. "Hey, honey," he said. "I have something for you." He leaned over and opened the drawer in the little white industrial table beside his bed and extracted a piece of paper. He handed it to me. I took it and read out loud.

Short Story

A four year old friend of ours, knowing of our interest in fiction, dictated the following:

FORSYTHIA SEAWEED

Forsythia Seaweed was a little girl. She had blowers. The blowers were supposed to eat oranges, but hers ate her elbows. She took them to be fixed and then they ate grapefruits.

"I tore it out of *The New Yorker*," my father said, "knowing of your interest in fiction," he added.

Did anyone else but my father know that I still secretly nurtured an interest in fiction? And how did he know? I folded the piece of paper and put it in my wallet. "Thanks, Di." I leaned over and kissed him.

The TV was on. The news aired of the mass suicide of the people of Jonestown in Guyana, the Peoples Temple, followers of Jim Jones. We both watched the helicopter view of the bloated bodies carpeting the ground.

"That's weird, huh?" my father said.

Don't die, I thought. *Don't die.*

My father had introduced me to artichokes. He'd taught me the joy of sitting on the porch in a thunderstorm. He'd shown me a thin, green snake delicately curled around a stalk of butterfly weed in his garden. He shook muscadines down from the vine growing in the tree and showed me how to pop the flesh out of each grape with my teeth. He made pancakes or waffles every Saturday morning for his children. In Alabama at his parents' house, he called me inside from the limbs of the magnolia tree because there was a movie on TV he thought I'd like. It was Shirley Temple, and we watched it together sitting on his mother's plastic-covered couch. He and I had sat together at the table after dinner, picking the marrow out of short-rib bones. "Ah, that 'delightful stage known as filling in the corners,'" he said, quoting *Winnie the Pooh*.

My father read. He read constantly. He read Tolkien's trilogy every winter. Another day I visited him in the hospital and found him there alone with a stack of small blue books spread across his bed. "What are you doing?" I asked.

"I'm re-reading all my favorite books, starting with these." He held up one of the small blue books. A McGuffey Reader, like the ones he'd gone to school with. "I'll work my way to the trilogy," he said.

I went home that afternoon and pulled my old childhood copies of the Little House books by Laura Ingalls Wilder from the shelf in the hallway. I began with *Little House in the Big Woods*. While my father reread his favorite childhood books, I read mine too. I read one after the other, and I found them comforting, and I still do.

When times get hard, I turn to *The Long Winter*, which was originally titled *The Hard Winter*. Hard indeed. The family nearly starved. The snow piled so high they tunneled through it to get to the barn. Laura's pa sang what Laura called his "trouble song": *Oh, I am as happy as a big sunflower that nods and bends in the breeze, Oh!* He was unable to play his fiddle for the family because his fingers were so stiff and cold and cracked. It had been a long time since I'd heard my father play the piano.

The weekend before my father died, I went to Lake Gaston to visit with my friend Laura, who'd been my maid of honor at my wedding. We met each other there, her driving alone from Virginia and her marriage and me driving alone from Chapel Hill and mine. I knew Di-Da was dying, but I needed the lake and I needed Laura and I needed to not be with Cal as I anticipated my father's death.

Laura and I pulled the mattresses off the beds and sat and talked in front of the fireplace in her parents' cabin, a place where I'd spent much of my childhood and junior high years. For old times' sake, we played Monkees albums on her little record player and danced. We ate hotdogs and potato chips and at night hugged each other before falling asleep. I didn't talk about my father, and Laura didn't ask. I didn't talk about my marriage either. I kept up an illusion of a good marriage, a mirage of having my needs met by Cal. To do otherwise would make me face facts, and I didn't want to face any fact that I could avoid, because the one I couldn't avoid, my father's death, waited for me in Chapel Hill.

On the way home, I stopped at the hospital. My sister and older brother and mother were all there. My other brother was at his home in Arizona. My father lay on the bed in a coma, his body curled into a parenthesis. I touched his shoulder. A nurse came in to check his vitals.

"Do you think he knows I'm here?" I asked.

She gave me a sweet smile. "I hope so," she said. She'd seen death before. She knew what to say and how to say it.

I went home to be with Cal. He was expecting me, and I didn't want to call him and tell him any different. He'd not been happy about me going off to Lake Gaston. He'd done his best to make me feel guilty. And now, I just wanted my own bed.

My sister and brother stayed at the hospital. My mother went home alone.

It seems cruel that I didn't spend the night with my mother. Perhaps we could have comforted each other, but I'd been avoiding her for years now, and I would keep on avoiding her. I'd received no counsel from her other than *obey God* and *read this book by Pat Boone*. How could I have sat in witness of her emotions with no one to witness my own? It seemed I'd spent my life in that state, unable to have my feelings received by anyone.

No matter. I fully intended to cry when my father died. I fully intended to let my tears come. I could feel the tears gathering like an army of grief. I would let them loose when the time came, and I would be home, in the comfort of my house with its rough walls and Masonite ceiling and uneven floors. I did not want to be with my family. I wanted to be with me, alone. Alone was something I knew and could depend on. Alone demanded nothing from me.

Cal would be in the house, of course, but I wouldn't ask

anything from him. He could ignore me. I would simply let my grief go and be held by my house. Eventually I would pull myself together enough to smoke a joint with Cal. This was all I expected, and it seemed so little.

When the phone rang, waking us up, I threw the covers off and climbed out of bed. I went into the hall to answer it. "Dad died," my brother said.

"Okay," I answered. "I'll see you tomorrow."

I hung up the phone and said into the darkness to Cal, "Dad died," then I sank onto the floor in the hallway, and the tears let loose. I wasn't sobbing. I wasn't hysterical. I'd hardly been crying anytime at all before I heard Cal throw the covers off the bed. I thought to myself, *My god. He's coming to comfort me.*

In that moment between hearing the covers being thrown off the bed and the time he arrived by my side, it felt good to know that Cal would be there for me. It was a momentous thing to lose a parent, and my husband would step into the occasion. He would kneel down and wrap his arms around me in the hallway and say, "I'm sorry, Bear."

The light in the bedroom went on. Cal's shadow fell across me and stopped. I looked up, expecting softness, expecting sympathy. It would have been so easy to give. He remained standing and said, "You had better get your shit together, Bear, because you—are—out—of –control." Separating each word. Emphasizing each word. He turned. The bedroom light went off. The bed creaked and the covers swished back up.

Even I was shocked. I'd expected nothing from him. I'd barely even begun crying. I was far from out of control. Cal could have done nothing, and I'd have been fine with that, but to do this? I wiped my eyes and stood. I went back to bed and climbed in. I lay there silent and still, keeping my body away from his. Soon he was asleep.

I tamped down as required. I stuffed my feelings into my-self until I felt like the snake we'd once seen in the woods, stuffed with squirrel, the bushy tail protruding from its mouth, unable to move.

I frequently took my wallet out of my back pocket and pulled out the tiny folded story my father had torn from *The New Yorker* for me. "Knowing of your interest in fiction," he'd said when he handed it to me.

Spring passed into summer and summer into fall.

One day Joel and I did not have any work on a construc-tion site, so he planned to use my labor to help him clear some saplings and small trees from his land to create a field. I drove to his house, and we walked together to the land he wanted cleared. He'd already cut down a few small trees and made a brush pile of them. He set fire to the brush and told me, "As I cut things down, you drag them to the fire."

I nodded, and Joel pulled the cord on his chainsaw and revved it up. He began closest to the fire, and as he cut, I hauled and tossed the wood on the flames. The flames grew with each sapling I threw on, and soon I didn't have to worry about the fire going out. Just keep up with Joel. Haul and toss, haul and toss.

Joel and I settled into the rhythm of the work, him sawing, me hauling. The sound of the chainsaw and the sparks rising into the air from the fire were all the communication we need-ed. After a time, it started raining lightly, but Joel showed no sign of letting up, so neither did I. It was good to burn things during a light rain. I knew that, and the rain wasn't much. At first a dampening of skin. A bit of moisture seeping into the bandana I wore over my hair. Soon though, it started raining in earnest, and still we kept working, Joel cutting down sap-lings and me hauling them to the brush fire. The rain came down even harder. I was drenched now, my braids dripping water, my clothes heavy and wet, my boots soaked. But we kept on going. Cut, haul, and burn. Cut, haul, and burn.

There was something wonderful about working in that heavy rain. I would keep working as long as Joel did. Stop-ping now wouldn't make me any drier. I wiped the water out of my eyes, grabbed some saplings Joel had cut, and hauled them to the fire. Finally, though, Joel cut the chainsaw off and held up his hand to signal to me. "All right," he said, "let's call it a day."

In his barn he handed me a dirty towel, and I sopped the water off my skin. "See you tomorrow," I said.

He nodded. "Yeah, see you tomorrow."

I climbed into the truck and drove home, windshield wipers slapping hard against the rain. Cal was at work, and I looked forward to being alone in the house in such a down-pour. I'd build up the fire, make a cup of tea, and sit in my rocker close to the heat. And I had a plan. I planned to try my hand at writing fiction again.

Once home, I stood on the porch and peeled off my clothes. We lived in such a private place, I could easily stand on the porch naked. I draped my sopping clothes across the porch swing. The rain thundered on the tin roof. I stepped into the house, leaving damp footprints on the floor. A hot shower, dry clothes, stoking the stove, and brewing tea, soon I was in my rocking chair with a spiral notebook in my lap. It was a full-sized notebook that I'd purchased at a drug store the week before.

"Just begin," I told myself. "Just write it. What happened that you cannot write a story anymore? You've got to begin."

I wrote a story that day from beginning to end, about two women who lived alone in the woods in a house like the one I sat in. One woman, the main character, was always a little scared of the woods. One day she came home and found the house empty. Her roommate had to work late, and she was there alone. She turned on the tap to make tea, and no water came out. This meant she had to walk down in the woods, turn the pump off at the well, let the pressure build up for about ten minutes, and then turn it back on.

This was a maneuver Cal and I had done often. Wildwood did not have enough wells for all its tenants, and on wells that shared houses as ours did, the water pressure sometimes dropped. The remedy, Mrs. Baker taught us, was to turn the pump off for a brief period of time. And of course, to use as little water as possible—put bricks in your toilet tanks and don't flush too often and water your gardens by hand.

Every summer at the start of a drought, Mrs. Baker came around wringing her hands and talking about conserving water. And just the weekend before, Cal and I had hiked into the woods, turned the pump off, and sat on a log smoking a joint while the pressure built back up. It wasn't something I'd ever done alone, but I knew how to do it. My protagonist had never done this alone either, and it was nighttime, and she was scared.

Nevertheless, she couldn't fix dinner without water, so she faced her fears. She got a flashlight and walked down to the well and cut the pump off and, as she waited for the pressure to build back up, she turned the flashlight off and sat in the woods in the dark, listening to the sounds and looking at the stars she could see in the clearing. She made friends with the thing she had been afraid of. She made friends with wildness.

What I remember about this short story does not come from its quality. I'm sure it wasn't very good. But it was a beginning, and since tearing up my writing six years earlier, I had not written anything more than tiny descriptions in my tiny notebook. Now I sat alone in my house with a large notebook in my lap, the fire crackling cozily, the dogs spread out on the rug at my feet, and above me the rain pounding loudly on the roof. I looked up at the Masonite ceiling and said a prayer to the god that lived there. "Please god, let me be a writer, and *I don't care who falls by the wayside.*"

I knew what I was saying.

I don't care who falls by the wayside.

There was not room enough for writing while I shared a home with Cal. Cal's creative life consumed us, and I loved it as much as he did. I loved the band practicing in our home. I loved hearing Cal idly picking his guitar. I loved the guitars themselves, leaning about the living room and in the practice room, the pedal steel sitting in the middle of the green rug, surrounded by amplifiers.

When I went with Cal to gigs, I went early and helped set up, and I stayed late to help break it down. At the gig we uncoiled miles of orange extension cords and duct-taped their paths to beer-stained carpets. While the music played, I collected money at the door or passed the hat. I sat with the other girlfriends and wives, and we danced together and drank beer.

The nights I chose to stay home were peaceful and quiet. The fire crackling if it was winter, sitting on the porch swing in the night if it was summer. Reading without interruption, without my mind having to divide itself between my book and paying attention to one of Cal's long-winded stories or trying to shut out music if the band was practicing. I enjoyed cooking and eating and cleaning up all in silence. I went to bed saying goodnight to no one. Sometimes, in the morning, I scribbled a tiny line about something in my tiny notebook. But I was ready for something more now.

I don't care who falls by the wayside.

I was telling God, or whoever lived in that Masonite ceiling, that I was ready to live without Cal, ready to nurse my interest in fiction. But other than my prayer and writing this one story, I did nothing to make it happen.

And what would I have done? If Cal and I were breaking up, and it was my idea, I would be the one having to leave. And leaving Wildwood was out of the question.

22.

When summer came, the band started getting more gigs at the beach and places east of us, sometimes a mini tour, with one gig followed by another the next night. They rented hotel rooms and piled in together, or else they were provided a place to stay, a ratty house somewhere inland. I mostly stayed home during these trips.

Cal seemed unable to avoid telling me about each mild flirtation he had at a bar. He came home from these gigs with stories of women sidling up to him during breaks, stories of sharing joints with women behind the bar before loading the truck and leaving, stories of every party they went to where he met a "nice girl." I wasn't sure about the "nice girl" part of the stories. The band played rough places now, solitary cinderblock buildings with nothing but a parking lot and broken glass surrounding them.

I listened to Cal's stories about women. I didn't shrug them off, but I didn't feed them either. I kept myself mild. I knew what it was to be attracted to someone outside of marriage, and I considered it quite normal. Hell, I was attracted to most of the guys in the band at one time or another. It wasn't something I mentioned to Cal, or anyone, because why would I? It would only upset him, and I had

214

no intention of acting on it. And neither did they. And if we occasionally shared a joint without our spouses, or flirted a bit, so what?

Cal and I had been babies when we married. Neither of us had many relationships before we started dating. I knew from experience that finding out you're attractive is potent. I thought Cal might be working this out for himself, and that these little dalliances were natural and not to be taken too seriously. And so, I listened and let them be what they were. Stories about the gig he'd just played, and stories about women. Maybe Cal wanted me to show jealousy. Maybe he wanted me to fight for him, to make clear to him that I wouldn't tolerate this.

But I wasn't going to make it my responsibility to keep an eye on him. I remembered his calls to me in the cabin, the way he policed me, his need to assert his presence on my days off. I remembered the way I'd kept myself small for him. I had no desire that he do the same for me.

Besides, I had better things to do. Moons to watch. Birds to listen to. A garden to weed. A fire to tend. Books to read. Dreams to remember.

During our eighth year as a married couple, Cal got lovesick for a girl he'd barely met. I found her phone number in the pocket of his jeans while doing the laundry. She'd not been a woman he'd mentioned, and he'd been mentioning women after every gig I didn't go to. So, who was she and why was her name and phone number in his pocket? When I asked him about it, he told me he'd met her at such-and-such bar, and that he wanted to go see her.

"Okay," I said. "Go see her."

Because really, what else could I say? When your spouse has gone so far as to say he wants to go visit another woman, you let him. Or you insist that he doesn't, and you become the warden of your relationship.

Cal packed up the truck with a few clothes thrown into an old suitcase that had belonged to my folks. He drove off to parts unknown. I didn't know where he was going, only that she lived east of us and he would be gone the weekend and that he hadn't called her to tell her he was coming. He merely drove to her. We made no arrangements for a phone call. This was Cal's big weekend without the ball and chain of marriage, and I respected his need for it. I stayed home alone in Wildwood, as I had been doing since I learned to drive.

And there loomed the wildest possibility of all, that I might, at the end of this weekend, no longer be married, and the house, Number Three Wildwood, would become mine alone. Because of course, if Cal wanted to end this, he would be the one moving out.

I walked through the house that weekend considering the rooms. I decided I'd make the band room into my bedroom and I'd set up a study in the other room. I'd have a desk overlooking the front porch. A typewriter and one of those old-fashioned rolling desk chairs made of oak that I loved so much. Never mind that I couldn't type. Never mind that a rolling chair would never roll on any of Wildwood's unevenly planked floors. I never let reality get in the way of a good fantasy.

Instantly, there was a man. A man who respected my writing. A man who ate food with onions in it and brownies with nuts. A man with whom I sat on the porch swing after dinner, who easily roped an arm across my shoulder. A man who danced with me in the yard under a full moon.

Some time back, Jackie had mentioned dancing one night with her boyfriend.

"Cal doesn't dance," I said.

"He dances with you at home alone, doesn't he?"

I shook my head. "No. He doesn't dance at all."

I longed for that. A sweet little spin across my braided rug with a man who loved me. Such a simple thing.

Cal came home Sunday afternoon. He pulled his truck beside mine. I met him with a joint on the porch. We sat down in the swing. I lit the joint and handed it to him. He took it, took a draw, and with his toke held in, said, "I didn't see her, Bear."

"Why not?" I asked.

He blew the smoke out. "I don't know. I got down there and just rented a hotel room and swam in the pool and came home."

"Oh well," I said, shrugging, because again, what could I say?

I didn't let go of my fantasy though. It wasn't a new fantasy. It was a fantasy I'd nurtured and fed and that had nurtured and fed me throughout our marriage.

It was a survival tactic to live in my head, and always had been. Cal might not be leaving. He might have lost his nerve when it came to visiting a woman he'd met in a bar. He might have chosen me over her, but his decision wouldn't affect my fantasy. Sometimes the boyfriend changed, but the place, this house in Wildwood never did.

"How's Scarlett?" Cal asked.

Of course. Cal and his beloved dog. Cal never asking how I was doing.

"Okay," I said. "Off running somewhere with Grendel."

"I missed her."

And this: Cal could never say he missed me. And maybe he didn't. It's not like I'd missed him. I nodded. We never spoke of that weekend again. The woman he'd been so taken with faded into a shadow in our history.

Jackie's boyfriend quit the band and was replaced by a young high school kid with a sweet face and rosy cheeks. His name was John, but I called him Little Johnnie Kilowatt, the electric drummer. John fit right in and brought a whole new group of younger people into our lives, friends of his from high school. Young, thinly whiskered boys, a lot like the boys who used to swarm into the living room of our first house years before. Those boys had grown up, but they still came around. Their whiskers were full now. Some had turned into fine young men I could have conversations with. Others had remained pretty much the same, and I still didn't like them, but I wasn't entertaining them every single night any longer. They had pads of their own now. The crew that John brought into our lives didn't, but they were there by John's invitation only. None of these boys swarmed into our house nightly, on their own.

The band went to the beach again, and I opted to stay home. When Cal returned, the rhythm guitarist arrived with him to help unload the equipment. I helped too. I was an old hand at this. I knew where the amplifiers went, the box of cords, the pedal steel guitar, all of it. After Eddie left, I asked Cal, "So how'd it go?"

"Alllll riiiiight."

When Cal came home from a gig, he was always eager to talk, eager to find Scarlett and scratch her behind the ears, roll a joint and relax. But after this gig, he didn't want to talk. He was grumbly about something, but I didn't know what. I persevered anyway.

"Was it a good crowd?" I asked.

"Okaaay I gueeess."

"Any problems? Any nice people?"

"I don't knooow."

"What's bothering you?"

"Noothiiing."

I shrugged it off. Cal and his moods. His surliness had been at the epicenter of my life for as long as I'd known him. His moods were like the tide. They came. They went. They flooded. They receded. I didn't take them on anymore. I drifted away to some other activity. I disengaged. Let him stew. This had nothing to do with me. Or so I thought. After a time, it became clear that it had everything to do with me.

After this weekend, Cal surpassed his own legendary capacity for being an absolute prick. He became surlier with me than he'd ever been before, and this says a lot. He was grumpier with me, and snappier with me, and it was over everything. Every single thing.

"Is this picture straight?" I asked the next day, hanging one of my thrift-shop finds in the hallway, before I knew not to ask him anything.

"I don't knooow." He snapped at me without even looking up from his guitar.

"Well, could you take a look?"

He looked, suffering my demands, obeying me as though I was his mother and he a teenage brat. "It's alllll riiiiight." He returned to picking his guitar.

I didn't know why he'd come home so grumpy, but I figured it would pass. Cal's squalls always passed. But not this one.

Over time, I understood that I had become an enemy, and Cal had set his targets. His contempt came at me like bullets, fired before I even knew I was being shot at. I had a bull's eye painted on my heart, aimed at by my husband.

I could not make sense of it. I could not fathom what I had done. His hatred of me, the suddenness with which it came on, the intensity of it, the relentless targeting of me that began that weekend, his ability to never let up, his unabating attacks on me, his athleticism and stamina when it came to keeping the pressure on, the thumbscrews down, his derision, his contempt, his loathing—all laid on thickly and consistently. He hated me like I was a smothering female who'd tricked him into this horrible life. He hated me like I was a shrew who'd stolen his manhood.

Yep, I had finally become the kind of woman Earl Johnson had warned him I'd be as soon as we got married. As soon as I got my claws into him. As soon as I got him by the short hairs. As soon as I put a ring through his nose. As soon as I got what I wanted from him. Yep, eight years later, just as that sage Earl Johnson had predicted.

I had always made myself small when necessary. In the face of Cal's moods, I could fold myself into drawers and cabinets inside me that I hadn't even known were there. But I'd never experienced this level of antagonism. His mood against me would not lift, not even for one second. Every day became more and more absurd as Cal escalated his crusade, and crusade it was.

"What's wrong?" I asked him over and over, because nothing changed. He grumped at me. He glared. He snapped. He barked. He snarled. He glared harder and harder every day. "What's wrong?" I asked again.

"NOTHING," he growled.

"Are you mad at me about something?"

"NOOOO."

"Are you mad about something else?"

"NOOOO."

"What then?"

"NOTHING."

"Okay. Should we go ahead and order some firewood before fall gets here?"

"I DON'T KNOW."

"Well, it's August."

"I KNOW IT'S AUGUST."

"Will you make the call, or shall I?"

"I'LL DOOO IIIIT."

The simplest things, things related to our survival, things we'd negotiated and done every year, were now cause for conflict. Each night when I went to bed, I moved my body away from his and he moved his away from mine.

I could have left. I was no longer dependent on him as I had been. I could survive without him. I could drive now. I could build a fire. I could chop wood. I could pay the rent and the bills. Technically, I could have easily left Cal, but undoing a marriage, even one that should be undone, is never easy. The emotional tangles are real, and they map through the heart in rills and runnels and inlets and bays and oceans.

The band still came and practiced at our house. The musicians I knew so well joked with me and smoked dope with me, bumped their hips against mine when handing me a joint, and it was such a relief that not everyone suddenly hated me now. It was clear though that they knew Cal and I were having troubles.

One day I was home alone, sitting on the porch swing, when two young girls came driving up. They introduced themselves as Bonnie and Mia, friends of John's.

"Is Cal here? Or John?" Mia asked.

"John doesn't live here," I said, "and no, Cal's not here."

I thought nothing of it. We had visitors all the time. We were the band house. People came and went, although I'd never met these two.

"Well, we thought the band might be practicing."

"No."

We sat on the porch and smoked a joint together. Mia wore a striped tube top. When she raised her arm, I saw the stubble of hair in her pit. I remember thinking of myself at her age, how uptight I was, how I would never have gone out of the house with armpit stubble wearing a tube top. I didn't think this judgmentally. I thought, *Wow. High school girls are a lot more comfortable with themselves than I ever was.*

They left after a time. I didn't tell Cal about their visit. Why would I? He'd just snap at me.

I started bringing up separation to Cal, but he was non-committal, nonprocessing, nontalking, nonreceiving, practically nonhuman.

"Do you want to leave?" I'd ask.

"I don't knooow," he snarled.

"Just tell me."

"I don't knooow."

"Well, what's wrong?"

"Nooothing."

There were many of these exchanges. He threw everything back at me. He was impenetrable. He was unchewable gristle. The psychological poisoning that he was doing was akin to constant doses of arsenic. I died a little bit each day.

I know now that the explanation was a simple one: he wanted another woman, and he knew that I wouldn't stand in his way if he told me that. He also knew, that if he said he wanted someone else, he'd be the one moving out, not me. Cal knew what was at stake better than I did. While I was trying to figure out what I'd done wrong, he was calculating his life without me. In Wildwood.

My sweet house with its uneven floors and its porch and its view of the woods was the custody battle I didn't know I was in. My sweet home with the woodstove that I, for the most part, solely tended. The whippoorwills and the moon and the woods and the walks I took, the butterfly weed growing along the side of the road, the vultures and hawks spinning in the air, Wildwood itself, all of Wildwood, which I loved more than I had ever loved anything, Wildwood, which had given me the self I needed. Wildwood's guardianship over me was the war Cal waged, and stupidly, I didn't know it.

His master plan was a page out of his lifelong playbook. Get me to make the decision. Get me to move. Glare me into leaving, just as he'd glared me into marrying him. The way to make room for what he wanted was to get rid of me, and the way to get rid of me without asking me to leave and without leaving himself, without ever admitting out loud that he wanted out of the marriage, was to demonize me. To turn me into an impossible shrew while he played the part of the put-upon, misunderstood husband. He was the man on the bulldozer, and I was the deer I saw standing in the churchyard one night during the clearing for Jordan Lake. Standing there in total bewilderment over the destruction of my habitat.

There was a house we used to pass by on our way home from the grocery store, back when I didn't drive. The house was a two-story frame house with a deep front yard. One day the front yard was piled with stuff. Clothes, gym bags, a weight bench, an easy chair. "Looks like someone got kicked out," Cal said, and we laughed.

No one came and got that stuff. It sat there for months, through all kinds of weather. It got rained on, and snowed on, and baked in the summer sun.

I thought about taking Cal's stuff and putting it out in the yard. His guitars and amplifiers, his records, *our* stereo (I'd be generous), his jeans and flannel shirts, his underwear and cowboy hat, his cans of Campbell's Chunky Beef Soup. All of it. I knew how to change a lock on a door. I could get a deadbolt. I could just be done with it. Make a statement. Force him to leave. He'd come home to find it all in the yard. He'd yell and stomp and load up his shit and drive away in a big huff. And then he'd be gone. Out of my life.

But I didn't have the heart for it. It seemed so public, and mean, and potentially costly for him. I knew the price of every guitar and amplifier he owned. I'd helped pay for them. And I knew how much they meant to him. I knew that if he didn't come get his stuff immediately, the weather would damage it. The heat. The rain. I could picture the record covers puffing with moisture. I could picture his pedal steel baking in the sun. The dogs peeing on his amplifiers. Lizards scampering across his flannel shirts and jeans.

I wasn't prepared for that soul-crushing act, but for years after, I wished I could have been that sort of woman. For years after, I've pictured his stuff piled in the driveway. I've pictured his anger. But he'd have taken it all. He'd have moved out. He wouldn't let anything happen to his guitars. He'd have taken Scarlett too. He wouldn't let anything happen to Scarlett.

I sank down in the shower and cried one day. And then I started laughing.

My life was absurd. I couldn't make sense of it. Every part of life was fine except when it came to Cal. The band still came over and practiced. The boys still joked with me. The house and Wildwood still held me. The dogs still swirled at my feet. The garden still grew. The vultures still spun in the air. But with Cal, everything was snap and glare and mud-dragged words.

His most potent tools. His only tools.

I could not bear to ask him once more what was wrong and have him snap at me in his all-caps way. I could not bear to ask him if he wanted to break up and have him throw up the brick wall of I DON'T KNOW while also dismantling our relationship. He created an impasse to get movement from me. Mission accomplished. I could no longer wait for his mood to lift. His mood would not lift. I could no longer wait for him to decide something. He would decide nothing, and I recognized that I had two choices. Stay and endure this misery or leave. But leaving had an asterisk, a footnote. I would leave only for a week. I intended to return. I was not banished from my house. I was merely absent for a brief period of time, and then we'd talk this over. Maybe he would even miss me.

He brightened instantly when I told him. The sun came out in his face. He smiled, and he had not smiled at me for months.

"Okay," he practically shouted with joy. "If that's what you think is best."

That fucking shithead. What an asshole. The decision would forever be known as mine. Not his. He'd cleared himself of any responsibility. He'd come out on top. He'd tell his mother with a hangdog face, "Nancy left me." But he didn't show a hangdog face to me. He didn't even bother to hide his delight. I was so hurt by his gleefulness over my leaving that I went down in the woods and sat beneath a pine tree and cried. He'd shown no concern for me. He hadn't even asked where I'd go or who I'd be staying with.

I had no idea the answer to that question, but I was determined to give him a week. The week was meant to force his hand. I fully intended to move back in, and then he, after a week without me, would have to tell me what he wanted to do. That was the plan. He could have some good solitary alone time to think this through. That's what I told him. Perhaps we should have discussed the terms, but as always, we didn't.

When I returned home after crying in the woods, Cal asked with a smile on his face, "Did you have a good cry?"

I shook my head at him, numbed by his sudden jubilation and magnified callousness. This level of prick-hood, even for Cal, was baffling.

"I cleaned the toilet while you were gone," he chirped.

You cleaned the toilet? You're happily telling me you cleaned the toilet after spewing contempt at me for months? You cleaned the goddamned toilet?

He hadn't cleaned the toilet once during our entire marriage.

"Let me show you," he said. I followed him into the bathroom, and he showed me how he'd used a chisel to get the hard-water buildup out of the bowl.

You probably scratched the porcelain, I thought, but didn't say. Why the sudden focus on getting the hard-water buildup off? We'd lived with it for years, both in the cabin and here.

The next afternoon I packed the truck. I took my sleeping bag and enough clothes for a week. Cal stood in the driveway and smiled and waved goodbye, chipper and happy. "See you in a week," he said. So happy. He was so fucking happy that

I was leaving, and I was so fucking hurt. I had no idea where I was going. I hadn't lined anything up.

I drove to the end of the driveway and turned left onto the dirt road, away from my home. Away from my garden. The dogs. My braided rug. The iron bed my father had slept in as a child. The morning glories. The porch swing Cal had gotten me for my birthday. I drove away from the vultures and the whippoorwills and the owls. I drove away from Wildwood. At the end of the road where dirt met the blacktop, I stopped. I did not know whether to turn left or right.

To my sister's house? To Jackie's house? To my mother's house?

No, not to my mother's house. I could not have endured her whining, "I hope you work it out," as though the tragedy was that I had left him and not what Cal had done to me, which I still couldn't describe in clear terms.

I could hear my mother saying, "Everyone has spats. I'm sure he'll take you back if you call and apologize."

Call and apologize to Cal? What would I say? *I'm sorry you mistreated me? I'm sorry you're an asshole? I'm sorry you hate me?* I couldn't go to my mother's house.

Nor could I go to my sister's house. I wasn't ready to process this with her. I didn't know what I was processing. I had no idea what any of this was except that I'd done nothing to deserve my husband's hatred and that I was giving him a week alone, hoping it would break the impasse.

I turned left, toward Jackie's house. I drove over the bridge that spanned what would become Jordan Lake, the bridge that spanned Seaforth, and the community of dirt roads I'd learned to drive on. The clearing and burning was done on this part of the land now, and below the bridge lay nothing but mud and bare dirt and a few sticks and puddles.

I followed the back roads to Morrisville, where Jackie lived. I crossed the railroad tracks, passed the general store at the corner, and turned into the driveway of her trailer. She was home, and she took me in. I'd arrived just in time for dinner.

After dinner, while her boyfriend Jake cleaned up, Jackie and I went across the street to a playground, where we sat in the swings and lazily spun, passing a joint in the dark and talking. I told her everything that was going on. The one thing I didn't tell Jackie was that I had no place to stay the next night, and when I showed up in her driveway, she wasn't home, and neither was Jake. I waited an hour and neither came.

It was seven o'clock, summer, and I needed a place to sleep. I left Jackie's house, still not knowing where I was going, but thinking it over as I drove the back roads toward Wildwood.

There was an old farmhouse that I knew of, close to Chicken Bridge, so named for the truck full of chickens that had driven off it into the Haw River once upon a time. The farmhouse was empty, but I knew the owners, and thought if Cal and I split up, one of us might move there.

I hoped it would be him, but I was facing the fact that if we split up, it would probably be me that moved. Cal would take no initiative. He would stay in the house in Wildwood like a troll under a bridge. If I tried to stay, he would continue his hate campaign against me. He would force me to leave. He had already forced me to leave. All these thoughts swirled in my head as I drove.

The farmhouse had been empty for a long time. There was a bed there though, and the electricity was on, and it was kept unlocked. It would need a good cleaning, whoever was going to live there, and I could stop by Wildwood, pick up some cleaning supplies, and go there. The cleaning would keep me busy and not scared as night came on. And eventually it would make me tired, and I'd be able to sleep. I'd pick up a pizza on the way.

I'd not told Cal that I wouldn't stop by our house if I needed something. Absolute banishment had never been my intent. I wouldn't have shown up and camped out, I wouldn't have even stayed and smoked a joint with the band, but if I needed something, I'd come get it. This was my house too.

No one was home when I pulled up. I let myself in. The first thing I noticed was that the house was eerily clean.

I went into our bedroom to get a blanket from the closet. Our closet had never had doors. Cal kept his clothes on one side, and I kept mine on the other. But now, hanging over my side in front of my clothes, strategically placed and hiding them, was one of Cal's plaid flannel shirts. My pocketbook, which Cal had made for me during a stint working in a leather shop, but which I never carried, was missing from its nail in the wall. I found it tucked on the shelf beneath one of the blankets. In the bathroom I discovered that my tampons, which I'd always left in plain sight and didn't need this week, had been hidden behind the rolls of toilet paper in the apple crate we used as storage. In the hallway, the pine plaque with our wedding invitation decoupaged onto it by Cal's sister was missing. Only the empty nail remained.

It was so clear to me, and so painful; I was being erased. Our history was being erased. Had I not been so hurt by this I might have thought more clearly. I might have seen that my mugs were still on display. The picture I'd bought at the thrift shop still hung in the hallway. My books were on display.

It was not me that was being erased, not exactly anyway. But it was anything that might say clearly to another person, a person who did not know Cal and our life together, *a wom-an lives here.*

To someone like that, someone very young, everything else in the house might have been all Cal. Maybe he hung the picture of flowers. Maybe he drank jasmine tea from the mugs he'd bought me. Maybe he read the Little House books left on the shelf.

All I saw was an erasure of me, this after years of folding myself into a tiny scrap to accommodate his needs, after years of reassuring him after he'd discovered my affairs, and now after months of being demonized and snapped at and glared at, every exchange weaponized and bayonetted in my direction. Goddamn him. I'd had it with him. I pulled a jug of wine from the refrigerator and started drinking and waiting.

There is no combination worse than drinking and waiting. I ripped one of the band posters off the wall of the practice room and tore it up. I moved Cal's shirt so that it no longer covered my clothes. I put my pocketbook back on its nail. I put my tampons back in plain view. When Cal showed up, I planned to tell him that if he wanted me gone so bad, I'd go. I'd just fucking go. For months I'd been his enemy, and now it seemed that I was so repulsive to him he could not stand to even be reminded of me. I still did not get it.

Finally, I went into the woods in front of our house and sat on a stump, drinking, while Scarlett whined and Grendel slept on the porch and Josh pushed his basketball at my feet.

After an hour or so, Cal came driving up. I watched from the woods, heard him say, "Uh oh, I'll be right back." And then I heard a nervous, girlish giggle.

"I'm right here," I said, stepping out of the woods. Mia was sitting in the passenger seat of his truck. "I know her," I said. "Good lord, Cal, she's sixteen years old."

"Uh, uh, uh," Cal said.

I tried to open her door to the truck. I don't know what I would have done, but she had wisely rolled up the windows and locked the doors. She looked out at me, wild-eyed.

"Her or me," I said. "Decide right now," inadvertently giving him an exit.

Cal jumped on it. "Uh, uh, uh, I'll be right back," he said. He got in the truck and drove off, leaving me to drink and wait some more.

An hour passed by. An hour and fifteen minutes. That was the max it should take him to get Mia back home, kick her out of the truck, and return. If he cared about our marriage, which is what I thought *Uh, uh, uh, I'll be right back* had meant, he'd make it quick. Finally, he drove up after two and a half hours.

"What do you want?" I asked.

"I don't knoooow." He hang-dogged his head. He would not look at me.

"Her or me?"

"I don't knoooow."

"Do you want me to leave?"

"I don't knoooow."

"Do you want to leave?"

"I don't knoooow."

"Cal, she's sixteen years old."

Finally, he looked at me, to give me one of his famous glares.

"Is this what you want? To be with her?"

"I don't knoooow."

"Do you want to break up?"

"I don't knoooow."

What choice did I have but to leave again? And again, he

did not ask me where I was going. And again, I did not know. I mattered nothing to him. Eight years together, during which time he'd flung his moods around like glitter, and now I was only something to get out of his way.

As I drove up the road, I imagined him sitting with Mia in front of her parents' house, telling her something about his troubles with me. I imagined her naivety. I imagined her nodding. Yes, she understood. *Poor Cal. Poor Cal.* He probably buried his head in her shoulder. He probably worked her for her sympathy. This was heady stuff for a high school girl. Exactly the kind of thing I'd longed for when I was her age. A man who needed me, who relied on my soft feminine nurturing, who longed for my understanding. A man who could not live without me.

I stupidly believed that I had become someone Cal could not live without. I stupidly believed he would choose me over a sixteen-year-old high school student. And why wouldn't he? I'd helped him build home after home. I'd chopped wood. I'd built and tended the fire. I'd kept the hearth warm. I'd taken the mouse traps out into the woods and emptied them of their victims. I'd taken down wasp nests from the porch because Cal was allergic to their sting. I'd baked brownies without nuts when we were stoned. But I greatly underestimated the willfulness of a man and his dick. With Cal, that willfulness came in the form of forcing someone else to make the decision in favor of what he wanted.

23.

At the end of the road, I sat, Wildwood to my back, once again not knowing where to go. I was too raw to inflict my company on anyone. I could not show up somewhere unannounced, weeping, drunk, filled with emotion and confusion—I couldn't do it. And I no longer wanted to go to the farmhouse.

I turned the car around. I drove back down the road, through the swamp, around the curve. I passed the first little house, the one that had charmed me all those years ago. I passed our driveway. The lights were on in our house, every one of them blazing as Cal always left them. I turned into a driveway, the driveway of the unfinished cabin, the cabin that would have been, had someone completed the work on the house, Number Five.

By the light of my headlights, I spread my sleeping bag inside the door of the cabin. Then I turned off the headlights and sat on the stoop to remove my boots. I climbed into my bag. The night closed around me. At some point I heard Cal playing his electric guitar. At some point I thought I heard him wail in anguish. Then I thought I heard it again. Or did I want his anguish so badly that I imagined it? Even if he had wailed in anguish, it could have just as easily been about a can of beer falling out of the refrigerator as about me. Or it could have been about Mia. After all, he was supposed be getting laid about now.

Eventually I fell asleep on the hard, unevenly planked floor. When I woke in the morning, I looked out to see Scarlett sniffing at the tires of my truck. "Hey girl," I said.

She looked at the figure in the doorway of the cabin and started baying at me.

"Scarlett, it's me."

She yowled. That loud, insistent Redbone-coonhound yowl.

I pulled myself out of the sleeping bag, thinking she needed to see me to recognize me, but she took two steps back and rose up on her hind legs and howled some more.

"Scarlett, Scarlett, it's me. It's me," I kept saying. I kept on holding out my hand to her. I thought she'd recognize my voice. I thought she'd come sniff my skin. I thought she'd come nuzzle me and lick my face. But Scarlett kept on backing away and bellowing at me.

"Come on, Scarlett. It's me."

She kept howling. She would not let up. She could not let herself recognize me. She howled and howled and howled and I worried she'd wake Cal up and he would come to investigate and, finding me here, he would accuse me of stalking him or spying on him.

"Scarlett, Scarlett, honey, it's me."

My voice would not do it. My scent would not do it. It was as though Scarlett had become Cal. I was the enemy, and now I was sure she would not only wake up Cal but the other neighbors as well. Wildwood wasn't exactly known for its early risers.

I pulled my boots on and tied them. Scarlett still bounced

up on her hind legs and wailed at me. I rolled up my sleeping bag and tossed it in the truck, my dog still howling at me. I drove away. I drove to my sister's house and let myself in. I woke her in bed, and she rolled over and held me as I cried. I stayed there a week and then asked Cal to leave Wildwood for a week so I could move my things to the farmhouse near Chicken Bridge, which I had arranged to rent for seventy-five dollars a month. I didn't ask where Cal was going, just as he'd not asked me.

I took care of the dogs during that week. Scarlett, that stubborn, dumb coonhound, never howled at me again. Whatever scent-detector dogs have for recognizing things and making sense of the world must have been absent in her. She should have smelled familiarity in my truck the night I spent in the unfinished cabin. She should have smelled familiarity in me. But she hadn't, and now that I was in my proper place, she happily scarfed up the bowls of food I put before her, happily accepted the Milk-Bones I handed her, along with rubs behind the ears.

I was more than fair to Cal. As always, he left the big decisions up to me. He did not participate in the division of possessions. I'd be the one to decide what to take or leave behind, and he could complain later if it didn't suit him or not even notice if it did.

I took the big iron bed that my father had slept in as a child, but I left the mattress and box spring, both of which I had in the farmhouse. I left the table we'd built out of pallet wood, even though I loved that table. But in the farmhouse kitchen there was a long table made out of a door and saw-horses, so I didn't technically need a table, whereas Cal, *poor Cal*, did. I left him the blankets and took only my sleeping bag. The farmhouse came with piles of quilts.

In the kitchen I took the food Cal would not eat—the jars of rice and oatmeal and beans. I took all the pans except the one he heated soup in. I split in half the collection of plates and bowls. I took the eighty-nine-cent wooden spoon I'd put in our shopping cart all those years ago.

I struggled over leaving the Ashley woodstove behind. I loved it, but to move it would require muscle power I did not have. It would also leave Cal without heat, and the farmhouse came with a box stove, just like the one Joel had provided for us to use in the cabin. I knew how inefficient it was compared to the Ashley. It would serve Cal right if I took the Ashley. But, in the end, I left it, partly because it would be so hard to move, but mostly because I doubted Cal would last the winter without me. And when he moved out, I fully intended to move back in. And the stove would be there, provided he didn't take it or sell it.

I made plans to this effect. I'd keep an ear out for any hippie gossip that Cal was leaving Wildwood. The minute I heard, I'd call Mrs. Baker and tell her I'd like to move back in. I'd contact Cal and offer to buy the stove from him. I had it all figured out. I was the keeper of the flame. I was the one who stoked the stove. I was the one who made that house a home.

He won't last the winter. He won't last the winter.

I chanted it to myself as I packed my belongings and said goodbye to the house. Goodbye to Wildwood.

A friend of mine came over with her truck and together we loaded my things into the beds. Together we unhooked the porch swing from its hooks and carried it to one of the trucks. I picked up Josh's basketball and tossed it into the cab of my truck and he jumped in. I said goodbye to Grendel and Scarlett. I locked the door. I looked around. My garden.

The yard. The porch. The stump in the center of the copse of trees I'd sat on the night he came driving up with Mia. I left.

I drove through the puddle in the driveway that was always there. I drove past the little curve where I always smelled honeysuckle in the spring. I drove up the dirt road, through the swamp, to the blacktop.

Suddenly I was let loose. I was out of this marriage. I was free. I could date. I could stay out late. I could write in my journal and leave it on the nightstand where no one would pretend to knock it off and accidentally read it.

I could do whatever I wanted, but all I wanted was to move back to Wildwood.

The farmhouse was a beautiful place, a large greying old house with wavy glass in the front door, a front porch, and a back porch off each side of the kitchen. The kitchen was as big as the entire house I'd just left. Outside was an orchard. Deer came to eat the fallen pears. There were no other houses around. I was alone there. I was terribly alone, because our friends—the people I'd opened my house to for years— steadfastly kept their social life with Cal and the band.

I think most of them liked me; I think most of them felt Cal was making a huge mistake, but it didn't matter. They no longer reached out to me. I was no longer a part of that scene. I was out of it. They would say hello if they saw me, and some of them would give me a hug, but that regular contact was over.

This shocked me, especially when it came to the women I'd hung out with. The wives of two of the band members, women I thought cared about me, weren't around anymore. They didn't call, and when I called them and asked them over, they declined. To be fair, one of them had two children and lived in Raleigh. But the other? Natalie? She was just gone.

While the band practiced, Natalie and I had deep talks sitting at my packing crate table in the kitchen, our hands wrapped around mugs of tea. We could talk so seriously about so many things. I knew the avoidance wasn't personal. I knew she was still my friend. I knew that if we ever got a chance to sit down and have tea together the conversation would flow once again. But Natalie wasn't going to make that effort, and it hurt.

One person did not leave me though. Trip. Trip, the boy who used to visit me in the bedroom while I watched TV in our first house, who told me that TV was an escape from reality, who had liked me all along. We started dating in the early fall. It was still warm. The leaves hadn't turned yet. He visited me in my farmhouse, and we sat outside and made out on a full moon. We smoked dope sitting on the porch swing, now hung on one of the back porches. We danced in the kitchen to the radio because I had no stereo and no records. I'd left all that to Cal. Music had once filled my home, and now it was gone, as absent as summer.

One day at Trip's house, the phone rang. "Hey, Cal," Trip said to let me know who it was.

"No, I haven't seen her," to let me know Cal was looking for me.

"I'll let her know, if I see her."

He hung up the phone and said, "Cal wrecked the truck. He wants you to go over there."

My heart seized up. I'd go. I knew I'd go. I was being a strong woman now. I could face anything. But Trip took me in his arms and said, "You don't have to go."

I nodded again, my face against his shoulder.

"Jesus," he said. "Your heart is beating like crazy. Come sit down." I did. "You don't have to go," he said again.

"I know. I'll go."

I'd been about to leave anyway, about to go to my farm-house, the beautiful, wild, lonely place that did not feel like home. I didn't like being alone there, as I had at Wildwood. At the farmhouse, the loneliness pressed down on me like a weight. The house was too big. It did not hold me. It did not cradle me. I wandered its ample rooms like a specter. I moved from one chair to another, restless and unmoored.

So, I would swing by Wildwood. I would see what Cal wanted. I'd let him see me, and then I'd leave. I think now that I felt summoned more by Wildwood than I did by Cal. I just wanted to see my house again. Did he have firewood stacked on the porch yet? I would have, I thought, although I didn't at my own house.

I drove into the driveway and saw his truck parked there. I didn't even see any dings on it. The wreck must not have been too bad. The door to the house was open. I stepped up onto the porch and knocked. "Come in," Cal hollered. I followed his voice to the band room. He sat in a chair with a crutch leaning beside him.

"Hey," I said.

"Hey," he said.

"Is your leg broken?"

"Naw," dismissing the injury, even though he'd called me at Trip's wanting me to come by, sounding urgent.

There are several things Cal could have said.

He could have said, "Thanks for coming. It's over with Mia."

Another option would have been, "I'm sorry."

He didn't say any of these things, and although I don't re-call exactly how the conversation progressed, I do remember a few things vividly.

At one point he said, slyly smiling, "You're not the only one with black lacy underwear."

So, you fucked Mia, I thought. That was the goal all along, wasn't it? Why did you have to dismantle everything to tell me I'm not the only one with black lacy underwear?

"I'm sure I'm not," I said, making certain to keep my voice even and mild.

He held up his left hand and showed me that he was wearing his wedding ring again. "I'm wearing my ring again," he said.

"It's not that easy," I replied.

At this, he pulled his ring off and threw it across the room. Never short on dramatics, he then pitifully got down on his knees to find it, scrabbling across the floor with his hurt leg.

"I'm going," I said.

As I was leaving, his mother drove up. She was bringing him some food. She laid her hand on my cheek while balancing a casserole with the other. "He needs you," she said.

"Clearly," I replied, and left.

Not long after this, Trip and I broke up. He was falling in love with me, he said, but I couldn't love anyone right then. Funny, how I'd longed so hard to be chosen by a man, and yet this choosing came at the wrong time. I was too raw. Too fragile. After Trip and I split, the farmhouse became a beautiful, wild prison.

Winter was on its way. I needed to prepare. I'd had slab wood delivered from the sawmill. This was the cheapest way to get firewood without gathering it myself, but it still required work. I would have to saw it into stove lengths. I'd been given a chainsaw. I knew how to use it. I could cut this wood up, and I'd be fine, but I wasn't fine. I was frightened of using the chainsaw alone. What if it slipped and I cut myself? No one would be here to help me. No one would know if I bled to death. I imagined my body freezing beside the woodpile, as the phone inside the farmhouse didn't ring. So, the load of slab wood sat there, unprocessed, the leaves falling on it, in hues of gold and red and brown.

It wasn't the bitter middle of winter yet, so I let the house be cold. I had a propane heater in my bedroom. I stayed in there, in the warm room, occasionally wandering the house, following the puffs of my breath from one beautiful, unusable room to another.

It was into this morass that Cal journeyed one night. It had warmed again. Like most North Carolina winters, the weather couldn't quite let go of one season to solidly enter the next. It was warmer outside than inside, even at night, and I had the door open. I thought I heard a car, tires crunching on gravel. I stood at the door looking out and saw headlights flickering through the trees.

Do men have any idea how scary it can be for a woman when they show up unannounced? It was dark. I was alone. None of my doors had working locks. Josh was a big dog, but he was more likely to push his basketball against an intruder than attack him, or even growl. I let out a deep breath of relief when I saw Cal's white Datsun King Cab pickup pull in beside my orange Datsun truck.

"Hey," he said.

"Hey."

"Can I come in?"

"What are you doing here?"

"I need to talk to you."

It had been days since I'd talked with anyone except at work. I let him in. He didn't mention anyone else's panties this time. He even said he was sorry.

I had been waiting years to hear Cal say these words, and I thought that maybe things could be better between us now that he'd sown his wild oats. I'd forgiven myself for my affairs, reminding myself what a child I'd been. I could forgive Cal too.

We ended up lying in my bed holding hands and talking into the night. I wasn't ready to jump back in with him, but I would consider it. I made that clear. "You hurt me," I said.

"I know. I'm sorry."

I nodded, leaned my head against his shoulder. He wrapped his arm around me. Why couldn't he do this all those times I'd needed it? When Yella Fella died. When my father died.

I wasn't stupid. I knew that Cal's contriteness had everything to do with what he wanted. He wanted me to come back to Wildwood, and I wanted that too. But I also wanted to know that this tenderness could last more than a night. Cal leaned over and kissed me. I kissed him back. I snuggled into his arms and said, "I can't make this decision tonight. You need to go. We'll talk tomorrow."

"No, let me stay."

"Call me tomorrow."

Winter is coming, I thought. If only he'll just leave and call me tomorrow. If only he'll not expect instant results. If only he'll prove to me, in the slightest way, that he's not here for instant gratification, then I can move back to Wildwood. I can be home again, not here, in this strange, remote farmhouse.

I only wanted a night. I did not want him to grovel or become a human doormat as I had done. I only wanted a night. One night to prove to me that he was sincere.

Cal didn't seem to understand that it wasn't him sleeping

with Mia that bothered me so much. That was an easy for-give-and-forget. It was not so easy to dismiss the way he'd treated me, the way he'd pushed me away, so meanly, so ut-terly, so maliciously, and so strategically. How could he have done that to me? He didn't have to tear me apart. He didn't have to force me out, make the disintegration of our mar-riage all my decision, so he could morally come out on top. All he'd had to do was say, "There's someone else."

I knew why he'd done it this way. It was the same rea-son I'd stayed with him instead of going home to my parents after my own affairs. Mother. He couldn't face going to his mother and saying he'd left me. He couldn't face making a decision that she would judge as morally wrong.

When I'd told my mother we'd broken up, she cried. Pre-dictably. She wanted us to get back together. The dissolution of our marriage was a tragedy, a tragedy it was up to me to fix. "I just want you to be happy," she trilled. She trilled this for years. "I just want you to be happy," she sniffed every time I saw her, as though happy could never be anything other than having a husband, even if that husband was Cal.

Cal was a man of convenience. Mia may have become in-convenient to him. Maybe I looked a little more convenient now. It would have taken very little work from him to con-vince me to return to Wildwood. I wanted it badly. I wanted to hang my porch swing there again. I wanted to stoke the stove. I wanted Wildwood's moon and Wildwood's vultures and Wildwood's road dipping through the swamp.

"Call me tomorrow," I said. "Just call me tomorrow, and we'll talk some more." I kissed him. If he could see potential at all, he'd have seen it in that. All he had to do was drive away, spend one more night alone, and call me the next day. I'd have gone back.

Instead, he drove off but returned shortly after. He got out of the truck holding his hand to his head. "I drove off the road and hit my head," he said. "Can I come in?"

Now I had my answer. He was as manipulative as ever. "I'll take you to the hospital," I said.

"Ohhh, nevverr miiind. Maybe I'll just go jump off Chicken Bridge and kill myself."

I didn't reply, and he drove away. I knew he wasn't going to jump off the bridge, and I'm not sure I would have stopped him anyway. I washed my hands of him that night. And just like that, Wildwood slipped away again. But I still held out that Cal wouldn't make it through the winter.

24.

It was a long, beautiful fall. The house was cold, but the weather outside was warm in the sun. I sat on my porch, moving my rocking chair into blocks of sun, nursing my fantasies about returning to Wildwood. I would hang my porch swing on the hooks still there. I would plant Heavenly Blue morning glories again. I would plant the garden again. I would add herbs along the edges. Come next winter, I would sit by the woodstove in my rocking chair, my braided rug spread on the uneven floor again. That rug covered the living-room floor of the farmhouse now, but when I moved back to the house in Wildwood, I would match every worn line of it with the floorboard it had worn against. I would put it exactly where it used to be, where it belonged. I would put me exactly where I used to be, where I belonged. All I had to do was get through the winter. And despite the beautiful weather, winter was coming. Somehow, I would manage.

The house was cold at night, but I didn't build a fire. Even if I'd bothered to cut the wood I needed, the box stove would have done little to warm such a large house. Nights were hard. I'd left the TV with Cal, as well as the stereo. No one called or came to see me. To avoid nights alone, I got a second job as a bartender at one of the dives Cal's band sometimes played at.

After working on the construction site with Joel, after tending bar, I came home late at night. I turned on the heat in the bedroom and fell asleep, and in the morning, I turned the heat off, got up, and went to my job on the construction site.

Cal's band was scheduled to play at the bar. Knowing my connection, the owner asked if I wanted to work that night or not. I said I did. I needed the money. But more than that, I needed to be seen. I needed to exist for these people again.

The band arrived early, as they always did. All the guys said hello to me, loose and easy, as though we were all still good friends, and I suppose in their minds, we were. I gave them beers, which they consumed while setting up. Natalie and Ava weren't there, and I hadn't expected them to be.

Apparently, Cal and Mia had gotten back together because she was with them. She wore a one-piece jumpsuit, and she marched past the bar where I was and stood in front of the stage and studied the lighting, as though she might have some opinions on how to improve it. It was an act meant for me, and I knew it.

I did not blame her for what had happened. I'd once been a child wanting a boy to choose me. I wanted her to know I had no hard feelings. I gave her a beer, even though I knew she was underage.

"I am of age," she said. "I just don't have my ID."

I cracked the pop-top and slid it to her. A peace offering. We, Cal's women, were both trying so hard to be cool.

I might have given Mia another beer had she asked, but she didn't. Instead, she sent Cal up to the bar, just to show she could. "Uh, uh, uh," he stammered, his shoulders drawn up to his ears. "Can I have two Coors Lights?"

I got them for him. He paid. I don't recall a tip.

During a break, the band and its entourage disappeared, including Mia.

I knew where they went. They went to a dead-end dirt road nearby to pass a joint around. At one time, I'd have been with them.

I made some new friends. A woman who'd lived in a house in Wildwood, her boyfriend, and their friend—a tall, beautiful, red-haired man—were coming to see me in my farmhouse one afternoon. The dead leaves were thick in my yard. I waited in the cold house. My new friends and I had nothing planned except drinking, smoking dope, and going out to dinner.

The phone rang. It was Natalie. She'd not called me since I'd left Wildwood. I was delighted to hear from her. "Hey," I breathed. In the brief instant, before she told me why she'd called, I thought our friendship might revive. I thought we might sit somewhere and drink tea and talk.

"I thought you'd want to know," Natalie said quickly, "that your house burned down."

"What?"

"It happened a week ago. Eddie told me not to call you, that you didn't care, but I thought you'd want to know."

The band had gone to a gig, she said, and came back and the house was gone. The fire already out. Scarlett was inside, she said. "She died. Grendel is okay. I thought you'd want to know," she said again. "Eddie says Jack or Paul took care of Scarlett's body. That's all I know. I thought you'd want to know," she said again.

"Thanks," I said. "I did want to know."

We hung up, and I stood there in the living room of the farmhouse next to the Christmas tree I'd put up, my breath puffing in the air. I could not fathom the news. I could not understand how it was possible that my house had burned down a week ago, and I'd not felt its absence. I'd not dreamed of those flames. I'd not heard Scarlett whining and howling as the house burned down around her. I'd not felt the heat of that fire on my skin. How was that possible? I didn't know the answer to that question, but it dug its claws into me, and if there was an answer, it lay in the ashes of Number Three Wildwood.

Wildwood pulled at me. I wanted to go there. I wanted to go to my house. I wanted to see for myself, but I couldn't. I was expecting company.

My new friends drove up. As they got out of the car, I came out of the house and onto the porch. In the yard, I blubbered, "My house burned down. And Scarlett died in the fire."

"Bummer," one of them said. "How about a beer?"

And the message was clear. Let's party. Partying solves everything. And so, I pulled it inside. I pulled it in as though I were swallowing a rope. I went through the night with them. We drank. We smoked dope. We went out to eat. We laughed.

The whole time, I watched the shell of my body pretending to enjoy herself. And the whole time, Wildwood called. *Come*, it said. *Come here. You are missed. You are needed.* The spirits cried.

I did not ignore them, but I had trapped myself into this night. I told myself, throughout the evening, that I would go to Wildwood in the morning when it was light. I would visit the house. I would lift the ashes in my hand and let them sift through my fingers. I would rub the ashes on my face, my arms, my breasts. I would roll in the ashes of Number Three Wildwood.

"Let's go to Tijuana Fats," someone said as we left the restaurant, and so we ended up at Fats, sitting at the bar, drinking highballs. My new friend slipped two tall, frosted highball glasses beneath her coat. Outside she gave me one. "To remember tonight by," she said, although a highball glass was not what I would remember it by.

I cursed myself for agreeing to travel in one car. I couldn't disengage. I couldn't leave. After hours of drinking, we returned to the farmhouse and got drunker and higher. "I need to go to bed," my female friend announced, "and I'm too drunk to leave." And so it was that she and I slept in my bed in the only room with heat, while the men slept in the kitchen and living room without heat.

In the morning the guys burst into our room and said they were cold. We moved aside, and they got into bed with us, and we warmed up. There was nothing sexual that went on, although perhaps they would have welcomed it. I don't know. If there were signs, I did not read them. I was only thinking of Wildwood. My house. The pilgrimage I needed to make. Rubbing the ashes on my body.

My friends wanted to go out to breakfast, and I did not speak against the idea. I wasn't strong enough to say no. I wasn't strong enough to say, "There's somewhere I need to be." Plus, I was hungover, and I needed food.

We drove separately this time. We went to Breadmen's, a popular restaurant in Chapel Hill. Again, I watched the shell of my body perform all the things a body must do. Order food. Eat food. Talk. Pay the bill. Hug the friends. I never saw them again. When I left, I drove to Wildwood.

As I approached our driveway along the dirt road, I tried to glimpse our house through the trees, but it wasn't until I turned into the driveway that I saw it. The blackened hulk of my home hunkered down on its little hill like a wounded animal. As soon as I opened the door to the truck, the smell of smoke punched me in the gut.

The roof was caved in, the porch was intact. An unfamiliar red car sat in front, close to the steps. I went around the red car and noticed it was singed on the other side, the side closest to the house. Serves you right, I thought. Too lazy to walk from the proper driveway to the house.

I put one foot on the first step leading up to the porch, testing it with my weight as Cal and I had done when we approached abandoned houses. It seemed solid. The second step seemed solid. And the third one. The porch floor seemed solid. The wall with the front door was intact, the door open. I peered in at my old living room. A mess of dark cinders and fallen rafters.

The willow bench Trip had lent us was completely gone. Strips of insulation drooped out of the walls. The woodstove lay on its side in the exact place where I'd sat in my rocking chair that rainy day and prayed to the god living in the Masonite ceiling to let me be a writer.

No god lived in the Masonite ceiling now. No mice lived there either. The Masonite ceiling was gone. The roof was gone. I was standing on what was left of it. Above me only sky.

My boots crunched across the living room to the kitchen, and I peered in. It was the most burned part of the house, but the cedar stump we'd built our table on was still there, laying prone and singed black, the tabletop burned away, and the two-by-four brace that had held it up gone. The back wall, where we'd cut the door and where I'd watched the goldfinch bathing in the puddle, was gone. The wall that held the sink and the stove that overlooked the garden was gone. Glass had exploded and covered the floor. Dark and glittery.

I turned back to the living room and went down the still-intact hallway to the bedroom. The mattress seemed fine. The green blanket was rumpled across it, stiff from the firemen's hoses and a week's worth of cold weather, frost on each peak like a mountain top. Cal's plaid flannel shirts still hung in the closet. They looked okay, and I wondered why he'd left them behind, but when I lifted one off its hanger, the scent of smoke poured off it. The drawers to the dresser yawned open, clothes spilling out. Pennies were glued to the dresser top with melted guitar picks.

I left the bedroom and went to the band room. The green carpet was singed dark, except for one circle. Something had been there during the fire. Perhaps one of his shirts had lain rumpled there. Or the towel he kept draped across his pedal steel.

I turned to face the door again, and as I did so, I spied something bright and blond against the blackness of the cinders. A little puff of air escaped my mouth as I recognized it. Our wedding invitation, decoupaged by Cal's sister onto a piece of pinewood. I remembered that it had been missing the day Cal had driven up with Mia in his truck. I picked it up and looked at it, the invitation still clear and readable. I didn't know how it could have survived, but of all the things I wanted from this house, this was not one of them. I dropped the plaque back into the cinders. And returned to the kitchen. The most burned part of the house. The wall gone. My garden just beyond.

Your soup's ready.

My call to Cal echoed eerily in the cinders of our home.

His soup plopping onto the stove, always turned to high, Cal always leaving the room.

Your soup's ready.

His reply from the living room.

Alllll riiiiight.

The fire originated, I heard, in the kitchen. A pot left on the stove.

Your soup's ready.

I heard that after the gig, after coming home and finding the house burned, Cal had started crying, and Paul the bass player, the man who'd dumped his rotating cast of girlfriends on me during practice, told him to get it together, the same as Cal had told me to get it together the night my father died.

At first, they couldn't find the dogs, and then they realized Scarlett had been inside and had died in the fire. One of the guys crawled into the wreckage and retrieved her body.

They called and called for Grendel, and finally he slunk out of the woods. He could not stop shaking. I pictured Cal kneeling down and hugging him to his chest, rubbing him behind the ears, burying his face in Grendel's fur, and telling him it was okay, even though it was not okay. It was not okay at all.

Story goes that Cal returned the next morning and searched the house for anything salvageable. Story goes that he had buried, among his T-shirts in the dresser in his bedroom, a chunk of hashish and a fifty-dollar bill, both of which survived.

My speculation had the pine-plaque wedding invitation buried in there too, buried before Mia came over that first time. Cal's T-shirts and jeans and the fact that it was in the least burned part of the house had protected it. I pictured Cal rummaging through the drawer the next day searching for his cash and his stash, tossing the wedding plaque into the hallway, where I'd found it. Tossing it as he had tossed me.

What was hard for me to believe the day I first saw the burned-up house, and for years to come, was that there was nothing there for me. There was nothing I could find, nothing to pick up and cherish, no life that could be resurrected. The house wasn't even ashes that I could run through my hands and rub on my body. The house was hardened cinder, a ghost of a house that I could walk through but never occupy again.

I had been right about one thing though. Cal had not lasted the winter in Wildwood without me, and winter came on with a vengeance that week. I ran the water in the farmhouse kitchen full blast hoping the pipes wouldn't freeze. I woke to an icicle protruding from my faucet. A friend came over to thaw the pipes, but they were frozen solid and busted. We turned the water off. I was too ashamed of this failure to call the landlord and have it fixed, so I didn't report it. I lived in the old farmhouse without running water. I shit outside in the cold behind a barn and peed in a jar, which I dumped in the grass.

Three weeks after the house had burned, two weeks after Natalie called to tell me, John, the drummer for the band, came into the bar where I worked. I was glad to see him and slid him a beer. He took a long thoughtful sip and then twirled the sweating can on the counter. Clearly something was on his mind. "What's up?" I asked.

"I don't think Scarlett's been buried."

"What do you mean?"

"I think she's still in that shed behind the house. Jack said he'd take care of burying her, and Paul said he'd take care of it. The night of the fire, we laid her in that shed in the woods, and they each said they'd come back the next day, but I don't think anyone has. When I ask, they both say the other took care of it."

I knew why John had come to me. He'd come to me because he knew I'd do something about it and Cal wouldn't. "Okay. I'll see to it. Thanks for letting me know."

John slid a dollar bill across the bar to pay for the beer, and I slid it back to him. He picked it up, folded it, and put it in my tip jar.

I went home that night to my cold, frozen house, turned the heat up in the bedroom, got in bed, and slept. In the morning, I pulled on my boots, loaded a shovel and a pick-axe into the back of the truck, and drove to Wildwood. I turned into our driveway and went past the burnt hulk of our house, the singed red car still sitting in front of the steps. I drove along a faded road through the woods to the shed.

There had been someone living in this shed when we'd first moved to the cabin. We'd taken a walk one day and gone past it, and she'd peered at us out of the grimy window. She didn't emerge to talk to us, and we never met her. I never knew her name. She must have moved out soon after, because the shed had been empty for years. We went there some days, just to look at it and stare at the phone numbers and messages the woman had written on the wall.

Call Janet
Bill—967-2732
Get hamburger.
Papagayos Tuesday 830

I backed the truck up to the door. Ever since John had told me that Scarlett's body might still be in this shed, I'd been considering how to do this. I planned a quick transfer of Scarlett's body from the shed to the bed of my truck. I planned to bury her in the yard of the unfinished cabin, where Cal had buried Yella Fella, and where Scarlett had yowled at me so relentlessly the morning after Cal came driving up with Mia. I'd brought a bandana to protect myself from the stench, and now I tied it around my face, bandit-style.

Three weeks is a long time in the life of death. Although I smelled nothing yet, I was sure I would. I didn't know if maggots fed on burned flesh or not, but I was prepared for it. I pulled a big black plastic bag from the truck and opened it, thinking I could shovel Scarlett's body into it if I had to.

I took a deep breath, held it in, and opened the door. There on the floor just inside lay a Scarlett-sized lump wrapped in our old orange electric blanket, singed and dirty. I touched the bundle, expecting sponginess and rot, but feeling only hardness. I reached under her body and lifted her up and realized she was frozen solid.

I let out my breath.

I held her against my chest, still swaddled in the orange blanket. What was probably her head rested on my shoulder. I laid her body in the back of my truck and pulled the bandana off my face.

I drove to the unfinished cabin and parked. I pulled away the grass, just outside of the cabin door. I took the pickaxe from the back of the truck and slung its blade against the earth. The strike reverberated into my arm, and one small ping of dirt came loose. I swung again, and again the same thing. The reverberation up my arm and another ping of dirt let loose. The ground was frozen. Frozen deeper than usual in the North Carolina piedmont. We never had winters like the one we were having now. I swung and swung and swung and accomplished only a button-sized indentation in the earth. I dropped the pickaxe and walked to the truck, slumping against its side. I wasn't going to be able to bury her. I had to figure out something else.

I climbed into the bed of the truck and moved Scarlett's body closer to the cab, where the wind was less likely to rip the blanket away. I tucked the loose flaps of the blanket around her body and propped the pickaxe and the shovel against her to keep it secure. I drove to the animal shelter in Chapel Hill. I told the woman at the desk that I had a dog that had died in a house fire in my truck, and I couldn't bury her because the ground was frozen. Could they incinerate her? The woman said yes. She pulled on her coat and followed me outside. I moved the pickaxe and shovel off Scarlett's body and lifted her and jumped down off the truck to the ground. I was holding her against me, ready to pass her to the woman, when she said, "We're required to unveil her. We're required to make sure this is a dog and not a child before you drive away."

"Oh," I said. "Oh, I didn't want to look at her."

I'd not wanted to see Scarlett's burnt body, the meat of her face seared away, her fur and flesh gone, and her bones showing. I'd deliberately not looked.

"I didn't want to do this," I said again, but I was a strong woman now. I pulled the blanket away. And there she was—in my arms—not burned. Not burned at all. Her red fur not even singed. "Oh, she wasn't burned," I said.

"I can take her now," the woman said.

"She wasn't burned," I said again. "She died in a fire."

The woman nodded. "I can take her now," she said, gently reaching and lifting Scarlett from my arms.

"I thought she'd be burned," I babbled. The woman walked away with Scarlett, the orange blanket flapping away from her face. Scarlett's eyes were closed. "I thought she'd be burned," I said again to the woman's retreating back. She opened a steel door on the side of the building and stepped inside. The door snicked shut behind her. "She must have died from smoke inhalation," I blubbered to the empty parking lot.

And now I knew what the unsinged circle on the green carpet in the band room had been. Scarlett had died there. She had curled up and breathed her last breath. I drove back to Wildwood. I went into the house. I knelt and touched the clear green spot on the darkened carpet.

25.

After our house at Wildwood burned, after I'd retrieved Scarlett's body from the shed and tried to bury her, I found comfort in the arms of cocaine and a man who seemed to have an endless supply of it. I moved in with him, quit my two jobs, and started running a paper route with him. One morning, after delivering papers, I took him to see my burned-up house in Wildwood. I think I hoped to share it with him. It had been so important to me, and now it just squatted on its little hill, empty and sooty. When he pulled his van into the driveway, I took satisfaction that the singed red car that had been parked in front of the steps was gone.

Richard walked around the house as I told him stories—about Scarlett, about the woodstove, about the big snow we'd had one winter and how snug the house was with the insulation of snow banked all around it and covering our roof. I pointed to the scruff of yard still surrounded by the fence I'd put up and spoke about my garden, how I'd like to have another one sometime.

All the time that I talked, he walked and peered at the house and said nothing. Then he dropped to his knees and opened the access door to beneath the house and peered in. "Hold on a minute," he said, and he went to his van and got a flashlight, which he shined under the house on the pipes that still snaked there.

"Damn, baby," he said. "We can take this copper and sell it."

"I don't want to do that," I said quickly.

"Are you kidding me? Copper brings a lot right now. There's a fortune down here."

"No."

"Aw, come on." He walked to the van, rummaged around, emerged with a hacksaw in his hand.

"Stop," I said. But he was under there, crawling across the dirt, then sawing on one of the pipes, then water was spurting out of it. "We got to get out of here," he said, scrambling out from beneath the house and heading for the van.

"You can't leave it like that."

He shrugged. "Come on. We don't want to get caught."

"These wells will run dry if we leave it like that," I said. "People here depend on those wells. This place has water problems."

I started to detail how Cal and I had to walk down to the well and turn the pump off, let the pressure build back up, and then cut it back on. "Every toilet on this road has a brick in it." I knelt down and watched helplessly as the water spewed from the pipe and pooled beneath my old house. "I told you not to do it."

"Come on. Let's go."

"I'm not leaving until you fix it."

"Come on." He climbed in the van and started it. I stood in my old yard, watching the water creep out of the access door, darkening the ground. I looked up at Richard, but the sun glinted off the windshield of his van so that his face was obscured. I shook my head. No. I would not leave.

"All right, all right," I heard him say. The van turned off. The door slammed. "Here." He handed me the flashlight. "Shine it under there."

I knelt on the ground, and Richard crawled under the house again and twisted the pipe to stem, and then stop, the flow. The knees of his jeans were soaked and muddy when he came back out. "Satisfied?"

I didn't answer. I continued to shine Richard's flashlight into the darkness. I watched for five minutes to make sure that the water really had stopped flowing.

"Come on," he said. "Let's get out of here."

"I want to make sure it's really stopped."

"I said it was, didn't I?"

Another few minutes and finally I stood and went to the van and got in, sullen and quiet.

"Hey," Richard said as he drove away. He reached over and took my hand. "It's okay, baby. No one saw us," misreading my mood completely.

I stopped snorting cocaine with him, although he continued to buy it and present it to me as though it was a gift. I'd watch him do it all in a night. He hit me once, and when I finally left, he stalked me, but once he'd found a new girlfriend, he stopped. Eventually he killed himself in her backyard by running a hose from his van's exhaust pipe to its window.

There were bills to pay left over from my time with him. I borrowed money from a friend to attend bartending school and learned to mix drinks using thinned paint and colored water to simulate the ingredients. I got a job in Raleigh in a place where the tips were pretty good. I chipped away at the bills, and to further save money, I moved into a thirty-dollar-a-month house in Apex, with no running water and no heat. I woke one night in a sweat and turned the electric blanket off. The next morning, I noticed that my sheets were scorched. In the spring I moved to an apartment I shared with my sister, then into another apartment alone. I got a job in Durham in another bar.

There were animals I could not take care of. Josh got hit by a car and died. A cat got killed by a car as well. Other animals came and went. In the bars I worked in, I learned to break up fights by stepping between men and their egos. I twisted one guy's balls to get him off someone. In one place there were whores giving blowjobs in the kitchen and a cocktail waitress with "Property of..." tattooed across her ass, which she showed me in the bathroom. There were lines of coke tapped out on a bar and a sleazy restaurant owner I was more or less required to dance with. There were comments on my ass and legs and every other body part I had. I smoked the hell out of some dope. I had boyfriends who came and went.

As a bartender, I worked nights and had days free. In my apartment complex, I drank my coffee in the mornings sitting at the kitchen table, watching all my neighbors leave for work. I fixed a second cup of coffee and rolled a joint and sat at the table some more. A whole day stretched out ahead of me. I was alone. On my own. There was nothing to do to distract me. Sometimes I wrote in my journal. I'd begun that practice again, and I kept my notebook next to my bed with a pen for late-night inspiration that never came, except in the form of lovesick poems about the boyfriend du jour.

Men were easy to attract. I still hoped to entice one to stick around. I still hoped to be chosen by one of the magical beings, although in person they did not seem so magical. They seemed troublesome and bossy and self-involved.

Once again, I blamed myself. I probably expected too much. I was probably too raw, too needy, hurting too deeply for any man to want to stick around.

One early spring day, sitting at my kitchen table smoking a joint and watching the apartment parking lot empty out as people left for work, I decided to take a drive. I made myself a thermos of tea and rolled a joint for the road. I set out for the country. I set out for Wildwood.

I turned onto the road that led off 15-501. I passed the cows in the field in front of the barn. I drove the curves and took note of all the landmarks I'd noticed on those early morning drives into town with Cal. The house in the big curve up on the hill. The Nature Trail Mobile Home Park. The house with the Cape Hatteras nightlight in its kitchen window. The house with the stained glass in its front-door windows. And then Farrell and Son's, where I turned right. I crossed the lower end of Jordan Lake. It was flooded now. When Cal and I lived here, there had been dumpsters along this stretch of road. Now there was water, although at this end, not much.

The green sign for Wildwood's dirt road came into view. The rickety row of mailboxes. My truck dipped down into the swamp, into the curve where I'd encountered the owl chasing the mouse. I drove past the field once filled with scruffy pine trees, now grown into a forest. Across the road from the field the empty trailer was no longer empty. I saw a grey car parked in its driveway. I drove up the little hill passing the first little house on the right. As I turned into the driveway for Number Three, I saw it. The blackened remains still crouched on its little hill. I pulled up next to it and parked.

I walked up the steps and onto the porch. I went inside to the living room. It had been years since it had burned, and nothing had changed. I crunched across the broken glass and embers into the kitchen. I stared at the hole in the wall over-looking my garden. I stared at the stump that had supported our handmade table. I stared at the insulation still drooping from the walls.

I returned to the living room. The woodstove was still there, still turned on its side. I went into the hallway. The pine plaque with our wedding invitation decoupaged to it still lay in the rubble, its blondness startling in the blackened soot. I kicked it aside. In the bedroom I stared at the blankets fossilized on the bed. I stared at the open drawers of the dresser. At the guitar picks and pennies still adhered to the top. Cal's clothes still hung in the closet. I left the bedroom and went into the band room. I knelt and touched the green circle in the blackened carpet where Scarlett had died.

I wondered if Cal ever revisited our house. I was sure he didn't. Once the hash and money had been retrieved from the dresser drawer, once he was assured someone would take care of Scarlett's body, although he never knew it was me, he left, and I was sure he didn't return. Cal closed emotional doors before he even opened them. I left this emotional door yawning wide open. I stood in the ruins of our house trying to push it closed. It would not close. It seemed insane that I was there. I wanted to take something with me. I wanted to hold something in my hand. I wanted a totem, and I remembered Cal scrabbling around on the floor, looking for his wedding ring after he'd flung it across the room, the day he'd asked for me to come over after wrecking his truck. The day he'd told me I wasn't the only one with black lacy underwear.

It would have been a poor totem, a lousy thing to take from the burnt house at Wildwood. But I searched for it anyway, hoping if I found it that it had melted and was a lump of gold. I could carry a lump of gold in my pocket better than I could carry his ring. I found nothing. I kicked around in the rubble, scuffing the toes of my boots into piles of charred rubbish.

Finally, I went outside and sat on the porch steps and smoked my joint and poured a cup of tea from my thermos. To have tea in that spot again nourished me. I could ignore the lost house behind me and look out to the view that I knew so well, the one I loved so much, the woods seen from the porch of our house. A truck dusted by along the road beyond. I recognized Bill, a neighbor in one of the last houses. He didn't see me. No one saw me. No one ever saw me when I visited the burned-up house, and I visited it often. I visited it hundreds of times.

I went two or three times a week. I went in all seasons and all weather. I never told anyone that I did this. I always went alone. I always took a joint and a thermos of tea. I always kicked through the rubble and sat on the porch. Over the years I did find things to take.

I riffled through the pockets of Cal's shirts and pants and took his change. Sixty-eight cents: a quarter, two dimes, three nickels, and eight pennies. I took a roach clip I found in a pocket of his jeans. I pried a bit more money up from the top of the dresser. I pried up melted guitar picks and shoved them into my pocket. I wanted none of this. What I wanted was my house. What I wanted was a time machine. What I wanted was to have been a cold, angry, unsympathetic bitch who moved all Cal's stuff out into the driveway and changed the locks. If I'd done that, I'd be sitting in my porch swing drinking from a mug instead of a plastic cup from a thermos.

I fished through the dresser drawers again and again, digging into Cal's underwear and socks and T-shirts. Nothing.

As always, Cal took everything, and left nothing behind except slop for someone else to clean up.

One day I backed my pickup truck up to the porch and wrestled the cedar stump that had supported our homemade table into its bed. I would recreate that table. I'd loved that table. I could build another one. I could find some packing crates and take them apart and sand the wood and stain it. I could do that. I didn't need Cal to help me, or anyone else for that matter. At home, I tugged the stump into my apartment, maneuvering it into the spare bedroom and leaning it against the wall with a piece of cardboard between the two so it wouldn't soot up the white paint.

For a long time, I eyed the Ashley woodstove, turned over and lying in the rubble. It seemed okay, although likely it was not. Its thermostat system, created by using a variety of metals that heated differently from each other, was surely ruined by the extreme heat of the fire. But maybe I could restore it. Maybe I could find a place in the country eventually and use it again. It wasn't made entirely of cast iron. I could probably move it. Foolishly I dragged it into the bed of the truck and took it home with me. I put it in one corner of the living room of my apartment and set a vase of flowers on it, just as I had done in the summers at Wildwood when it was not in use.

I started seeing a man I liked. He told good stories, and unlike Cal, he didn't take forever in the telling. All the same, he filled the air with himself, but as long as he was entertaining, I didn't mind. I found it convenient. I used his need for attention as a shield. I asked him leading questions. I let him talk. If Brad was talking, there was nothing I needed to add. All the same, he'd asked enough questions and allowed enough space that he knew a few things about me.

He knew I'd been married to a musician and lived in a house close to Jordan Lake that had burned down. And one afternoon, after driving out to the lake and sitting on the shore together, I asked if he'd like to see where I once lived.

It was summer. The trees were leafed out and thick. I'd visited the house the week before, and everything was as it usually was. I'd sat on the steps, slapped at mosquitoes, drank tea, and smoked a joint, hearing but unable to see a vehicle dusting down the road.

Now, it was that little copse of trees, the leaves solid and green, that prevented me from seeing that there was a blue-and-white bus with a stovepipe sticking out from one window parked beside the burnt house. I pulled all the way into the driveway, shocked to see it, and shocked to see that the woman living in it was sitting on a cinderblock used as a makeshift back step, eating a peach, a cat lazing at her feet.

I stopped. I threw the truck into reverse and drove out fast.

"I'm sure she would have been perfectly nice if you'd stopped to talk to her," Brad said.

I nodded. "Probably so," I managed.

Inside I felt mute. It was her yard now. It was her place. I couldn't tell Brad what this meant. I couldn't tell him that, while he was at work during the day, I drove out to Wildwood and sat on the steps of my old house. I couldn't tell anyone that. It would seem crazy to do such a thing. I couldn't tell anyone that in some ways, I still lived there, I still lived in Wildwood. I was a real live ghost to a life I'd once had.

I'd recognized the woman. Her name was Jeri, and I'd met her on a construction site when I worked with Joel. I remember her startled look as I sped into her driveway as if

I owned the place and sped out just as quickly, as though I'd been caught in a robbery.

I started having dreams about Wildwood. The dreams came repeatedly, and unpredictably. In the first dream I was driving into the driveway of the cabin. I woke and thought, *Wildwood. I was in Wildwood.* I closed my eyes and tried to return to that dream, but didn't.

Over time, the dreams became more and more elaborate. Sometimes I dreamed of the first day I saw Wildwood, only Cal wasn't in the car with me. I don't know who was driving, but I was sitting in the passenger seat, and there was the first house, then the second, and the third, all the way to the end of the road. Other times I dreamed there was another dirt road branching off the original that I had never seen before, and down that road were more houses built in the same funky style. Sometimes I dreamed I was moving into one, cleaning its windows, unpacking my belongings.

I always woke, knowing I'd been there again, feeling the place. Feeling the cold of winter or the summer heat. Hearing the crackle of a fire in the woodstove or the whir of a fan in the window. Smelling woodsmoke or smelling honeysuckle.

Now that I could no longer haunt Wildwood, Wildwood haunted me.

My mother also haunted me. I found myself driving somewhere and unconsciously chanting, *I want my mama. I want my mama. I want my mama.* Then I would snap out of it, surprised to realize I'd been saying this. My mama was not dead. She was still alive, living in a nursing home now, confined to a wheelchair.

When I went to visit, she looked at me, gasped a bit, and then said, "I wish the boys were here." If we got around to anything else besides the missing boys, it was that my sister and I were not married. "I just want you to be happy," she'd say.

I was never what she wanted me to be, and we could never meet with each other on the plane of two grown women who knew a few things about the world. She would perpetuate the narrative she'd grown up with to the bitter end. Boys and men were sacred. Girls and women were just God's tools to be used by boys and men.

I had always wanted my mama.

We tell ourselves to forget things. We tell ourselves to move on, and we try. But what is moving on but pretending and functioning until pretending and functioning become habit? Because no one knew I had haunted the burned house at Wildwood, no one knew the void it created when I found Jeri living in the bus beside it. It was as though I'd had a secret lover who died. I couldn't speak of it. Wildwood, except for the lingering dreams, was gone from me now.

There were two things that remained though. One was pot, the other writing.

I partook of one daily and dabbled with the other. I managed to take a few writing classes at a place called The ArtsCenter in Carrboro. I still couldn't type, but I purchased a tiny Brother word processor that had a tiny screen showing eighteen letters before printing. This allowed me to make corrections, but a screen showing only eighteen letters was not nearly enough to take care of my clumsy typos and poor spelling. Still, I managed to eke out a pretty good short story written from the point of view of a child born to hippies, a child who grew up on a commune in a house that later burned down.

Like creative people everywhere, I was trying to figure out how to become the thing I was not yet. I had an idea of what being a writer meant. I lived in an area with lots of writers. I saw them. They lived public lives. They did not seem to work the kinds of hard, physical jobs I worked, and I judged myself by it.

I wanted to become the kind of writer who could live off her royalties and recline in diaphanous gowns all day, not that I'd ever worn a diaphanous gown in my life, or ever would, but I wanted the option. Besides, it wasn't the wardrobe that mattered, but what the wardrobe represented. Leisure. Another story effortlessly flying off my fingers onto the typewriter, emerging in pages that needed no revision, no corrected spelling or typos. I did not know how hard creating a story, especially one after another, could be.

By now Brad and I had broken up, and I'd quit bartending and worked nights in a bakery. The baker made the bread dough and shaped the loaves. He slid the trays onto racks and left me alone to bake it off, let it cool, slice it, and fill orders for restaurants. Sometimes I didn't leave until the sun was rising.

I was always in the bakery when the bars let out. The windows were steamed from the oven. No one could see in, but I could see the shadowy forms of people walking by. I could hear their laughter. The smell of bread enticed some people to try the door and shout, "We want bread. The people want bread."

"Let them eat cake," someone else said. And they drunk-giggled down the road. Or once, they stood on the sidewalk singing to the steamed-up windows lit from within.

I'd worked hard all my adult life—stocking shelves and unloading trucks, toting lumber and kegs of beer, and now hauling fifty-pound bags of flour and shoving trays of bread into a hot oven.

What was standing in the way of me being a writer? As far as I was concerned, the answer was easy. Time. And what took up my time? Work. And why did I have to work? To pay rent. To pay bills.

A friend submitted my short story to a literary magazine without my knowledge, and they accepted it, my first published piece of writing, and this gave me incentive. I had to put writing at the forefront of my life, and I made a plan. I reasoned that I was never going to make money to buy myself time, so I would have to come at the problem from the other end. Cheap living was what I needed. I needed to get out of the apartment complex. I sold everything I owned, including the chainsaw, which I'd never used, the maul for splitting wood, the old crosscut saw Cal and I once used on the land now under Jordan Lake. I sold most of my clothes and all my books. I chunked the old Ashley woodstove and the cedar stump that had been the base of our table into a dumpster, and I moved into a fourteen-foot travel trailer I bought used. It contained a couch at one end that converted to a bed, a dinette, a tiny kitchen, a bathroom, and a closet. Jackie's mother let me park it on her land for free.

After I had it moved, I called the electric company to get the power hooked up and was informed that they did not hook up power to trailers until the county had inspected the structure. I called the county and was informed they did not inspect trailers under thirty-two feet. I called the electric company and was told the same thing again and went back to the county, and so began the loop-de-loop of bureaucracy in which no one would budge. Everything I owned had been sold. I had nowhere to go. Finally, a friend of mine stepped in, climbed the pole, and hooked up the power.

Without paying rent and without paying for electricity, my living expenses plummeted. I only had to pay for gas to heat and cook with, plus my phone bill. But I soon learned that writing needs not just time, but also psychic space. A large amount of my brain was now taken up with struggle, struggle with my new home.

The bed was too short for me. My clothes were crammed into a slim closet. Come winter, every night I unhooked the hose that provided my water to keep it from freezing. I had two dogs that took up all the floor space at night. If it rained and they were wet, the little trailer steamed with their damp fur smell. Plus, my plan of gaining time backfired. I added hours to my shifts at the bakery just to avoid being home. I wasn't writing. I wasn't doing anything but working and smoking dope and avoiding home.

I'd lived in the travel trailer a few months when the literary magazine that had chosen to publish my short story finally came out and held a publication party at a local bookstore. I bought a new dress from the thrift shop for the party. It had to be held together with safety pins, but with a belt covering the pins and a pair of funky leather boots, I felt pretty satisfied with my appearance, and off I went to my first literary party.

I was to learn, at this literary party and many more, that the primary opening into a conversation with a writer is, "Where do you teach?" Meaning, what university are you affiliated with? Telling people at literary parties that I worked in a bakery, or later worked in a grocery store and cleaned houses, never helped me make friends. A strange silence fell when I revealed how I made my living.

The next question was, "Where did you go to school?" Meaning college. The college I'd refused, and this, too, caused uncomfortable and awkward moments. I didn't teach any-where, and I hadn't gone to college, so who was I to be at-tending a literary party? Who was I to think I could write? I felt as though I was an imposter, a fluke. It was a chance en-counter with pen and paper that had gotten me here. Surely, it wouldn't happen again.

They wouldn't have been far off in this assumption. I didn't apply myself to writing. My short story had been a chance encounter. And it might not happen again.

But I always told myself in every weird situation that it was probably me. I was probably reading the vibes wrong. I was probably too uncomfortable with myself. After all, I was probably the only one at this party wearing a dress purchased at a thrift shop, held together with dime-store safety pins.

I attended the party alone. I'd brought no one with me to take the social edge off. I stood close to the table with the cookies, holding a plastic cup of ginger ale. Since my drunk-en night with my temporary friends, the night I found out the house at Wildwood had burned, I'd shunned alcohol, but I did love cookies, so I shoveled a pile onto my plate. It gave me purpose to eat those cookies, and something to do with my hands. Occasionally people drifted into my sphere, asked where I went to school, or where I taught, and then gaining the answers, drifted away again. At one point I felt the safety pin holding my dress together pop, the sharp point digging into my waist. I went to the bathroom to fix it and returned to the party. Soon I abandoned my plastic cup of ginger ale and plate of cookies and slipped out, without saying goodbye to my editor or anyone else whom I'd met.

The first thing I noticed when I drove up to the travel trailer was that the lamp I'd left on in the window was off. The light bulb must have burned out. Well, crap, I thought.

This meant going into one of the benches that formed the dinette seating. There was lots of hidden storage there, not easily accessible. It's where I stored my crockpot and my light bulbs and an extra pair of hiking boots.

I turned the headlights off and then noticed that the outside light next to the exterior door was also off. I checked the surrounding houses and saw that their lights were on. I knew what this meant. I'd been busted by the power company for pirating electricity. I turned my headlights back on, and by their shine made my way to the door, where I found the expected note hanging on the knob.

I fumbled with the key, found a flashlight, and made my way back to the truck to turn the headlights off. There was a number to call. How the hell was I going to explain this?

I felt a little woozy from the party and the sugar in the cookies. I hadn't had any protein, and I found a jar of peanut butter and a sleeve of crackers, which I made into a meal. I had no electricity. No candles even. Just the one flashlight. But my heat and cookstove ran on propane, and the water still ran from Jackie's mother's well. I was warm enough for the night. I could brush my teeth and make a cup of coffee in the morning. The dogs settled on the floor, and I crawled into my sleeping bag. I'd deal with this tomorrow. By the time the sun rose, I knew what I had to do. I had to find new digs.

Wildwood, I thought. *I wonder if there are any houses for rent in Wildwood.*

26.

Through the hippie grapevine, I'd heard that the Bakers were infirm now, and their daughter had reluctantly taken over the business of collecting rents first of the month. It had been seven years since I'd left Cal and the house had burned. I might have contacted the Bakers earlier, but I was always worried they blamed me for leaving Cal and the loss of their house to fire. After all, Cal was prone to spinning stories of victimhood and blame, and I was never sure what he'd told them. In my mind, and possibly theirs, the end result of my leaving him was that the house had burned down. It would have never happened had I not left. I think everyone knew that, maybe even Cal.

But now, I realized, I'd not have to deal with the Bakers at all. Only their daughter, who need not know I'd had any-thing to do with the house that burned. If only there was a place for rent. I would start by driving down the road.

Just before the driveway to my old house, I slowed the truck and peered through the copse of trees, surprised to find a large grey house in the place where mine had stood. I saw Jeri, the woman who had lived in the bus, marching to a pile of lumber, a measuring tape clipped to her belt. The bus was still there, but the burnt shell of my house was gone.

And then I was past it and driving by the cabin with the deep porches, and then the unfinished cabin where I'd spent the night, and then Number Six, the cabin where we'd first lived. The other houses went by to my right. Different neighbors now, with the exception of one man who I knew still lived in the house he'd built so many years ago. At the end of the road, I turned around and drove back, slowing again at the driveway, seeing Jeri carrying a board inside. And then I was past again and driving down the hill, into the swamp, up the other side of the hill, and to the blacktop.

I drove to Farrell and Son's and bought some gas, a Coke, and a pack of Nabs. "Hey, Nancy," Mr. Farrell said. "Haven't seen you in a while."

"I've been around," I said, surprised he even remembered me.

I sat in the parking lot drinking my soda and eating my crackers, thinking, and making up my mind. I dusted the crumbs off my jeans and drove back to Wildwood. At my old driveway I turned in. Jeri was sawing a board on a table saw. She finished and looked up as I parked the truck.

"Hey," I said. "I don't know if you remember me. We met a while ago on a construction site. Nancy." I pointed to my chest. "Peacock. I used to live here."

"In the house that burned?"

"Yeah."

"Sorry about that. It must have been a bummer."

"It was."

I didn't mention Scarlett, or that I'd haunted the place, or that I'd driven up one day to find her living in the bus and had been so shocked and stunned and hurt that I'd hightailed it out of there without speaking. If she recognized my truck, she didn't say.

275

"You bought the land?"

"Yeah."

"It's a great piece of land. I loved living here."

"Did you plant the garden?"

"Yeah. And I put up the fence."

"We're going to plow it up and plant next spring."

"It gets good sun," I said. And then I got on with it, the purpose of my visit. "So, I'm looking for a place to live. Do you know if anyone's moving? Anything coming open?"

"Good timing," she said. "Kathy and I have been living in the cabin next door while we build the house. We expect to take occupancy in a couple of weeks. I'm just finishing up trim work. Do you want it?"

"The cabin?" I looked over at it. The deep porches. The cedar trunk posts at the corners.

"Yeah," Jeri said. "The cabin," as though it was the most natural thing in the world for me to drive into Wildwood, wanting a house, and having one handed to me.

"Yeah, I want it." The words breathed out of me.

"Mrs. Harold, she's the Bakers' daughter, would be happy to know we found someone. Do you want to see it?" Jeri asked.

"Yes." I'd been in this cabin, but I'd never been upstairs.

I followed Jeri across the shared driveway, up the gullied road that led to the deep front porch. I placed my foot onto a large, curved stone that served as a step. There were several of these stones scattered about the houses of Wildwood, serving as steps. The Bakers, I heard, had salvaged them from a building at Duke University that was being torn down. How they moved them was beyond me. Each one was the width and length of a dresser and eight inches thick.

From that stone, I stepped onto the porch, and from the

porch I followed Jeri through the hand-built door painted red. The door was wide but short. I had to duck to get through.

"We've moved the furniture already," Jeri said, "so it's a little empty."

We entered a room that served as both living room and kitchen, the kitchen area tucked into the far corner. A table sat in the middle of the room. In the kitchen area, open shelves lined one wall, and a narrow gas stove was shoved in next to the sink. The sink was large, cast iron, with a drain board. At one end of the drain board was a chest of drawers, and in the corner next to it, a woodstove, a large homemade barrel stove that sat on a hearth of bricks.

I'd seen these stoves in other houses in Wildwood. A man in Chatham County made them from discarded hot water heaters. They were reputed to be very good stoves, holding a fire overnight, and large enough to pack.

"The woodstove was here when we took the place over," Jeri said, "so I guess we'll leave it behind."

"That'd be great."

Silently I thanked the gods of the electricity company for cutting my power right when they did. The cabin in Wildwood and a woodstove too. I could move right in when Jeri and Kathy moved out. My mind busily calculated the things I'd need to get. Firewood. A refrigerator. A stove.

"We don't need the stove or fridge," Jeri said. "You can buy them if you want. They work fine." She shrugged. "Twenty bucks?"

"Sure," I managed.

"Kathy will be so relieved. We were just going to take them to the thrift shop and weren't looking forward to moving them. This table too," Jeri said. She touched the edge of the plain square table. "We don't want it. Kathy pulled it off the side of the road, just to tide us over until we got the house built. You can have it if you like."

"I could use a table. I've been living in a travel trailer. I don't have anything."

This didn't surprise Jeri. She'd lived in a bus, after all.

"Well, the table is definitely yours."

"Can I see the upstairs?"

"Sure. Go on up. I'm going to call Kathy." Jeri walked to the phone that sat on one of the steps leading upstairs.

I climbed the narrow stairs. Halfway up, a window with a deep ledge looked out over the rutted driveway. At the top of the stairs was an open closet. To the left, a hallway with a bedroom on one side, and further down, another bedroom. The wall dividing the two rooms was made of plywood. Jeri and Kathy's bed was in the bedroom overlooking the front entrance. The back bedroom had built-in shelves with glass fronts and a built-in desk. The window was low and over-looked the roof of the back porch, which was as large and deep as the front porch. Downstairs I heard Jeri talking on the phone to Kathy.

"Nancy Peacock," she said. "I remember meeting her from a long time ago. I think she'd be a good neighbor. She's buy-ing the stove and fridge, and we can just leave the table too."

I heard her conclude the phone call and hang up. I went back downstairs. Jeri had pulled a pad of paper from some-where and was writing things down. "Here's the landlady's number. Mrs. Harold."

I nodded.

"And here are the numbers for utilities."

Jeri handed me the slip of paper.

"Thanks. And when are you moving again?"

"Two weeks. We'll be in by Christmas, but you can take over in January. That gives us time to mop up the loose ends. Your timing is good," she said appreciatively. "We told Mrs. Harold we'd be out by the end of the next month, but things haven't taken as long as we thought. We were planning on paying one more month's rent and then giving it up to her in February. You'll save us a little money."

"Very good timing," I agreed. "What's the rent?"

"Two hundred."

Up by seventy-five dollars since I'd lived here, but still a deal.

"We replaced the stovepipe first of winter because we didn't know how long we'd be here. So things are looking good in that department. Now, listen, with Mrs. Harold, don't sign a lease if you can help it. She'll be here first of the month for the rent. It's a job she didn't want, so be here. Don't piss her off. And she doesn't want to fix anything."

I smiled at hearing the same advice Tom and Karen had given Cal and me when we'd first moved to Wildwood.

Out on the porch, Jeri nudged her foot against a pile of firewood stacked against the wall. "We can just leave what we don't burn in the next few weeks. I don't think we're going to feel like hauling it next door, and you'll need something to start you out."

I thanked Jeri and left. It was December. Christmas trees glowed from picture windows. Plastic Santas waved from porches and yards. Back at the travel trailer, by flashlight, I called Mrs. Harold and introduced myself. I told her I was interested in renting Number Four after Jeri and Kathy moved out. I did not tell her I'd lived in Wildwood before, that I'd been married to the person whose house burned down, that I knew her parents, and that, if marriage counted as kinship,

I was distantly kin to her, still married to Cal because we'd never gotten a divorce, although I'd ceased using his name as soon as I left him.

Mrs. Harold asked a few questions. Where did I work? Would I be able to provide the rent on the first of each month? "I don't want to come but once for the rent," she said.

"That's understandable."

"I live all the way in Bear Creek."

"Yes ma'am. That's a long way off. If I can't be there, I'll leave a check. We can decide on a place to leave it."

"Well, all right," she said. She never mentioned a lease, and I never asked.

During the week, I went to a party held by a friend in her house out in the country far north of Chapel Hill. I was less awkward at this party than I'd been at the literary party, but still, large groups of people who seem to have no problem being sociable with one another always make me nervous, and part way through I walked out to the pond behind the house and sat on the bank. It was warm that night, one of those surprise spells of warm North Carolina winter weather.

The moon was full. I remember the way it glistened on the water. Behind me the party roared on, music and eruptions of laughter, the clinking of glasses. Out here an owl hooted in the woods.

"Nice, isn't it?" a voice said behind me. I turned around. A handsome man with a beard, thin and tall, walked up to me. "Mind if I join you?" he asked.

"No, please do."

He sat down beside me and pulled his knees up to his chest. "I'm Gregg."

"Nancy."

I don't know what Gregg and I talked about out there beside the pond, beneath the moon, but when he found out I lived in a travel trailer without electricity, he asked me over to his house for dinner, and to take a shower if I wanted. I accepted.

Gregg cleaned the bathtub before I arrived and set out clean towels. Dinner was simple. Soup and bread. I'd already told him about the cabin I would be moving into after Christmas. He told me he'd be leaving the next day for the holiday with his family in Anson County, but he'd like to see me when he got back.

"I'll be in the cabin," I said. "I'm not sure if the phone will get cut on by then, but here's how you get there." I drew a map on the back of an envelope, with landmarks—Farrell and Son's gas station, and beyond it, Jordan Lake indicated by scalloped lines. "If you reach the deep end of the lake, you've gone too far. Lystra is the name of the road. Don't confuse it with Old Lystra."

Gregg nodded. "I know those roads."

"And here's the entrance to Wildwood. I'm Number Four. It's the second driveway on the right, shared with a big grey house. The house is to the right on the driveway. My cabin is to the left. You'll see it."

Gregg took the envelope, folded it, and placed it in the pocket of his shirt. He kissed me. "Merry Christmas," he said. "I'll see you next year."

Next year was only a week away. I'd already called the power company to have the electricity put in my name on January 2. I tried to come clean with them over the pirated electricity I'd used for the travel trailer. I owed them money, I explained, and if they'd tell me how much, I'd send them a check. "We have no way of tracking that," the woman on the other end of the line said.

If I'd thought it through, I'd have not said anything. I'd have realized they had no way of knowing who lived in the travel trailer with the illegal hookup. But I didn't want trouble with them. Even though I'd confessed my crime, I still had good credit with the company, and they required no deposit. The water department was a different story.

Gone were the dysfunctional wells Cal and I had dealt with, the pumps we'd had to cut off while waiting for the pressure to build up again before cutting back on, the bricks in the toilet tanks, and cautions about watering your garden. The Bakers and the residents of Wildwood had lobbied for county water and won the privilege. Each house was now hooked up to a meter. It was a good thing, but the water department was a demanding entity. They required a deposit in cash before they'd cut your water on, no matter who you were. I planned to drive to the county seat on January 2, the day the bureaucracies opened their doors for business after the holidays.

On Christmas day, I made an obligatory visit to my mother. There was no joy in it.

"I wish the boys were here," she said when I walked into her room.

"I just want you to be happy," when the subject of me came up.

I stayed a while, made excuses, left. In the parking lot I opened the glove compartment and took out the joint I'd rolled for the aftermath of my visit and smoked it driving back to the travel trailer.

When the holidays finally ended, I threw the foam from my bed into the back of my truck, along with my clothes and cookware. I opened the door to the cab and motioned for the dogs to jump in. And I headed to Pittsboro to pay my water deposit. It was cold, and the weather forecast was for snow.

Snow in the North Carolina piedmont is no small event, and by the sounds of it, this was a sizable storm, with an estimated ten inches accumulation. As I drove, I kept the radio on for updates. School closings were reported, one after another. The newscaster warned us to buy bread and milk and go home. People in the North laugh at the South's freak-out when it snows, but things are different down here. Roads thaw during the day and refreeze at night, making driving more treacherous. Plus, sand and salt aren't a big budget item in any municipality, and roads don't get cleared until the snow has stopped falling. I knew from experience that the dirt road of Wildwood would be the last in the county to get plowed. And if the power went off, we'd be the last to get it cut back on.

My plan was to pay the water deposit, get groceries on the way to the cabin, and then bunker up once there. I could sleep on the floor, cushioned by the foam from the travel trailer. I had my sleeping bag. I'd have food in the fridge. And I'd have the woodstove.

There had been a little firewood on the front porch of the cabin when I'd last been there. Before now, the weather had been warm. I guessed that Jeri and Kathy had not burned much during the last few weeks. The supply they were leaving me would last a few days, I thought. And maybe the storm wouldn't be too bad.

My biggest concern was the water. I doubted that with the amount of snow predicted the water department would get my water turned on the day I paid the deposit as promised. But to find out, I had to pay the deposit in cash and in person.

The snow began falling as I drove. The flakes were large and gathered thickly in the air. Within minutes the grass along the side of the road turned white. The road itself turned white. The snow fell harder. The whiteness on the ground thickened, and I had a choice to make: go on to the water department or turn around and get food. There was a good chance that if I prioritized the water department, there wouldn't be much food left in the grocery store. I'd seen empty shelves before—white metal where bread and cans of soup had once been plentiful, frosty freezer doors with nothing behind them. I pictured being snowed in at the cabin without any supplies at all. I turned around and went to the grocery store and stocked up, and then drove straight to Wildwood.

Jeri and Kathy had left the key on the window ledge beside the front door. I unlocked it and ducked through the short doorway inside.

It was cold. Of course. I flipped the light switch and got darkness, which I was prepared to deal with, knowing that even if the power company switched the electricity to my name today, without interruption in service, as promised, it was likely to go out in the storm.

With the snow falling fast and furious now, I had a pretty good idea what I was in for. This was no light dusting. I wasn't going anywhere, and nothing was coming in. I had the woodstove, but no furniture to absorb the heat, or sit on. I had a cooler and the candles I'd used to tide me over in the travel trailer during my last weeks there. To eat, I had the food I'd just hurriedly purchased. The grocery store had been crowded with people but not completely void of food. I had bread, bologna, cheese, butter, eggs, peanut butter, mayonnaise, cans of soup, and a few apples. Dog food. Jugs of water. And a copy of the *New York Times*, not for reading, but to use for building a fire.

While the dogs wandered the yard, I hauled my piece of foam inside and upstairs to one of the bedrooms. I made the bed with sheets and my sleeping bag. I put the perishable groceries in the cooler on the back porch and left the rest on the kitchen counter. I brought in the pots and pans and my clothes and dumped it all on the table Jeri and Kathy had left for me. I had to get some kindling together before every stick in the woods was covered. I roamed about picking up sticks, dusting the snow off, snapping them to the right size, dropping them into the paper grocery bag I'd just brought home.

Inside the cabin I built a fire, coaxed it to a good flame, cut the dampers down when the fire seemed ready, hoping for a nice bed of coals to keep me warm through the night. I lit a candle, dripped some wax onto a plate and adhered the candle to it, then blew it out. I didn't need it yet. I placed the matches beside it. I hauled my clothes upstairs and hung them in the closet. I arranged my pots and pans and dishes on the shelves in the kitchen. Then I sat on the bottom step of the stairs. It was dim in the cabin, but not dark yet.

The snow was beautiful. To see it falling outside the windows of a cabin in Wildwood thrilled me. To be here again, to be so close to the house that had burned, the one I'd been so sure I'd return to, was a miracle. I just needed to get through this snowstorm. I'd be all right.

The cabin slowly warmed. I shed my coat and eventually my knit cap. My breath ceased to puff in front of me. I stepped outside for more firewood. There wasn't as much as I'd hoped. I'll be all right, I told myself. I can scrounge up dead wood. I'll be all right.

As I gathered an armload of wood, a truck turned into the driveway, its tires tracking through the snow to the cabin. Gregg parked behind my truck, got out, and said, "I thought you might use some help." He reached into the bed of his pickup and held up a black plastic box covered in snow. "I got a chainsaw for Christmas. What a great place," he added, looking around. "I got something else you might need." He reached into the magic pickup truck and lifted out two lawn chairs.

A knight in a shining pickup truck. "Thank you!"

We carried the chairs inside, and Gregg glanced around. "I want a tour later," he said, "but we should get you some firewood before nightfall."

We spent the rest of the afternoon in the still-falling snow, kicking through the four inches already on the ground, combing the woods for fallen trees, hauling what we could to the porch, where Gregg cut and I stacked.

"Stay for dinner?" I asked. "All I've got is soup and sandwiches." We both knew dinner would mean staying the night, and given the snow, maybe longer.

"Sure." Gregg smiled and opened the short red door for me, and I ducked inside. He opened the two lawn chairs and placed them around the woodstove.

"You can look around," I said, and he did while I opened a can of soup and made a couple of sandwiches.

"Great place," he said again, coming downstairs.

It was dark now. Gregg lit the candle. We ate pulled up close to the woodstove. "I take it the utilities never got cut on? Not even the water?"

I laughed. It was so obvious. "Nope. It's not going to happen until the snow's over. No water. No lights. I was on my way to pay the deposit at the water department but decided to turn back and get groceries instead."

"Good call," he said, holding up his sandwich. "You'll be all right."

I nodded.

He pulled a joint from his shirt pocket. "Want to smoke?"

Of course, I did.

Gregg stepped out to pee before we went upstairs to bed. He opened the door and said, "You should come out here." I pulled on my coat and boots without lacing them and stepped onto the porch. The electricity for all of Wildwood had gone out. The night was dark, the snow still falling, softly pattering onto the trees and the ground. Through the woods I could see dim spots of light, candles and kerosene lamps burning inside the little houses. "It is so fucking beautiful," Gregg said.

We snuggled that night on the narrow piece of foam, sharing the sleeping bag and pillow. The next day we stepped outside on the porch. The snow had stopped falling, leaving ten or twelve inches on the ground. To relieve ourselves, we each plowed separate paths off the back into the woods and tromped down our own personal circles.

We took a walk that morning. The little cabins and shacks looked like pictures out of storybooks, smoke drifting comfortingly from the stovepipes, firewood stacked on porches, boots left beside doors. No cars or trucks coming or going. No sounds from the outside world. The road was a solid plane of white with nothing but our footprints.

During the next week Gregg and I wandered up and down the road and met the neighbors. We took walks in the woods. We cooked and then cleaned the dishes by melting snow on the woodstove, conserving our precious jugs of water for drinking and cooking. We gleaned more firewood from the surrounding forest. We smoked dope and made coffee. I swept the cabin with an old broom left behind. We slept under my sleeping bag on the narrow foam mattress. In the mornings we followed our separate paths behind the cabin to our personal circles of tromped-down snow.

One morning Gregg stepped outside for firewood and then tucked his head back in to tell me it looked like Jeri and Kathy had some lights on in their house.

"Really?" I stepped out onto the porch, and sure enough, the light in Jeri and Kathy's house looked different. It looked as though there might be electric lights. But it was hard to tell.

"I'll walk down the road and make sure," he said.

He pulled on his boots and coat and trudged out, soon returning, and reporting back that, yes indeed, Wildwood had power.

Because my electricity had not been cut on yet, the end of a power outage for my neighbors did not mean power for me.

"Maybe I can call them," I said. I pulled on boots and coat and walked over to Jeri and Kathy's house. They let me use the phone. This was a time when you could get a human being on the other end of the line during a power outage, and I explained my situation to the man who answered.

"We're not taking orders for service right now," he snapped. "We've got thousands of customers still without power."

"I've already placed the order for service," I said. "It was supposed to be cut on the day it started snowing."

"We're not taking new orders," he repeated.

"Listen," I told him. "It's not a new order. I placed the order. It's Number Four Wildwood. Nancy Peacock. I know there's a switch somewhere that you can flip to get me power, and all I'm saying is if you can find it and flip it, I'd really appreciate that. That's all I'm saying."

There was a long pause on the other end of the line. "I'll see what I can do," he said. "I'm not making any promises."

"I understand. Thank you."

I hung up the phone.

"You know," Kathy said, "we have the tool you need to turn the water on. We had to cut the water on and off so often while we were building that we just bought one. And we have a hacksaw. You could cut the lock and turn the water on. They're not going to get to that anytime soon. We should have thought of it earlier."

"Well, it sounds like a good idea now," I said.

Jeri and Kathy gathered the tools, and we tromped out to the road and kicked around in the snow looking for the meter.

"I think it was around here," Kathy said, pushing her boot into the snow and moving it off to the side.

"Found it!" Jeri said.

We pried the cover up, but no, that one was the meter for their house. We pushed the snow aside next to it and found the one for the cabin, with a padlock preventing the water from being turned on. I took the saw and began. Gregg came out and joined us. We took turns sawing at the padlock until finally it broke free. Kathy handed Gregg the tool for turning the water on, a sort of specialized wrench that only fits a water meter. Gregg applied it and turned.

"Go see if it's on," he said.

I ran back to the cabin, stomped the snow off my boots, and went in without taking them off. In the kitchen I turned the faucet. Water. In the bathroom, water. I flushed the toilet. Water.

"It's on," I hollered to the group gathered at the road.

Three hours later, the cabin surged to life with electricity. Two nights later we heard the snowplow grinding down the road. We went outside and stood on the porch, watching it through the woods.

"Well, I guess this is it," Gregg said. "I should go home."

"I don't want you to leave," I said.

He did leave, but he came back with his clothes and his books.

A few days later I took the cut lock from the meter to the water department and confessed that I'd cut it off during the snowstorm.

"That's a crime," the woman said. "You're not supposed to do that."

"I know," I said. "Throw me in jail if you have to, but I'd been without water and electricity for over a week. I'd put in the order for the electric and was on my way here to set up an account when it started snowing." I pulled bills from the pocket of my jeans. "Here's my deposit. I was desperate to get water. To flush the toilet. I'm sorry, but it seemed like an extreme situation."

She gave me a long disparaging look. I'd not dressed for court. I wore what I always wore. Blue jeans. Boots. A knit shirt. My old green army jacket.

"Let me talk to the supervisor," she said. She took the broken lock and knocked on a door, entering and closing it behind her. A moment later she emerged and told me they were not going to press charges, but I'd need to pay for the lock.

"That's fair. Thank you." I turned over my money and received a receipt.

Finally, we were up and running at Wildwood. Gregg had been living in someone else's house, and he owned as little furniture as I did, so we picked up pieces bit by bit from thrift shops and sometimes the side of the road. One unit of a plaid sectional couch fit in the small space beneath the stairs. An orange upholstered chair was perfect for pulling up close to the woodstove. A rocking chair was perfect for the porch. Gregg had a bed, which we hauled upstairs.

But it was not to last with Gregg.

What happened with Gregg is what happened to me with a lot of relationships. I wanted to be alone again, and come spring, Gregg moved out.

27.

I made a lot of dramatic attempts at quitting dope. Several times I threw my stash away in a roadside dumpster, along with my rolling papers, my roach clips, my pipe, and whatever groovy little velvet or satin stash-bag I was carrying at the time. I'd go a week, sometimes two, but then I'd want to smoke again, and I'd supply up once more. But it wasn't as much fun as it used to be.

I didn't like getting stoned with people anymore. Even people I'd been getting high with for years. Even Jackie. I no longer felt that I could yuck it up like I used to. When I did get stoned with someone, I wanted them to leave so I could ride out the waves of paranoia by myself.

Alone, I could feed my fears like bears in cages, throwing them the meat of my worries every day. Had I said the wrong thing to that person? Had I done a good job with that task? What was the weird look in that customer's eye as I sold her a bagel? Was I okay? Was I okay? Was I okay?

No, I wasn't okay. I was hurting. I was ungrounded. Even back in Wildwood, I was unmoored.

Maybe it was the ghost of Scarlett's puppy buried in the lot next door. Maybe it was the ghost of Scarlett, left wrapped in the orange blanket in the shed behind me. Maybe it was the ghost of my marriage. Maybe it was the ghost of my house gone in the fire. Maybe it was the ghost of myself. Whatever it was, something haunted me, and it haunted me hard. It haunted me relentlessly. Every day I swam through its vapors and fumes. It clung to me, and in many ways, I clung to it.

I left the bakery and started my own cleaning business. I worked alone, which suited me. Every day I entered the strange world of suburbia and let myself into other people's houses while they were at work. I scrubbed their toilets and bathtubs and mopped their floors. I washed their sinks and made their beds. I vacuumed their carpets, zigzagging the machine back and forth as I backed out of the room, leaving no footprints, no trace but fresh vacuum tracks.

One day Jeri and Kathy walked over and said, "We're thinking about hiring you to clean our house."

"Weekly or every other?" I asked.

"Every other."

I pulled an estimate out of my head. They accepted it. "Wednesday afternoons okay?" I asked.

"That works," Jeri said. "We won't be here. Here's a key."

And so it was that I began spending time alone in a house built in the exact same space where my house once stood. I scrubbed a new stainless-steel sink where my old cast-iron sink used to be. I gazed out a window at my old garden. I dusted shelves built around a piece of wood that had once held up my porch. I sat on the new porch sometimes, in a new porch swing, looking out on the view that I'd loved so fiercely.

One day, Jeri came home early just as I was finishing up. She offered me strawberries, and we sat outside eating them and flipping the stems off the edge of the porch.

"What happened to the old foundation?" I asked.

"The foundation of your old house?"

"Yeah. Did you haul it away?"

"No, it's still there. We wanted to use it, but the building inspector wouldn't let us. We built around it. Want to see?"

Of course, I did. I wanted to see anything that was left.

We walked into the yard beside the garden. Jeri unlatched the access door built into their neat and plumb cinderblock foundation. I knelt on the ground and peered inside, and there was the bumpy rock foundation of my old home. I reached out and touched its hardened cords of cement.

My heart broke in that moment. The young girl I had been showed herself. She came out and dug the garden. She stoked the Ashley woodstove. She braided her hair. She creaked the porch swing into motion. She gazed up at the moon. She listened to the whippoorwills and the cicadas. She sat by the woodstove with rain thundering on the tin roof and prayed to a god that may or may not be living with the mice in the Masonite ceiling. She was beautiful, and she didn't know it. She was smart, and she didn't know it. Bless her. She placed her hands on my cheeks and asked me who I was. It was an excellent question.

Winter came as it always does. I stopped smoking dope. It wasn't hard to do this time. I didn't want it anymore. I came to understand that I had to make a choice. I could be either a pothead or a writer, but I couldn't be both. I chose writing.

Since uttering my prayer to the Masonite ceiling of the now burned-up house, I'd written exactly two short stories, maybe six poems, and a shitload of crap in my journal. That's where most of my writing energy went. To the journal.

I'd read somewhere that Anaïs Nin's psychiatrist had told her that as long as she was writing in her diary, she would not write anything else. All her writing energy was going there, it seemed, as was mine. I couldn't imagine living without my journal. I needed it. I needed to let loose on the page so all the things inside of me did not accumulate like a colony of biting ants. I needed to record things to survive. But did I need to keep those recordings?

I had three fat, spiral-bound, five-subject notebooks, each page filled with my tiny script reporting the events of my life. I took the notebooks off the shelf in the upstairs room with the built-in desk and thumbed through them. I read random passages reporting my struggles, my yearnings, my musings over one man or another or the next.

I could not bear this stuff. I could not bear to face how I'd spent my time, mooning over men, and then hiding myself from them. Breaking up with them, pursuing them, spending nights with them, never wanting to see them again, wishing they would call.

The ballpoint ink weighted the paper and made it crinkle as I turned the pages. It reminded me of the journals I'd torn up after Cal found out about my affairs, how I'd enjoyed the same sound before I destroyed them, how I used to love the feel of the ink. I still did, but I didn't enjoy the content. I wanted to burn these journals, but was this another act of self-destruction? Was I trying to hide away again?

No.

No, this was a purging. A cleansing. An acquittal, an exoneration, not for having had affairs with men, but for having made that fact, and the fact of my marriage, more important than I'd made myself.

Before I went to bed, I banked the woodstove, I lifted the pile of logs with the poker and shoved one fat notebook beneath it. I let the fire catch, turned the damper down, and went upstairs to sleep. In the morning, I opened the stove door and raked the ashes, as I always did. And there among the glittering coals was the glowing red-hot spiral coil that had held the notebook together. I raked a bit more, and scraps of my burned journal emerged. I caught glimpses of ghost-words left behind. Occasionally a man's name appeared, but I was pleased to see that other words had been left behind too.

Dirt road. Squirrels in the attic. Lizard. Hawk. Vultures.

For three nights I burned my journals, and every morning it was the same.

Burned house. Foundation. Woods. Sunset. Falling star.

The red-hot coil, and the snippets of paper with their phantom words.

Truck. Firewood. Stovepipe. Spider.

I signed up to audit a creative writing class with Lee Smith at NC State University in Raleigh. I was the oldest person in the group. I brought in a short story about an incestuous couple. Lee called me to a conference in her office one day. She said that the students had come to her to complain about my story. It disturbed them. "Writing is about making people emote," she said. "You disturbed these students. It's okay to disturb someone."

I went home to my cabin and sat in the rocking chair. I'd disturbed people with my writing. I let that soak in. I'd disturbed total strangers.

I'd like to say that I threw myself into stories, that I started writing every day, but after the class with Lee Smith ended, I stopped. There were no assignments anymore. Nothing making me do it. No classmates to disturb. The one short story of mine that had been published felt like a one-off. I remembered that literary party, the cookies, the popped-open safety pin digging into my skin, the polite questions: *Where do you teach? Where did you go to school?*

I bought a copy of *Writer's Market*, thick with listings of places to submit. But I was putting the carriage in front of the horse. The problem wasn't submitting. It was writing. I just didn't, except in a new journal, another fat five-subject spiral notebook that I planned to fill and burn in the woodstove.

But the stovepipe in my cabin was a dangerous problem. Most of it was outside the cabin. There, it was warmed by the smoke from my fires and cooled by the winter air, creating a buildup of creosote. I'd begun my first winter with the new stovepipe installed by Jeri and Kathy, but the creosote combined with moisture in the air caused the metal to degrade and become thin and hazardous.

Joel and I had replaced portions of the stovepipe several times. The thing to do, he told me, the safe thing to do, was get double-walled stainless-steel pipe to replace all the outside pipe. I counted the sections. There must have been ten. Double-walled stainless-steel stovepipe was expensive. I could not even come close to affording it, and I could not keep on asking for Joel's help replacing the pipe.

Instead, I borrowed Jeri and Kathy's extension ladder.

The side of the cabin with the stovepipe had been chinked by the Bakers' son and his friends. They'd scratched their names in the cement up close to the eaves, just as Cal and I had scratched ours in the cabin two doors down, close to the foundation. I raised the ladder and leaned it against the name Tubby. I climbed up with a can of stove cement in one hand and a spatula tucked in my pocket. I sought out the troublesome spots, the developing holes, the thin places, and I smeared the stove cement on.

Being up close to the stovepipe, I saw just how much trouble I was in. Whole sections were brown with rust. Touching the spatula to some parts, I felt the metal crinkle against the pressure. When I borrowed the ladder again to do some more patching, old stove cement flaked off. With every cold night the creosote built up and increased the chances of a chimney fire.

I'd never experienced a chimney fire before, but I'd heard stories. How the creosote ignites and travels up the flue and roars. How the fire can't be extinguished. A chimney fire burns until the creosote is finally consumed, for hours sometimes. The only thing one can do is to make sure the rest of the house is safe, which was an impossibility in the cabin. The thin stovepipe with its flaking patches could not contain a fire. I imagined the flames tonguing out in twenty places, licking at the dry walls of my cabin, catching it on fire, burning it to the ground next to the loss of my previous house.

I couldn't avoid building a fire. The cabin would freeze. The pipes would freeze. More than once, I woke up in the middle of the night sure I heard a roar. I lay in bed, listening, my heart pounding. No, it seemed okay, but I got up to check. I made it through the winter, but that summer, when I was offered another place to live, I took it. I left Wildwood, willingly this time.

28.

My mother died. We never made peace with each other. I'd disappointed her, and I had hated going to see her. I cringed when she said, "I wish the boys were here." I clenched my fists when she said, "I wish you'd find someone."

"I'm fine, Mom."

"I just want you to be happy."

And on it went. Every single time. The subject of men defined our relationship. She wanted a husband for me. She wanted the boys to visit. Her world orbited around the magical beings God had allegedly made in his image. We circled each other like magnets that could not click.

But I have three memories of my mother that I cherish, things that occurred when I was very young, before we moved to Chapel Hill, when we lived in Alabama in a long brown house with rattlesnakes in the front yard, where I was never allowed to go alone.

The first memory is of a blue dress my father bought for her for Mother's Day, a gift that was supposed to be from all of us. I was enchanted by the idea of giving my mother a surprise gift, by the big department store box, and by the blue dress with its built-in bosoms nestled in tissue paper. I made my father open the box and show the blue dress to me again and again.

The second memory is of a warm summer day and a stick on the paved driveway. I made up my little four-year old mind to step right in the middle of that stick, just because I could. I was barefoot, and the concrete driveway was warm and pleasant. The other children were home, tasked with looking out for me while our mother was inside taking a shower. But when I stepped on the stick, I discovered it was a sleeping snake, enjoying the warmth of the concrete. Each end of the snake flew up and bopped me on my leg. I screamed, and my mother rushed out of the house wearing just her girdle and bra, holding my brother's BB gun. By then the snake was gone.

My third and most treasured memory: On a late spring day, close to summer, while my siblings were in school, my mother took me to a gathering in another housewife's back-yard. There were no men or other children. The yard was private, closed in by hedges, invisible to the outside world. I ran around the women's legs as they sipped iced tea and chat-ted. The weather was hot. Southern hot. Alabama hot. Hu-mid. The women decided to shed their blouses and bras, and in that circle of lawn chairs I suddenly had breasts blooming like peonies all around me.

I had seen my mother's breasts, but I had never seen the breasts of other women. I remember being amazed. They were huge and beautiful, and I circled and looked, and no one told me I was being impolite. Not even my mother.

Many years later, after leaving Cal and before my moth-er moved into the nursing home, I decided to ask her about these memories. They were strong in my mind, but equally strong was my doubt about the last two. Had my mother charged out of the house in her girdle and bra when I screamed? Had she joined a circle of women in stripping down half naked in the heat?

I opened with the blue dress in the department store box, nestled in tissue.

"I remember that dress," she said, smiling.

"Do you remember coming out of the house with a BB gun, wearing just your girdle and bra? It was when I stepped on the snake."

"I did no such thing," she snapped.

I don't know why I asked. Of course, she would deny ever being outside in her bra and girdle, wielding a BB gun. But even though I fully expected denial, I forged ahead with the third memory. I wanted to know my mother as someone besides the woman who'd leaned over me and hissed when I "took the Lord's name in vain." I wanted to know her as someone besides the Pat-Boone-pushing churchy woman she had always shown me. I wanted this so badly that I told her my memory of the circle of women intentionally disrobing on a hot day in Alabama.

"Certainly not. Absolutely not. No. I would never. Where do you get such notions?"

She denied it so vehemently and so quickly that I felt it must be true. But God, that celestial interloper, was listening in. It was as though he was waiting for my mother to screw up so he could pounce and deny her entrance to heaven, sending her to hell instead. Because no matter how careful you were, no matter how much you tried to be good and to please him, he was always on the lookout for one tiny little slipup.

I wanted my mother to admit to being the woman who had sat in a lawn chair with other women, drinking iced tea and finding relief from the heat by baring her breasts, but she would never admit it. To the bitter end she, and other women I met, wanted to clasp the fetters of womanhood, the fetters of *good girl* onto me.

One year I went to the nursing home to take my mother to Easter service in the chapel there. I dressed up: A nice skirt and blouse, hose, high heels, clothes I hated. Clothes that tugged at me and confined me and restricted my movement. I dressed up so as not to embarrass my mother, as she'd wanted me to during my adolescence when we'd battled over what I would wear to my forced attendance to church.

At the nursing home I wasn't prepared for the effect one daughter's appearance at Easter would have on the other women there. Before the service had even started, they noticed me and came up to me. Uninvited, they laid their soft hands on my cheeks. They looked me in the eyes and said, "It's good you're here."

"You're such a good girl."

"I hope you visit your mother again."

"You're such a good girl."

"A good daughter."

"God bless you for being here."

"What a good girl you are."

They didn't mean for their comments to be so relentless and assaultive, but like my mother, they wanted the world to bend the way they'd been told it would bend. They wanted the reward they'd been promised. They'd all been good. Done good things. And now that they'd raised their children and buried their husbands, they were alone in this place with other women who had also raised their children and buried their husbands. It was not how it was supposed to be. It was so far from the glorious promises made to them by clergy and church that they could not reconcile with it.

Oddly enough, my mother had never pressed me to have children. She balked if I said I did not want children, which I had done once before marrying Cal, but she never suggested afterwards that we should start a family. I wonder if deep down she knew what a disaster that would be, with Cal as a father and me as a mother. I wonder if deep down she knew we couldn't and wouldn't rise to the occasion. Maybe she knew Cal would abandon me. Maybe she knew I would feel the burden of children, just as she had. Or maybe she felt that getting me out of the house and under the care of a man was enough. It meant she'd done her job. It meant God could get off her back about this.

These women in the nursing home, gathered around me, patting their soft hands against my face, telling me what a *good girl* I was for being there, deserved recognition. They deserved awards and easy old age, but in that absence, their neediness for it pulled me down deep into the world they wanted me to occupy. I could feel their disappointments projected onto me. I could feel them needing to believe I was a good girl, carrying on a tradition and thereby proving that their lives had not been in vain. That they'd not taken a wrong turn. They'd not drunk the Kool-Aid of the patriarchy. They'd not been lied to. They'd not been manipulated. They'd not carried forward a tradition that was killing women's spirit.

My mother and I sat in the front row of the church to accommodate her wheelchair. The minister stood and faced us and droned on about Jesus dying for everyone's sins.

How dare God, I thought, to judge my mother for protecting a child while in a state of undress, or for disrobing on a hot day. How dare he judge any of these women for any of the other millions of things they'd done in their lives to raise their children and relieve the pressures put on them. But this empathy I had didn't change anything between my mother and me. After the service was over, she said, "I wish the boys were here." And, "I wish you'd find someone." And, "I just want you to be happy."

I wanted to leave so badly. The women surrounded me again and told me how good I was. I ate lunch with my mother in the cafeteria. I carried her tray for her. I wiped her mouth. I returned her to her room. I fielded more of the same—the absent boys; my sad, husbandless life; my unhappiness as she saw it. And then I extricated myself from her. As I walked through the halls, I felt the tentacles of traditional womanhood all over me, grabbing and pulling and not letting go. I reached my truck and started it and drove away.

I drove to the woods, to Duke Forest, a large tract of land open to the public, surrounding New Hope Creek.

I'd not had the foresight to bring clothes to change into or shoes for walking, but I was determined that I get down to that creek. I needed that creek more than anything right then. In the truck, I pulled off my high heels and peeled off my pantyhose and began the mile-long trek barefoot down the graveled road to the water.

At first it was painful. I crept along, cringing and jumping each time a rock poked into the arch of my foot. But after a while, my feet became used to it. I felt my soles stimulated by the poking rocks. When I finally reached the creek, I loped along a cool dirt path to my favorite boulder. I stuck my feet in the water. It was cold, and finally I felt the resurrection. My own.

I know my mother loved me. I know she loved me fiercely, and I suspect that she was as much of a nature worshiper as I was. While the other children went off to school in

Alabama, I stayed home with Mama. I remember scattering torn pieces of bread on the picnic table and standing at the picture window with her watching a cardinal peck at them. I remember picking honeysuckle blossoms in the ravine down front and sucking the nectar from the tips, my mother's eyes bright with pleasure.

During the spring, when all the dogwoods bloomed in Chapel Hill, my mother, driving me to Franklin Street or the library, would gasp at their beauty. She never wanted me to pick wildflowers for her, because she thought they should stay in the ground. Once, when the lot through the woods from our house was sold and a bulldozer arrived to clear it, she stomped through the trees and stood in front of the machine, stopping the man from working.

I wonder if, without God in the way, we might not have gotten along.

My mother left me a little money, with which I bought a computer. With a computer I didn't need to know how to type perfectly. With a computer I could make typos and misspell words and fix them later. I could move text around, pattern things, go back and change a character's eye color or hair color or name. With a computer, I could write the "history novels" my mother had once declared to be a good goal.

But even after making this investment in my writing life, I still went about it haphazardly. I worked intermittently. I sometimes sat down at the desk as though I was ready to write "the great American novel," and when it didn't arrive, I wouldn't return to work for a week, or two, or three. I didn't write every day. I didn't commune with the story, as I now know I need to do. Instead, I communed, once again, with a new boyfriend, a man I thought I loved. He knew of my writing. He knew of my aspirations. He was a musician, and one day he said, "How are you going to feel when I make it and you haven't?"

I laughed.

There was a time when I would not have laughed. A time when I would not have pointed out his ludicrous language. A time when I'd have taken his prediction of his success and my failure as absolute. Predetermined. My destiny. But that time had passed.

"Listen to yourself," I said. "Listen to your wording. '…when I make it and you haven't?' What sort of horseshit is that?"

He explained, of course, that he hadn't meant it the way I'd taken it, and it only proved his point. I was too sensitive, a critique I've heard too often.

The problem was that I was not sensitive enough. Even though I laughed at him, even though I spoke up for myself, I still thought I was in love with him. I thought he might eventually ask me to marry him, and I wanted to be free to say yes, and I wasn't free.

For twenty years Cal and I had been separated but still married. I'd always known I'd be the one to bring divorce to the table, and the one to pay for it. Cal would initiate nothing and pay for nothing. He would wait me out, just as he'd waited me out when I became his inconvenient wife, an obstacle to fulfilling his desire for Mia, applying the thumbscrews of misery to get me to move. And I still blamed myself for moving. For not chucking his stuff out into the driveway and changing the locks. For the house burning down due to his stupid Campbell's Chunky Beef Soup, the burner set on high.

Your soup's ready.

Alllll riiiiight.

But Cal wasn't in my life anymore. I didn't even know where he lived. I could find out through his mother. I had some money now. If I wanted a divorce, I could get one.

I found a lawyer who would handle a no-contest divorce for a small fee. When I met with him, he asked several times if I was sure there would be no contested property.

I snorted at this, thinking of Cal's plaid flannel shirts hanging in the closet, smelling of smoke, the coins I'd culled from his pockets, the melted guitar picks I pried off his dresser. I thought of the stump from our packing-crate table, and the burnt Ashley woodstove chunked in a dumpster. I thought of the pine wedding invitation plaque, weirdly bright against the dark embers of our floor. I thought of the green circle in the sooty carpet where Scarlett had laid down to die.

"It all burned up," I told him. "There is no mutual property left."

I called his mother to find out where to have papers served. "Send them in care of me," she said, resigned to our divorce after our long separation.

"There's no need for him to attend," I told her. The last thing I wanted was to see Cal in the courtroom. I was afraid he'd throw me a curve ball, claiming property that didn't exist, complicating our simple divorce with some new Cal-as-victim narrative.

"I'll tell him," she said.

"He doesn't need to come," I repeated.

"I understand."

"I'll take care of everything," I said again, as if that was ever in doubt.

"I'll tell him. Just send the papers care of me."

Our divorce came through the day the Gulf War started. In the courtroom, the easy cases were tried before the others, and mine was called first. I took the stand, scanned the faces in the courtroom looking for Cal, and was relieved not to see him.

Before the judge got down to business, he asked me if I was aware of what had happened overnight.

"Do you mean bombing Iraq?" I asked.

He nodded.

"Yes," I said. "I heard of that."

He then asked me questions pertinent to the matter at hand. I testified that I was who I said I was, that I'd been married to Calvin Powell since 1972, and that I was suing for a no-contest divorce and wished to legally take my maiden name back. And it was decreed. The judge's hammer told me so. It was both surreal and anticlimactic. As I was leaving the courtroom, I heard the judge asking the next witness if he'd heard what had happened the night before.

I walked to my truck alone, weirdly aware of how my dress swished against my calves as though I was watching a character in a movie. I was surprised that I wanted someone there with me. Even Cal would do. Maybe we'd go out for a hamburger. Maybe we'd shake hands and hug. Maybe there would be closure, something as final as the burnt-down house. Instead, I went to work. I changed in my client's bathroom from my divorce clothes to my work clothes, and I cleaned the house.

I cleaned two houses that day, then I went home, changed clothes again, and drove to Raleigh to meet the two friends I'd asked to celebrate this occasion with me. Ava, the wife of one of Cal's band members, and Jackie.

In the bar we ordered margaritas and nachos. It was early, that time after work when employees gather at bars and belt a few down before going home to their families. I recognized the vibe from my years of bartending. The loosened ties. The high-heeled shoes dangling off stocking-clad feet. The developing flirtations.

Over everyone's heads, in every direction, large-screen televisions played the bombing of Baghdad over and over. The streaks of light seemed uselessly pretty and reminded me of the Perseid meteor shower I had watched with Cal while tripping in the driveway of the cabin. But this wasn't a meteor shower. It was the bombing of a city.

It would create a neat symmetry in storytelling to say that after leaving the bar, after saying goodbye to Ava and Jackie that night, I returned to a house in Wildwood. So neat that it's tempting to lie about it, tempting to write that I built a fire and snugged up close to the woodstove. To write that Wildwood held me as I squirted a few tears over the critical intersection of divorce and war. But the metaphors weren't writing themselves anymore, as they had the night I agreed to marry Cal as the train went by in front of us. I didn't live in Wildwood. I returned to the trailer I now lived in, and the next day I cleaned houses again.

Still, Wildwood reached for me. Wildwood was like a mother who would always welcome me home, who never blamed me for my own hurt, never cried over my return because I had failed at something, never wished I was someone else. The next month, in April, the boyfriend I thought I would marry left me for another woman, and this coincided with Jeri and Kathy telling me that a house along the dead-end dirt road that I loved so much was coming up for rent. The house was at the very end of the road. Number Eleven Wildwood. I moved in.

29.

Things had changed a lot in Wildwood over the years. Some of the tenants passing through were not the domestically blissful hippies who had previously been my neighbors. The people who had just vacated my new house left a lot of clues as to who they were and how they lived.

The yard and surrounding woods were scattered with discarded furniture, trash, and motorcycle parts. On the back porch, they'd left boxes of greasy, heavy machinery and wet clothes and rags draped across a broken chair. In the bathroom, the floor was greasy, black-stained plywood, and more motorcycle parts filled the bathtub. In the window one pane of glass was missing, a piece of yellow cardboard duct-taped in its place.

But the house teased me with possibility, as all the houses in Wildwood had. This one was a one-story shack with front and back porches, another woodstove made from an old hot water heater left behind, with a stovepipe that rose straight up from the top of the stove to exit out the low-pitched roof. I was pleased to see this. No turns and elbows and very little stovepipe outside meeting the cold air. This meant the stove would draw well, and that keeping the pipe clean and safe would be manageable.

I roamed about the yard and woods, hauling the junk and trash and broken furniture into a pile at one corner of the front porch. I added the junk from the back porch and the junk from the bathtub. The pile grew taller than me. I hired a man with a backhoe and a dump truck to pick it up and haul it away. I measured the missing pane of glass in the bathroom and had a piece cut to size, pointing it, and glazing it in. I covered the greasy bathroom floor with adhesive tiles. I borrowed a ladder and stove brushes from my immediate neighbor, a man who'd lived there when Cal and I had first arrived. I climbed onto the roof and cleaned the stovepipe, replaced the cap, and smeared some roofing tar around one of the tin panels that seemed to be leaking.

In the kitchen, there were three perfectly round holes in the floor, places where someone, working on something, had not bothered to place a board beneath a drill. I planned to close them up, but before I got around to it a snake came in. I never saw the snake, but I came home from work to find its moist skin draped across my clean dishes. I nailed the lids of tin cans on top of the holes.

Sometimes cars full of people would come park at the dead-end road to drink beer and party. I'd be home alone, but I'd make a big show of turning on the porch light and opening the door and then hollering inside to no one, "I don't know who it is. Get the flashlight, and let's find out." Then I'd close the door and get a flashlight and turn it on, letting it trail across the windows a few times. Sometimes I'd have to open the door again and holler, "Hurry up, will you?" But usually, the car and the people would be gone by then.

I was alone, very alone, the condition I'd always longed for but had been lured away from by a man. I needed aloneness, I decided. I needed it to write.

For years I'd been futzing around with a novel. I wanted to expand my only published short story written from the point of view of a child of hippies into a longer story. I continuously dabbled at it, backed away from it, procrastinated on it, started over, and then started over again and again. How did anyone ever get this done? How could anyone write a contiguous story in increments of time between work and cooking and gathering firewood and stoking a woodstove? It didn't seem possible, yet I knew it was. I had novels on my bookcase to prove it.

One night I went to town for some chow, and after eating, I wandered into a bookstore on Franklin Street. In the paperback section, I happened upon a book called *Writing Down the Bones* by Natalie Goldberg. I opened it up and thumbed through the pages.

"Give yourself permission to write the worst junk in the world," I read.

Set a timer and write nonstop for a certain number of minutes, Goldberg suggested. Don't worry about it. Don't fret. Just write.

What? It was unheard of to just write. To just see what comes. To not know where you're going. To just write for ten minutes.

Buy those funny notebooks with silly pictures on the covers, Goldberg suggested. It helps, because they're not thick, you can fill them fast, and it's hard to take yourself too seriously when you're writing in a notebook with Goofy on the cover.

I bought Goldberg's book, and before I drove home to Wildwood, I stopped at the drugstore and bought a notebook with a picture of Mickey Mouse and Minnie Mouse dancing to a jukebox on the cover. The next afternoon, I set my kitchen timer for ten minutes.

"Give me the room you're in," Goldberg wrote.

It seemed simple enough. I described my house in Wildwood. The uneven wooden floors, how one plank was higher than another in places, how this wore lines in my rug. I described the concrete blocks that the woodstove sat on. I described the collection of things I'd placed across the "mantel"—cap blocks I'd purchased to create a shelf on top of the cinderblocks behind the stove, stacked to protect the wall. On that makeshift mantel I'd placed a deer antler found in the woods, a turtle shell, a vase of feathers, and the single woman's shoe from beneath the fallen-down house in the woods that I'd once walked to.

I'd thrashed my way through the woods one day, down to the stream and up the bank, to find that old homestead. I described kneeling down and reaching under the collapsed roof for the shoe, and how a marble rolled out of its toe. I wrote about how I could not separate that shoe from its marble, how the marble likely belonged to the child of this woman whose husband had a pile of discarded liquor bottles behind a shed in back and a belt hanging from a nail. I wrote about how that shoe lived on my makeshift mantel now, with the marble sitting on its toe. One thought led to another until it didn't.

"I don't know what to write," I wrote. "I'm stuck, I'm stuck, I'm stuck."

My hand hurt. Thankfully, the timer went off. I rubbed my wrists. The next day, I did it again.

The spirits of Wildwood were always looking out for me. I think they heard the prayer I muttered to the Masonite ceiling on that rainy day in Number Three before I left Cal.

Please, God, let me become a writer, and I don't care who falls by the wayside.

We can help you become a writer, the spirits said. *But you're going to have to do something in return. You're going to have to write.*

Even though it was uncomfortable, even though it made my hand hurt, I put a stake in the ground and wrote every day with the timer ticking away in another room so the sound wouldn't bother me. I made this my practice. I applied Natalie Goldberg's techniques to my approach to writing the novel. I set a timer. I made myself sit at the desk for an hour each morning. Five days a week, I told myself. You just have to do this five days a week. You don't have to write on weekends if you don't want to.

It turned out I did want to write on weekends. It turned out that if I did not write every day now, I was unmoored. The desk I sat at every morning took on the same sacred quality as a hearth when heating with wood.

I began getting up early, before I went to work cleaning houses. I'd fix a cup of coffee and sit at my desk and open the computer, and when I did so my subconscious received a signal.

Oh, we're writing now. Fun, let's go.

At the time there was no internet. There was nothing else but writing that the combination of coffee, desk, and computer could possibly mean. It could not mean I was putzing around on YouTube or checking headlines or answering emails or responding to something on Facebook. When those things came about, the computer became a pool of quicksand for me. The more I struggled, the deeper I sank. But when I wrote my first novel, when I found the chutzpah to barrel through a first draft, the computer was nothing more than a well-loved tool.

Thirty-five pages was a milestone. Fifty was amazing.

Seventy-five was a watershed moment. One hundred was unimaginable, but I reached it.

I vowed not to begin revising until I'd completed a draft. And then I vowed not to read it for three months, but I could not wait three weeks. Nor could I read the entire thing. I read the first few chapters and knew I needed to put it in first person and stick closer to the short story I'd written years earlier.

I joined a writers' group. They read and commented on my novel while I sat mutely, not allowed to talk. The next day I cried. One woman said I needed to double the length of the novel. No one would want such a short novel. Another said I needed to focus on the relationships of the children, rather than the relationship between the narrator and her mother.

I waited another week, then read over the comments, and very quickly, if something did not resonate with me, I dismissed it. I was especially puzzled by the comment on the novel's length. It seemed so random. A novel had to be a certain length. A publisher would never want such a short piece of work. But I knew that making the novel longer could muck up the story, and I would be doing it for an editor who only lived outside of me, if even that. She was imaginary and mythical.

How long does a novel need to be? I asked the spirits of Wildwood.

It needs to be as long as a piece of string, they answered.

I ignored the advice to lengthen my book. I ignored the advice to focus the storyline around the children. And with those decisions made, I began a third draft of my novel, to clear up what I thought were legitimate points, things that had resonated with me. Things that I felt in my body, yes. Yes, that's right.

The novel I wrote got published and reviewed in the *New York Times*. It was chosen by that paper as a notable book. I was relieved that my mother was not alive to see it, relieved that I did not have to field her asking me how I knew so much about pot. I imagined my lies. "I talked with someone who smoked it once, and he told me what it was like."

It would have been an obvious lie, and she would have believed it, because she'd never wanted to know the truth about me.

One night, while living in the last house in Wildwood, I sat in the front room reading, only the screen door between me and the night. Outside the crickets were chirping, the bugs making their Southern-nighttime-soundtrack. I hadn't heard a whippoorwill along the road in years, but the bugs were constant once the weather warmed up.

There was a gap between my screen door and the floor. There were many gaps in the houses in Wildwood, many cracks, so much porousness where the outside came inside. I'd had lizards walk in through this gap beneath the door. They roamed the house and left. Bugs, of course, showed up through this entry and others. The mice just lived here. On this night, an enormous spider walked in. I saw it out of the corner of my eye.

"Okay, buddy," I said. "Just stay right there." I went to the kitchen, slinking along the wall so as not to scare it, not to startle it into scurrying off and hiding somewhere out of reach. I got a jar and a piece of stiff paper. I quickly placed the jar over the spider and slid the paper underneath it.

But something happened to the spider as I did so. It seemed to splinter and split into hundreds of tiny dots. The tiny dots swarmed over the glass. I raised it up to have a look. The spider wasn't so large after all. She'd only seemed fat because she'd been carrying all her babies on her back. Hundreds of spider babies surged all around the sides of the glass. As I held the jar and watched, they returned to her and settled on her back again.

To dump her out, fling her into the leaves as I usually did, would panic her babies and scatter them. Not wanting to do that, I took the glass outside and slowly removed the paper from the top, and slowly turned it on its side so she could leave with her family intact.

And this is what finally made me cry over my relationship with my own mother. When I was a baby, malleable and dependent, she'd carried me, nurtured me, and kept me alive. And then as I grew older, with a will and thoughts of my own, we began to clash, and every clash we had was generated by something outside both of us. Religion. Expectations. The patriarchy. I could never be who my mother felt I should be for whatever reasons she imagined: my own safety, to avoid hell, to make her look better in the eyes of God. And she could not see me for who I was: smart, creative, pretty, capable. And of course, I could not see myself that way either. But those things were there all along, and Wildwood gave them to me.

I still dream about Wildwood, and when I wake up it's with a warm feeling all around me. Even if I can't remember the dream's details, I know I've been there again. I know the dirt road, and the cabins, and shacks, and the owl, and the deer, and the swamp. I know the smell of woodsmoke, the smell of honeysuckle, the sounds of bugs and birds. I know the vultures spinning in the sky. I'm grateful to all of it for birthing me, for giving me to myself, for placing my tiny soul into my arms like a baby, for laying her in my arms for me to see and hold and nurture. I am grateful to the wildness and grateful to the spirits that live there.

Amazingly enough, Wildwood remains. Most of the original houses are still there, made of logs and rough-cut lumber, salvaged windows, and rusty tin. They are individually owned now. The road is paved. Many parts of the surrounding farmland and countryside are developed. Many of the beacons and markers I used to look for in the early mornings as Cal drove me to my parents' house are gone. The farmhouse with the stained-glass windows has been razed. The house in the curve and high on the hill is gone. The nightlight shaped like the Cape Hatteras lighthouse is gone, although amazingly enough, the house is still there, as is the Nature Trail Mobile Home Park. The field with the cows in front of the barn is still there, different cows to be sure, but otherwise looking the same. The bridge we used to cross heading toward town has been named for James Taylor. A Food Lion is just a few miles away from Wildwood now, as are a Subway and a pizza place, and just through the woods from our dead-end road is a gated community.

I remember those woods. I remember the old homestead with the piles of liquor bottles behind the shed and the woman's shoe with the marble in it. I remember the junkyard filled with those old, clunky cars, the ghosts of journeys, the ghosts of prayers and desires and desperation held within their glove boxes. I remember the little stream I jumped. I remember the girl I used to be checking her Cinderella watch to make sure she was back at the cabin in time for her husband's phone call.

I will never leave her alone again. I applaud that girl. I applaud her grit and gumption, her bravery and stamina. I applaud her spirit and intuition and prayers. And even though she can't hear me, I whisper to her: *It's going to be all right. You're beautiful. You're worthy. You're strong. You're smart.*

One day, I whisper, *you're going to write about this.*

AUTHOR'S NOTE

A memoir is not fiction, nor is it nonfiction. A memoir is a story teased out of a life, and a life is made up of many stories. To shape this memoir, I have had to make choices. I've left some things out, I've changed names, I've rearranged events, and I've even made a few things up—details that contribute to the magic of story. I have not invented events. Naturally, with one or two exceptions, I don't remember exactly the conversations recounted here. But I stand by the gist of things, the gist of this story as I recall it. It shaped my life, and I hope you find meaning here.

ACKNOWLEDGMENTS

I want to thank these people for being a part of my writing journey.

The Iron Clay Writers: Agnieszka Stachura, Claire Hermann, Rebecca Hodge, and Barrie Trinkle, thank you for being there every Wednesday night for years, and for providing honest feedback and encouragement, as well as laughter and excellent cake.

I thank my husband, Ben, for lots of discussions, emotional support, and excellent editing.

I am grateful to my friend and fellow writer Anne Anthony for sharing and letting me share so much more than writing.

Thank you to Susan Emshwiller and Chris Coulson of Pinehead Press, Susan for saving this story from the dustbin and both of you for being fellow rebels on the literary trail and for helping me dodge falling empires.

Thank you to Nora Gaskin of Lystra Books and Literary Services for caring so strongly about this story and helping me through my tech-phobia. I am also grateful to Kelly Lojk for excellent book design and copy editing.

And finally, I want to thank my larger writing community, including everyone who has ever attended my prompt-writing groups, written with me, shared their works with me, and held me up with their spirit and energy.

NANCY PEACOCK is the author of several novels and a book of essays. She served as the NC Piedmont Laureate in 2018. She has also had poetry published in *Poets Reading the News, Southern Arts Journal,* and upcoming in *Atlanta Review.*

Nancy runs writing groups online and for over twenty-five years has facilitated a popular, free prompt writing workshop. Her website is www.nancypeacockwrites.com